Luke-Acts and Empire

Princeton Theological Monograph Series

Luke-Acts and Empire

Essays in Honor of Robert L. Brawley

Edited by

DAVID RHOADS,
DAVID ESTERLINE,
and
JAE WON LEE

PICKWICK *Publications* · Eugene, Oregon

LUKE-ACTS AND EMPIRE
Essays in Honor of Robert L. Brawley

Princeton Theological Monograph Series 151

Pickwick Publications
An Imprint of Wipf and Stock Publishers
199 W. 8th Ave., Suite 3
Eugene, OR 97401

www.wipfandstock.com

ISBN 13: 978-1-60899-098-6

Cataloging-in-Publication data:

Luke-Acts and empire : essays in honor of Robert L. Brawley / edited by David Rhoads, David Esterline, and Jae Won Lee.

Princeton Theological Monograph Series 151

x + 176 p. ; 23 cm. Includes bibliographical references.

ISBN 13: 978-1-60899-098-6

1. Bible. N.T. Luke and Acts—Criticism, interpretation, etc. 2. Religion and politics—Rome—History. I. Brawley, Robert L. II. Rhoads, David M. III. Esterline, David. IV. Lee, Jae-Won. V. Title. VI. Series.

BS2589 L81 2011

Contents

Preface

It is our distinct pleasure as editors and contributors to honor our colleague and friend Robert Brawley on the occasion of his retirement. Any who have entertained scholarly discussion with him, participated in his classes, shared personal conversation over a meal, or sat on the same academic committees know that Robert is a fine human being. In order to elucidate this observation, we would like to take this brief preface as an opportunity to lift up some of his salient traits.

Above all, Robert is a thoughtful and careful scholar. When he has presented at scholarly meetings or when he poses a question to another presenter, it is as if he is taking the measure of a gem, carefully turning the issue or the text around and looking at all sides. In his classroom, he is never in a hurry, always eager to linger on a text or on a historical conundrum to see what can be made of it and where we can draw appropriate conclusions. His books, articles, papers, reviews, and lectures all manifest the same respect for the material and the same high regard for the role of the interpreter.

It should also be noted that Robert has been a wide-ranging scholar. Most of his work has been on Luke-Acts, a fourth of the New Testament. He has also published articles on each of the other Gospels, three letters of Paul, and the Letter to the Hebrews. The breadth of subject matter in the books he has reviewed and the courses he has taught attests to broad interests. He has also encompassed many different methodological approaches: narratology, intertextuality, social identity, theology, and ethics. These approaches reflect cutting-edge disciplines in New Testament studies.

One of the traits we most admire is that Robert writes with moral purpose. Much of his work in Luke-Acts seeks to overcome the problem of anti-Judaism that has plagued New Testament studies. Furthermore, his work in intertextuality demonstrates the early Christian rootedness in Judaism. His studies of morality in the formation of character deal with many moral issues of the early church. His outstanding leadership in the study of ethics in the New Testament writings—in academic seminars, in works he has edited, and in the classroom—has contributed significantly to contemporary ecclesial discussions of sexuality and gender identity.

Robert has spent his professional career in theological education, focusing on the formation and training of women and men for leadership in communities of faith. He is an outstanding preacher; his frequent sermons provide a model of faithful integration of the text, scholarship, and the most difficult issues of our local and global contexts. He is a theological educator committed not only to ideas, but also to the nurture and development of faithful leaders.

We have often heard Robert described as a gentleman. Indeed, it is an accurate depiction. He is gracious, kind, loyal in friendship, eager to listen as well as to question, and thoughtful to colleagues and students alike. He has worked hard at communicating with his students in the Spanish and Korean languages. He has promoted the work of others through the translation of two significant volumes in German. He is generous with compliments.

This volume on Luke-Acts and Empire is testimony to the fact that Robert is always eager to learn more, pioneer into new territory, address topics of substance and relevance, and foster fresh contributions to the field of New Testament. We are proud to offer it in his honor.

Contributors

MICHAEL BACHMANN is Universitätsprofessor für Evangelische Theologie, University of Siegen, Siegen, Germany.

WARREN CARTER is Professor of New Testament, Brite Divinity School, Fort Worth, Texas, USA.

RICHARD J. CASSIDY is Professor of Sacred Scripture, Sacred Heart Major Seminary, Detroit, Michigan, USA.

JAE WON LEE taught, as Assistant Professor of New Testament, at McCormick Theological Seminary in Chicago for eight years.

RAYMOND PICKETT is Professor of New Testament, Lutheran School of Theology at Chicago, Chicago, Illinois, USA.

BARBARA REID is Professor of New Testament Studies, Catholic Theological Union, Chicago, Illinois, USA.

STEVE WALTON is Senior Lecturer in Greek and New Testament Studies, London School of Theology, Northwood, Middlesex, United Kingdom.

KAZUHIKO YAMAZAKI-RANSOM is Professor of Biblical Studies, Revival Biblical Seminary, Aichi, Japan.

Luke and Empire

An Introduction

Raymond Pickett

THIS FESTSCHRIFT FOR ROBERT BRAWLEY IS A COLLECTION OF ESSAYS
that deal with how Luke-Acts depicts and negotiates the reality of the
Roman Empire. Although New Testament scholarship has long recognized the importance of the Greco-Roman context of New Testament
texts, a thoroughgoing focus on how these documents envision and
challenge imperial ideology and structures is relatively new. In some
ways, then, these essays mark a distinctive turn in Lukan studies. As
an introduction to these essays, I would like briefly to set them in the
context of New Testament studies generally and in the context of Lukan
studies in particular, and then to suggest ways in which recent studies
of Luke-Acts contribute to the emerging body of scholarship that evaluates the early Christian movement and the documents it produced as
responses to the Roman Empire.

Luke-Acts and Judaism

Scholarly interest in the relationship between the New Testament and
the Roman Empire is quite recent and has acquired enough momentum
in the past decade or so to be regarded as a paradigm shift. Although
certain interpretative issues have long been considered in the light of
Roman history, law, and certain imperial practices, the current interest in political interpretations of New Testament texts has resulted in
a variety of new lenses that have transformed the landscape of New
Testament studies. This paradigm shift has followed on the heels of

another major development in New Testament studies initiated more than thirty years ago—namely a through re-examination of the Jewish texts and contexts that served as a matrix of early Christianity. Both began in Pauline studies.

I want to consider the development of these two paradigm shifts and the connection between them, because how Luke-Acts is perceived to negotiate the realities of the Roman Empire depends to some extent on how Luke-Acts is situated vis-à-vis Judaism.[1] In the early 1970s, what has come to be known as the "new perspective on Paul" was initiated with the work of Krister Stendahl, E. P. Sanders, and others who built on their insights. The "new perspective" had implications beyond Pauline studies because it was really also a new perspective on Judaism. Stendahl maintained that Paul remained a first century Jew. However, since the Reformation, Paul's conversion and gospel were construed in terms of constructions of the individual person that were alien to early Judaism.[2] Sanders' seminal work was distinguished by the fact that approximately seventy-five percent of his book on Paul was devoted to a study of Judaism as a pattern of religion on its own terms.[3] This new view of Paul's Jewish background catalyzed a re-examination of Jewish texts, which has resulted in a more complex and variegated portrait of Judaism that continues to become even more richly textured and debated. It also exposed the fact that New Testament scholars had been operating predominantly with a stereotypical and misleading caricature of Judaism that was predicated on the Gospels' depiction of Pharisaic Judaism as a legalistic religion.

The new perspective on Paul and the subsequent corpus of scholarship on Jewish texts begged the question of what was meant by Judaism(s). This reconsideration of Paul and Judaism in turn then paved the way for a revival of the view that early Christianity was a messianic sect within Judaism. Previously, the Jewish character of the New Testament documents was gauged against a relatively monochromatic depiction of Judaism and found to be lacking. But the more diverse and

---

1. Robert Brawley has made important contributions to the conversation about the depiction of Jews in Luke-Acts and its relationship to Judaism. See Brawley, *Luke-Acts*, and "God of Promises," 279–96. For an overview of scholarly perspectives on Luke's treatment of Jews and Judaism, see Tyson, *Luke*.

2. Stendahl, "Paul," 78–96.

3. Sanders, *Paul*.

robust portrait of early Judaism that continues to emerge opened the way to conceive not only of "Pauline Judaism" but also other forms of "Christian Judaism."[4] As early Christianity became a predominately Gentile phenomenon, Judaism increasingly served as the foil against which Christian groups defined themselves. Nevertheless, the movement spearheaded by Jesus in Galilee as well as the network of messianic communities that emerged throughout the Roman Empire after his death and resurrection perceived themselves and indeed were probably seen by outsiders as expressions of early Judaism. Unfortunately the view that "early Christianity" in the first century was in some sense separate from the Judaism out of which it emerged has persisted in both scholarship and the popular imagination.[5] This view is probably more the case in scholarship on Luke-Acts than on any of the other Gospels, because the myth of the origins of "Gentile Christianity" is predicated on a particular reading of Acts that differentiates the mission to Gentiles as an early and discrete epoch in the history of salvation.[6]

The story of what has come to be known as the "parting of the ways" between Christianity and Judaism is both complicated and contested. From the earliest years when the Jesus movement began to spread throughout the Roman Empire, Acts suggests that Gentiles were more responsive than Jews to the message of a crucified messiah raised from the dead. An historical assessment of the percentage of Jewish and Gentile believers is difficult to make. It is apparent from the New Testament documents that Gentile believers were socialized into communities of Christ that also included Jewish believers and that these

---

4. "Christian Judaism" is a designation used frequently in Matthean scholarship, but could also be applied to assemblies of Christ in various regions that included Jews and Gentiles and whose identity and practice continued to be shaped by Israel's Scriptures. Mark Nanos has proposed the term "apostolic Judaism." See Nanos, "Paul and Judaism."

5. The term "early Christianity" is anachronistic and hence in quotation marks because its use reinforces the perception that these communities were distinct from Judaism. Given the diversity of "early Christianity," as well as early Judaism and Greco-Roman society, it seems best to imagine assemblies of Christ in different geographical areas that functioned within a network of relationships with communities of believers in other regions and also maintained some relationship with local Jewish communities.

6. The reasons for this perspective are complex, but it is perhaps most clearly articulated in Conzelmann's *Heilsgeschichte* schema. One significant consequence of this view is that Luke is the one Gospel consistently thought to be written by a Gentile. See Conzelmann, *Theology*.

communities were predominantly Jewish in ethos. Baptism into the community of Christ entailed becoming monotheists in a polytheistic world, and we know from Paul's letters that these former pagans paid a social price for their exclusive devotion to the One God of Israel (cf. 1 Thess 2:14; Gal 3:4; Phil 1:29–30).[7] Moreover, the practices and beliefs of these early communities of Christ were grounded in the Scriptures of Israel. So for all intent and purpose, the earliest assemblies of Christ appeared from every angle of vision to belong to a Jewish messianic sect that continued to be related in some respects to local Jewish communities throughout the Mediterranean world. The separation of what eventually became a predominantly Gentile messianic movement from its Jewish roots was much more gradual and probably occurred much later than has been previously thought.[8] This notion of a gradual and later separation of Christianity from Judaism is an important observation for the essays in this volume, because how one perceives the outlook, milieu, and purpose of Luke-Acts vis-à-vis early Judaism has a direct bearing on how one perceives the ways in which Luke-Acts negotiated the realities of imperial society.

Luke-Acts, which begins with Jesus' birth and ministry in Galilee and culminates with Paul preaching in Rome, depicts the early Christian movement as a form of messianic Judaism. Luke was written between 80 and 110 CE, so its response to the Roman Empire must be assessed in terms of Jewish imperial relations after the Roman Judean War of 66 to 70 CE. The destruction of Jerusalem by the Romans in that war fundamentally redefined not only Judaism but also Jewish relations with the Roman Empire. The fact that the Romans did not allow the Temple to be rebuilt revealed a special prejudice against Jews and was a major cause of conflict over the next 65 years.[9] Roman policy toward the Jews impacted the reconfiguration and development of Judaism after the destruction of the Jerusalem Temple in 70 CE, and this included those groups that acclaimed Jesus as messiah and Lord. The view that that one of the purposes of Luke-Acts was to present "Christianity" as a legitimate religion (*religio licita*) in the Roman Empire is predicated on a corresponding premise that "the Way" was a religious movement

---

7. I translate ἐπάθετε as "suffer" in Gal 3:4.

8. See Becker and Reed, *Ways*; and Dunn, *Jews*.

9. Goodman, *Rome and Jerusalem*, 428.

distinct from Judaism. To track the transition to a different view, we turn to a brief consideration of Lukan scholarship in recent years.

Luke's View of the Roman Empire in the History of Scholarship

By and large Luke-Acts has been regarded as one work of two-volumes in which the narrator continues the story of the ministry and mission of Jesus in Acts by recounting the history of the early church.[10] There is clear continuity. Acts takes up several of the themes in the Gospel of Luke, and there are many instances in which characters in Acts exemplify the teaching and practices of Jesus.[11] Much has been written on the genre of both the Gospel of Luke and Acts, but the designation of Acts as an *apologia* has fundamentally shaped the perception of Luke's perspective on the Roman Empire. Some of the most influential Lukan scholars, namely Cadbury, Conzelmann, and Bruce, argued that Luke's primary purpose was to persuade Roman officials that Christianity was not a political threat to the Empire.[12] A variation of the apologetic perspective suggests that the two-volume work served to present the early Christian movement as a legitimate religion (*religo licitia*) within the Roman Empire. According to this view, Luke wrote an *apologia pro imperio* to address "a church harboring anti-Roman sentiment" and to convince the church that the Roman Empire was not a threat to them.[13] Other scholars have maintained that Luke-Acts was written as a defense of Christianity against Judaism or paganism, or a defense of Paul. Nevertheless, the proposal that Luke-Acts was written as a political apology has become the default view in the majority of Lukan scholarship. As a result, a prevailing opinion is that Luke-Acts reflects a positive stance toward the Roman Empire and hence is politically innocuous.

The view that Luke presents a positive or at least an uncritical portrait of the Roman Empire has mostly gone unchallenged until quite recently. More than thirty years ago Richard Cassidy proposed a political

10. Two works that raise questions about the unity of Luke-Acts are Parsons and Pervo, *Luke-Acts* and, more recently, Walters, *Authorial Unity*.

11. See Talbert, *Literary Patterns*.

12. Cadbury, *Luke-Acts*, 308–15; Conzelmann, *Theology*; Bruce, *Acts*, 15–44.

13. Walaskay, *Rome*. See a survey of the apologetic readings of Acts in Esler, *Community and Gospel*, 205–19.

reading of the Gospel of Luke in *Jesus, Politics, and Society: A Study of Luke's Gospel*. Cassidy was ahead of his time inasmuch as thoroughgoing political readings did not begin to impact New Testament interpretation until the early 1990s. We will return to that shift shortly. First, however, it is necessary to demonstrate why it is untenable to adopt the view that Luke takes a positive stance towards the Roman Empire. Although Luke-Acts does not overtly criticize the Roman Empire as such, neither does Luke-Acts consistently portray the Roman Empire in a positive light.

In his 2002 essay "The State They Were In: Luke's View of the Roman Empire," Steve Walton summarizes and critically engages five perspectives on Luke-Acts.[14] Walton offers counterpoints to those who attribute to Luke a pro-imperial point of view. He points out that even though Luke is the only Gospel to set the story of Jesus and the Jesus movement on a political stage by naming the Roman rulers and officials (Luke 2:1–2; 3:1–2; Acts 18:12–17; 21–22; 23:31—24:6; 24:27—26:32; 27:1, 11, 31), the benefits of the *pax Romana* are never explicitly mentioned.[15] Furthermore, the characterization of Pilate and the Roman judicial system in the trial of Jesus is critical to any understanding of Luke's attitude to the Empire. Those who claim that Luke reflects a positive stance towards the Roman Empire take Pilate's threefold declaration of Jesus' innocence as putting him in a favorable light. But, as Walton observes, Pilate executes Jesus even though he concedes he has done nothing wrong according to Roman law. This portrayal makes Pilate all the more culpable.[16]

Luke's depiction of the Roman Empire's officials, soldiers, and justice system continues in Acts where the evidence is a little more ambiguous. On the one hand, John's instructions to those being baptized (3:1–10) are compatible with Augustan ideals for the groups mentioned. Moreover, Luke does provide an affirming depiction of Roman officials, especially centurions (Luke 7:1–10; Acts 10:1—11:18). On the other hand, in Acts, Paul frequently finds himself before Roman officials or in prison. As was the case in Jesus' trial before Pilate, the fact that Paul is pronounced innocent and generally cooperative does not necessarily

14. Walton, "State."

15. Ibid., 16.

16. Ibid., 20. Walton points out that the verb παραδίδωμι is used at least twenty times by Luke to mean "giving over" in persecution, arrest, betrayal or execution.

mean that the Roman officials and their judicial system acted with fairness and impartiality. Walton and others have pointed out that "Luke presents Roman officialdom 'warts and all,' and does not hesitate to tell of failings and corruption."[17]

What is evident from a consideration of Luke's attitude towards Rome regarding its officials and its judicial system is that Luke-Acts is neither straightforwardly pro nor con. If Luke's purpose was to present the Roman Empire as a hospitable habitat for the church at a time when it was coming to terms with the delay of the *parousia*, then he does not make a very persuasive case, for there is much about the portrayal of the Empire in Luke-Acts that would be cause for concern among followers of Jesus.[18] Nevertheless, one would be hard pressed to read Luke-Acts as issuing a direct challenge to the Roman Empire and imperial authorities. This begs the question, then, of Luke's purpose(s) in writing, as well as the question of the scholarly methods used to ascertain his aims.

There is no consensus about the purpose(s) or situation of Luke-Acts. However, the frequency of "apology" language does suggest that at least one of the reasons Luke wrote was to offer an apologetic defense of the Jesus movement.[19] In her essay "The Acts of the Apostles as an Apologetic Text," Loveday Alexander reviews and evaluates speeches and sermons in Acts according to five different types of apologetic texts. A key insight in her analysis of Acts is that disputes between followers of Jesus and the Jewish community take up a large portion of the narrative, with a number of formal trial scenes providing occasions for apologetic speeches.[20] Moreover, she observes that Luke's narrative presents numerous opportunities for Paul's self-defense before Roman magistrates in Philippi (16:11–24), Thessalonica (17:1–8) and Corinth (18:1–17). Nevertheless, in Philippi Paul needs to defend himself as a Jew before fellow Jews who brought him before city authorities.[21] In Corinth, Paul is charged in a Roman court with persuading people to worship contrary to the law. But the Roman proconsul Gallio was of the

---

17. Ibid., 23.

18. This is the view articulated by Conzelmann in *Theology*.

19. The verb ἀπολογέομαι occurs in Luke 12:11; 21:14 and in Acts 19:33; 24:10; 25:8; 26:1, 2, 24. The noun ἀπολογία occurs in Acts 22:1; 25:16.

20. Alexander, "Acts," 195.

21. Ibid., 198.

opinion that it was a matter of Jewish rather than Roman law that was at issue; and he dismissed the case in Rome (18:13).

In the dramatic scene in which the Roman judicial system hears Paul's case in Caesarea (Acts 24–26), Paul is presented as innocent of the charge on which he was tried, which was in fact an offence against Jewish law.[22] Alexander makes the important point that while Paul's final speech is made in Rome before a Roman tribunal, the bulk of the defense is addressed to a Jewish audience and answers charges concerned with matters of Jewish rather than Roman law.[23] Based on the fact that the greatest number of lines in the speeches and sermons in Acts are addressed to Jewish audiences, Alexander maintains that the Jews in Acts bring in the Romans as external arbitrators in disputes about Jewish custom and law. Alexander's close reading of the speeches leads her to posit that an ongoing intra-Jewish debate between church and synagogue was the situation being addressed by the apologetic of Acts.[24]

The Audience of Luke-Acts: Jews and Gentiles

A thoroughgoing and constant engagement with Jewish characters, institutions, and Scriptures in Acts as well as in the Gospel of Luke would seem to suggest an ongoing connection with Judaism. However, the dominant view in scholarship has been that Luke was writing for a Gentile community of Christ believers who no longer had any connection to the synagogue.[25] Is it possible that the implied audience of a work that seems to be so deeply rooted in Judaism was a community of Christ believers that did not include the Jews and did not have some relationship with the Jewish community? Esler presents a detailed argument for the view that Luke was writing for a mixed audience that included Jews and Gentile "God-fearers."[26] This view is consistent with the emphasis in

22. Ibid.

23. Ibid., 199.

24. Ibid., 205.

25. See Esler, *Community*, 31, who attributes the "virtually unanimous belief among New Testament scholars that the Christians for whom Luke wrote were predominantly Gentile" to the influential commentary on Acts by F. C. Overbeck published in 1870.

26. Esler, *Community*, 44. Significant is the fact that throughout Acts the evangelists who preached in the synagogues are described as winning converts among Jews as well as God-fearers. In Esler's view, however, Luke's community had acquired a sectarian status in relationship to Judaism (53–70). According to Esler, Luke presents

the narrative itself on the history and scriptures of Israel. Ninety percent of the words in the first two chapters of the Gospel of Luke come from the Septuagint, and both Luke and Acts are saturated in the language and imagery of Israel's Scriptures. The hopes and promises for Israel's restoration found in Israel's scripture are featured so prominently in the infancy narratives and threaded throughout the Gospel and Acts that they provide a key to ascertaining the larger purpose of the narrative. The canticles in the birth narrative invoke the covenants with Abraham (1:55, 73) and David (1:27, 32, 69); hence, they set up Luke's story of Jesus as a fulfillment of Israel's hope of restoration and salvation.

More than any other text in the New Testament, Luke-Acts tells the story of Jesus and the early church as a story of salvation. The noun σωτηρία occurs in Luke 1:69, 71, 77; 19:9; Acts 4:12; 7:25; 13:26, 47; 16:17 and 27:34.[27] Especially in the context of the birth narrative, the language and imagery of "salvation" invoke the sovereignty of God and stir up national hopes of deliverance from oppression. Two important themes emerge from Luke's use of salvation terminology. First, Mary's song of salvation announces a socio-political reversal by depicting God as "savior" who "has brought down the powerful from their thrones, and lifted up the lowly . . . filled the hungry with good things, and sent the rich away empty" (1:52–53). In addition to a reversal of fortunes, Mary's Song also announces a re-distribution of resources. Political overtones are also evident in Zechariah's prophecy that God will raise up a "horn of salvation" from the house of David, so "that we would be saved from our enemies and from the hand of all who hate us" (1:71). The phrase "rescued from the hands of our enemies" occurs again in 1:74 and raises the question of the identity of Israel's enemies. The fact that Luke alone

---

Christianity as the legitimate development of Judaism (65). If Luke is writing in the 80's, as Esler suggests, it doesn't seem necessary or likely that a definitive separation has occurred. Rather, it seems preferable to regard the "sect" or movement as still within Judaism, even if on the margins. Mikeal Parsons says that Acts clearly presents the "Christian" movement as one Jewish sect among several. See Parsons, *Luke,* 8. Parsons cites Tiede, who says that Acts reflects an intra-family struggle among Jews which, in the wake of the destruction of the Temple, was deteriorating into a fight over who is really the faithful "Israel." Jervell is one of the few scholars who maintains that Luke is primarily addressing Jewish Christ believers who have left the church and returned to the synagogue. See Jervell, *Luke* and *Theology.*

27. The verb σώζω occurs in Luke 6:9; 7:50; 8:12, 36, 48, 50; 9:24; 13:23; 17:19; 18:26, 42; 19:10; 23:35, 37, 39; Acts 2:21, 40, 47; 4:9, 12; 11:14; 14:9; 15:1, 11; 16:30; 27:20, 31. The term σωτήρ occurs in Luke 1:47; 2:11; Acts 5:31; 13:23.

among the Gospel writers explicitly sets the stage for this story of Jesus and his followers by identifying Augustus and the governor Quirinius as imperial powerbrokers (2:1–2) may be a way of naming or alluding to Israel's "enemies."[28] Taken together, the references to salvation encompass deliverance from oppression, poverty, illness, demons, and anything or anyone else opposed to God's purposes.[29]

The other important theme in the infancy narratives and throughout Luke-Acts is the universal scope of the promise of God's salvation. From the beginning of the Gospel of Luke, salvation is said to include all the "nations," including Israel. In Luke 2, Simeon, a "righteous" and "devout" man "looking for the consolation of Israel" (2:25), acclaims: "for my eyes have seen your salvation, which you have prepared in the presence of all peoples, a light for revelation to the Gentiles and for glory to your people Israel" (2:30–32). This hope for the redemption of the nation of Israel is expressed again at the end of the Gospel of Luke (24:21) and at the beginning of Acts (1:6). These passages refer to the promise of universal restoration that God announced long ago through God's holy prophets (Acts 3:19–21), and they serve as an interpretive key for the entire two-volume work.

According to Tannehill, the narrator of Luke-Acts believes that events are moving in a single direction toward the fulfillment of God's purpose of inclusive salvation.[30] Acts concludes with Paul speaking to the local leaders of the Jews in Rome and serving notice that "this salvation of God has been sent to the Gentiles; they will listen" (Acts 28:29). Although the Jews in Acts are frequently depicted as having rejected the message of salvation through Jesus (e.g. Acts 3:17–21; 4:11–12; 5:30–31; 7:51–52; 9:28–29; 13:44–47; 14:1–7), the hope of salvation still includes the restoration of Israel.[31] Nonetheless, the narrative requires audiences

---

28. The use of εἰρήνη three times in Luke 1:79; 2:14, 29 and throughout the Gospel and Acts (Luke 7:50; 8:48; 10:5; 11:21; 12:51: 14:32; 19:38, 42; 24:36; Acts 9:31; 10:36; 12:20; 15:33; 16:36; 24:2) would likely have been heard as contrasting God's promise of "peace" or *shalom* with the *pax Romana*.

29. Jesus' discernment and enactment of "God's purpose" and opposition to God's purposes are important motifs in Luke-Acts. See Green, *Theology,* 28–35.

30. Tannehill, "Story," 325–39.

31. Jervell, "God's Faithfulness," 31–32, rightly underlines the fact that the promises of *salvation* are given to Israel and never taken away from them. The history of Israel never comes to an end, but continues without breach in the church. The church in Acts, then, "is nothing but Israel—not a new Israel, but the one and only people of God, Israel in a new phase of history, namely, that of Jesus."

to revise their expectations of what this restoration will look like and whom it will include, namely the Gentiles. Moreover, the narrative is designed to inspire followers of Jesus to yield to the power of the Spirit by embracing the vision and enacting the practices through which God will bring about this restoration.

From a narrative critical point of view, there is common agreement that the central purpose of Luke-Acts is to depict the fulfillment of God's promises recorded in Israel's scriptures to "save" and "restore" the people of God. The main point of contention about the purpose(s) of Luke-Acts centers on its historical, religious, and social context and the rhetorical strategy of the narrative as a whole. As we have seen, there has been a general lack of appreciation for the Jewish character of this narrative and of the Jewish elements of the audience it presupposes. Another point of contention has been the tendency to construe Luke's depiction of God's purpose(s) in theological terms. Walton rightly criticizes Conzelmann for placing Jesus within a Jewish "religious" framework that attempts to show Christianity as politically neutral. He points out that Conzelmann was operating with a division of "religion" and "politics" untenable for the first century, a view that has nevertheless persisted in Lukan studies and in New Testament interpretation generally.[32]

In the context of the Roman Empire, phrases like "kingdom of God," "son of God," and Davidic messiah were freighted with political significance. Moreover, the promise of and hope for salvation for God's people and for the restoration of Israel are unambiguously political. It is common in Lukan scholarship to characterize Luke-Acts as a story of God fulfilling promises of salvation for Israel and the nations. But in an imperial context, the salvation of Israel from her enemies and the restoration of Israel as a nation, as well as a messianic mission to the "nations" (ἐθνῶν), are literary and scriptural themes that clearly have political force. What does it mean in the context of the Roman Empire for Luke to affirm that Jesus is a Davidic messiah who will reign over a restored and united Israel that now includes non-Israelites?[33] In antiquity, religion, politics, and economics were inextricably linked, that

32. Walton, "State," 17.

33. See Wolter who maintains that Messiah Jesus will restore the βασιλεία for Israel (Acts 1:6); and that he will reign forever on the throne of David over the house of Jacob (Luke 2:32–33). Wolter, "Israel's Future."

is to say that they were all seen to be aspects of the same social fabric of everyday life. A good example of this on a more local level is Paul's exorcism of "a slave girl who had a spirit of divination and brought her owners a great deal of money by fortune-telling" (Acts 16:16–24). When the girl's owners realize her diminished capacity to make money, they brought Paul and Silas to the magistrates and accused them: "These men are disturbing our city; they are Jews and are advocating customs that are not lawful for us as Romans to adopt or observe"(16:21). This is example in Luke-Acts where acknowledging the sovereignty of the "Most High God" causes friction in the narrative with imperial society. In attempting to ascertain perspectives on and responses to the Roman Empire in Luke-Acts, we need a more integrated and nuanced approach that can discern the social, political, and economic implications of theological themes.

If Luke's inclusive message of Israel's restoration and salvation from her enemies encapsulates the purpose of God and the narrator, then the narrative is opposed to whatever stands in the way of its realization. Therefore, while Luke-Acts may not directly challenge the Roman Empire *per se*, it can be said to be counter-imperial inasmuch as it presents a wisdom or strategy for renewal that is set in contrast to key claims of Greco-Roman society. In Luke-Acts, Jesus is depicted both as prophet engaged in teaching and healing in Galilee and as risen Lord of the church who mediates the sovereignty of the One God of Israel. So, for example, when Peter refuses to comply with the Sanhedrin's injunction against teaching in Jesus' name because "we must obey God rather than any human authority" (Acts 5:29), this means any Jewish or Roman authority that would impede the enactment of God's purpose through Jesus and "the Way." More than that, the Divine sovereignty to which Jesus and his followers answer also *authorizes* specific practices and a communal form of life that are in many respects contrary to imperial culture. Jesus' teaching to love your enemies and lend without expecting anything in return (Lk 6:27–36) as well as Luke's emphasis on almsgiving (Lk 11:41; 12:43; Acts 9:36; 10:2, 4, 31; 24:17) and the sharing of possessions (Acts 2:45; 4:3237) are but a few examples of behavior that was uncharacteristically Roman.[34]

34. Most of what would be regarded as counter-cultural to Greco-Roman values and norms in Luke-Acts has its roots in Torah and the prophetic tradition. So, the counter-imperial message of Luke-Acts is inextricably tied to the counter-imperial

Luke-Acts as Alternative Social Vision to the Roman Empire

When Luke-Acts is interpreted in the light of the more intricate and diverse portrait of early Judaism that began to emerge with the new perspective on Paul, it becomes apparent that what is being narrated is an account of a messianic movement that spread throughout the Roman Empire with a view to encompassing all the nations.[35] Luke-Acts addresses a community that should be regarded as a Jewish group engaged in intra-Jewish dialogue with other Jewish groups about the future of Israel after the destruction of the Jerusalem temple in 70 CE. Therefore, Luke's perspective on and response to the reality of the Roman Empire needs to be evaluated in terms Jewish-imperial relations. However, as we discovered with early Judaism, a more complex model of the Roman Empire is needed. In the 1990's, Pauline scholars began to take a closer look at Paul's gospel and letters in terms of their critique of Roman imperial ideology.[36] Much of that work focused on increased awareness of the importance of the imperial cult in the Roman provinces and the inherent tension between Christological claims in the New Testament and competing claims made by and on behalf of the emperor. It is well known that κύριος and υἱοῦ θεοῦ were titles also ascribed to the emperor. More recently, there have also been attempts to examine the significance of these terms in Luke-Acts vis-à-vis the imperial cult.[37]

What can be somewhat misleading, however, is the claim, whether implied or explicit, that New Testament writers were primarily interested in challenging the Roman imperial ideology. Except for the brief period of Hasmonean rule, post-exilic Judaism had existed as a temple state in Jerusalem and as a *politeuma* in the Diaspora under successive imperial regimes. Only under extreme circumstances and in response to par-

---

character of early Judaism. For a contrast and comparison of the Jewish and Roman ways of life, see Goodman, *Rome and Jerusalem*. Seth Schwartz has recently argued that Judaism fundamentally rejected the reciprocity-based social dependency and the emphasis on honor that were characteristic of Mediterranean society in general and Roman society in particular. Schwartz, *Jews*.

35. On the importance of Jerusalem and the table of nations in Luke-Acts see Parsons, *Luke*, 86–95.

36. See Horsley, ed., *Paul and Empire*; Horsley, ed., *Paul and Politics*; Horsley, ed., *Paul and the Roman Imperial Order*.

37. See Rowe, "Luke-Acts"; and Howell, "Imperial Authority."

ticularly egregious acts of disrespect or violence by the *imperium*, such as was the case with Antiochus IV, did Jews directly challenge imperial authority. For most of Jewish history during the Second Temple Period, fidelity to the one God whom Jews venerated as the sovereign creator of the universe was not regarded as incompatible with acknowledging the sovereignty of the ruling authorities.[38] Roman relations with Judaism changed, however, after 70 CE. The war itself and the fact that Roman authorities would not allow the temple to be rebuilt marked a shift in policy that indicated extraordinary prejudice against Jews; and this was a major source of conflict for the next sixty-five years.[39] The centrality and symbolic significance of Jerusalem in Luke-Acts is noteworthy in this respect, and may reflect the strained relationship between Judaism and the Roman Empire in a post-70 world.

The prominence of Jerusalem and the temple in Luke-Acts is inextricably linked to the theme of the restoration of Israel set out in the first two chapters of the Gospel and reiterated at both the end of the Gospel and at the beginning of Acts.[40] Zechariah's prophecy that Israel would be delivered from the hands of her "enemies" (1:70, 74) would more than likely have conjured up for hearers memories of the destruction of Jerusalem and Roman oppression of Jews. The birth canticles and the numerous other citations from and allusions to Israel's scriptures raise the audience's expectation that Luke's story of Jesus is a story of God rescuing the people of God from imperial abuses of power. The birth canticles pass judgment on an imperial world structured contrary to God's purposes and announce God's alternative reign.[41] The political force of the promise of salvation in the context of a narrative with numerous references to Roman rulers and their collaborators is

38. According to Shaye Cohen, the prophecies of Jeremiah provided the model for the political behavior of Jews who lived under foreign rule in antiquity. From Jeremiah's perspective, the fall of Jerusalem and the triumph of Babylonia were the consequence not of sin and punishment but of immutable fate. The conviction underlying this view was that God controlled the destiny of nations and empires. The hope was that God would restore Israel to political independence, but in the meantime Jews were exhorted to support their conquerors and pray for the welfare of the countries in which they lived (cf. Jer. 29:5–7). Cohen, *Maccabees*, 27–30.

39. Goodman, *Rome and Jerusalem*, 428.

40. On the "restoration of Israel" *topos* in Luke-Acts, see Ravens, *Luke*.

41. In their interpretations of the canticles in Luke 1–2, the articles in this volume by Barbara Reid and Warren Carter both emphasize the announcement of God's alternative reign.

evident. But in the aftermath of the Jewish wars and the destruction of the Temple it begs the question of how this promise will be fulfilled and what salvation might look like during a time when Judeans still live under Roman rule.

The question of how the overtly political hopes evoked by the birth canticles acclaiming the restoration of Israel will be actualized and how the imperial order will be transformed is really a question of how the sovereignty and purposes of God are manifest. However, Divine sovereignty and purpose are actualized not only within the narrative world of Luke-Acts, but also in and through those impelled to embody Luke's story of Jesus and the community of his followers. The rhetorical strategy of Luke-Acts is to empower audiences to enact this story of Jesus and his followers in their life together. In other words, the impending transformation proclaimed in Luke-Acts occurs not only within the narrative world of the text, but also in the social world in front of the text as individuals and communities perform the vision of life set forth. Hence, Luke-Acts is not interested in critiquing imperial ideology as such, but rather in inspiring audiences to adopt life-giving values and practices that are set in contrast to the imperial way of life.

Although religious rituals, inscriptions, and other visual representations extolling the glory of the Roman Empire were ubiquitous throughout the provinces,[42] these did not impact the quality of ordinary people's lives as much as did the imperial socio-political system that levied taxes, controlled resources and administered justice. It is within this more local and practical sphere of influence that we would expect to find Luke's two-volume narrative negotiating the realities of imperial society with a view to shaping the beliefs and behavior of hearers. So in addition to the characterization of Roman officials and their collaborators throughout Luke-Acts, it is also important to consider how Luke's representation of the imperial system serves as backdrop against which the practices and patterns of life characteristic of God's reign are depicted in the narrative. Throughout Luke-Acts, Jesus and the community of his followers mediate and embody divine power in ways that cause them to act contrary to the imperial cultural system and those who represent it.

It is this connection between power and form of life that is crucial to understanding how Luke engages the imperial system. Martin

42. See Zanker, *Power.*

Goodman has emphasized how important it was to the elite living in the imperial world to live in what he calls a "Roman way."[43] Luke's Jesus is a prophet who challenged a Roman social system that benefited a select few in whose hands power was concentrated at the expense of a majority of people who were beholden to them. Moreover, as a teacher, Jesus set out core values and practices that served as the basis for a counter-imperial pattern of life in community, which in Acts is called "the Way."[44] Luke-Acts does not just set up a contest between Divine sovereignty and imperial power as such, but rather sets up an alternative world where God's purpose and power find expression through characters and behaviors that improve the quality of life of those who were marginalized and dispossessed by the imperial system.

A case in point is Jesus' teaching on the economy of God's kingdom in Luke 6:32–36 and his direct assault on the patronage ethic upon which imperial society was founded. Patronage was a system of reciprocal relationships of mutual benefit based on inequality. Luke writes for people who live in a world where a handful of elites controlled almost all of the resources as well as the social and political structures that determined peoples' lives. The majority of people were clients who were dependent upon and controlled by patrons who required their undivided loyalty. Approximately ninety percent of people in the Roman Empire lived around subsistence level.[45] So the majority of people were preoccupied with basic needs of food and shelter. It is precisely this experience of life under Roman rule that is alluded to in Mary's Song: "[God] has brought down the powerful from their thrones, and lifted up the lowly; [God] has filled the hungry with good things" (1:52–53). In his inaugural sermon in Nazareth Jesus uses the words of Isaiah to describe his ministry as one of liberating people from captivity. The mention of the "poor" picks up the theme of Mary's Song. The "year of the Lord" refers to the "year of jubilee" and the restoration that served to relieve the plight of the poor (Lev 25).[46] As a whole, the passage signals to the audience that the ministry of Jesus will address issues of economic distress. This is an emphasis throughout Luke's narrative;

43. Goodman, *Rome and Jerusalem*, 150.

44. On Luke's depiction of Jesus as prophet in the Gospel of Luke, see Croatto, "Jesus" 451–65.

45. See Friesen's poverty scale in "Poverty"; and "Injustice."

46. See Ringe, *Jesus*.

and the strategic location of the Nazareth speech suggests that the hope of salvation should be understood, at least in part, as deliverance from imperial oppression (1:52; 6:20; 7:22; 14:13, 21; 16:20, 22).

The Greek term for "release" (ἄφεσις) in Luke 4:18–19 in both its verbal and noun forms is used repeatedly along with other related words in the Gospel of Luke to call attention to the action of releasing or freeing people from something. In fact, Jesus' ministry in Luke could be succinctly characterized as a ministry of release. But since Luke casts Jesus in the role of prophet and teacher, he depicts Jesus' ministry as more than a series of episodic moments of "release" strung together. Rather, as prophet, Jesus also addresses the underlying causes of economic oppression. Jesus' teaching in his second Galilean speech further elucidates his practical approach to liberating "captives" (Luke 6). In 6:30 he recommends a specific practice to deal with the problem of poverty in Greco-Roman society: "Give to everyone who begs from you; and if anyone takes away your goods, do not ask for them again." Then in 6:32–36 Jesus elaborates on and provides theological grounding for the exhortation not to request repayment.

> If you love those who love you, what credit is that to you? For even sinners love those who love them. If you do good to those who do good to you, what credit (χάρις) is that to you? For even sinners do the same. If you lend to those from whom you hope to receive, what credit (χάρις) is that to you? Even sinners lend to sinners, to receive as much again. But love your enemies, do good, and lend, expecting nothing in return. Your reward will be great, and you will be children of the Most High; for [God] is kind to the ungrateful and the wicked. Be merciful, just as your Father is merciful. (Luke 6:27–36)

In addition to offering a practical strategy for assisting the poor, Jesus here also opposes the patronage model of reciprocity and power that governed interpersonal relationships in Greco-Roman society. Releasing others from debt and obligation subverts a patronage system that kept people beholden. Instead, he recommends a practice of divine generosity that would encourage solidarity and mutuality.

In Luke 6:32–34, the word that is translated as "credit" in the NRSV is χάρις. In the New Testament χάρις is usually translated as "grace," but it was also widely used to denote a gift or benefit conferred by a patron as well as the client's response of gratitude.[47] By telling followers to give and to do good without expecting anything in return, Jesus both invokes and subverts the foundational pattern of reciprocity in Greco-Roman society that kept people obligated and submissive. Patron-client relations were characterized by inequality and reciprocity; but, more than that, patronage was a totalizing cultural system that encompassed every dimension of life. In the Roman Empire, patronage was a dominant and generalized form of institutionalized resource allocation.[48] As Halvor Moxnes has noted, the central concern of first-century Greco-Roman economy was to have power to control the economic system and to expropriate surplus.[49] This economic system was founded on a reciprocity ethic that kept masses indebted and ingratiated to patrons. Moreover, these patronage ties fostered a sense of loyalty, obligation and indebtedness that undermined social forms of solidarity and equality.[50]

If Jesus' teaching in Luke 6 is seen as part of the narrative arc that began with the poetic description of salvation and restoration set out in the canticles, then it serves as the foundation for an alternative social vision that is mediated and modeled by Jesus and other characters in the Gospel. The early references to the covenants with Abraham and David foreshadow Jesus' proclamation and formation of an inclusive and nonhierarchical community that operates according to economic principles and practices that challenged the reciprocity ethic characteristic of Greco-Roman society. In telling followers to give without expecting anything in return, Jesus is doing more than encouraging individual followers to be charitable. Just as the canticles in the birth narrative announce that the sovereign creator is about to effect salvation and restoration on behalf of the world, so Jesus is here succinctly proposing a strategy for how this salvation and restoration will be enacted by the covenant community living out a kingdom economy predicated on Divine generosity. Salvation and restoration are actualized as those who hear Jesus' words and do them (6:46) release one another from indebtedness and obligation and embody the beneficence and mercy of the sovereign creator in their dealings with one another (6:35). In other words, by refusing to participate in the reciprocity ethic, the covenant

47. Danker, *Greek-English Lexicon*, 1079–80.

48. See Johnson and Dandeker, "Patronage."

49. Moxnes, *Economy*, 27.

50. Johnson and Dandeker, "Patronage," 223–24.

community is "released" from a patronage system that was at the nub of their oppression in order to enact an alternative way of life that privileged and empowered those who had been socially and economically marginalized.

The realization of God's promises of salvation announced in Scripture and actualized through the power of the Spirit by Jesus and his followers is the main plot of Luke-Acts. However, the emphasis on salvation and restoration throughout the two-volume work indicates that the Roman imperial world reflected in the narrative is a harsh world for many and hence in need of transformation. It would appear that Luke-Acts was written to promote an allegiance to a Divine kingdom that was at cross-purposes with the imperial world order. Throughout the narrative, Luke often describes how Roman society works, only to contrast it with the values and practices of Jesus and his followers. The universal scope of the vision of Luke-Acts suggests that the hope of the renewal of Israel set out at the beginning of the Gospel has become nothing less than a strategy for reforming society as a whole or, better yet, creating an alternative one, through those who embody the character of the sovereign creator.

The Essays in Luke-Acts and Empire

The essays in this volume all deal with some aspect of the ways in which Luke-Acts engages the reality of the Roman Empire. In "Singing in the Reign: Performing Luke's Songs and Negotiating the Roman Empire (Luke 1–2)," Warren Carter appeals to the performative function of African-American Spirituals and protest songs in the context of slavery and Apartheid to read the canticles in Luke 1–2 as performative songs. He contends that these songs serve to name contexts of oppressive suffering, bestow dignity on those who were dishonored, and foster hope for improved living conditions. Over against an elite-dominated social order maintained by the emperor, Luke's songs foster communal solidarity in the struggle against imperial hegemony and celebrate the inauguration of a socio-economic transformation.

Barbara Reid also focuses on the first chapters of the Gospel of Luke. In her essay, "Women Prophets of God's Alternative Reign," she calls attention to the manner in which Luke sets the stage for his story of Jesus by naming the Roman rulers and the Jewish leaders who collaborated with them. The numerous references to these officials in Luke keeps the reality of Roman imperial rule and its dominance over every aspect of life before hearers of the Gospel. As part of Luke's strategy for resisting this imperial ideology, the angelic and prophetic figures in the first two chapters of Luke—Gabriel, Elizabeth, Zechariah, Mary, Simeon, and Anna—articulate God's alternative reign. Mary as a prophetic figure features most prominently in Reid's essay. In the Magnificat, Mary challenges Roman imperial power by singing about a leveling of the distribution of goods and power. Furthermore Luke's depiction of Mary challenges the portrait of the ideal Roman woman. Mary is portrayed as an empowered person who chooses to serve God.

In "Jerusalem and Rome in Luke-Acts: Observations on the Structure and the Intended Message," Michael Bachmann joins the ranks of Robert Brawley and others who have argued against "the standard reading of Luke-Acts as a triumph of gentile Christianity over Judaism."[51] He offers an in-depth analysis of the continued significance of Jerusalem and the Temple in Luke-Acts, and he explores the relationship of Jerusalem and the Temple to Rome. In tracking the movement of Luke's narrative toward Rome, Bachmann points out that in addition to being the political capital of the Empire, Rome had religious significance. He claims that Luke describes the movement toward Rome in a way that features Jerusalem and the Temple as symbols that keep alive the Jewish hope of restoration and salvation. Bachman makes the interesting observation that Stephen's speech in Acts 7 presumes the existence of a "heavenly sanctuary," and that Paul's journey to Rome is legitimized "from above." This leads Bachman to interpret the final climactic scene of Luke-Acts in Rome as a matter of keeping alive Jewish hopes connected with Jerusalem and the Temple, a hope now shared with Gentiles. In Luke-Acts, Rome replaces neither Jerusalem nor worldwide Judaism.

Jae Won Lee utilizes a postcolonial lens to consider "Pilate and the Crucifixion of Jesus in Luke-Acts." Her thesis is that Luke portrays Pilate as part of a system that makes a travesty of Roman (in)justice. Lee's postcolonial reading focuses on issues of imperial dynamics and sheds light on some of the complexities of imperialism. She points out that people in Galilee and Judea had an indirect experience of the Roman Empire, because it was hidden behind governors, client kings, and local elite Judeans. Moreover, Lee emphasizes that collaboration among

51. The quote is from Brawley, *Luke-Acts*, 159.

colonized people is always a matter both of resisting and supporting the colonizers. Luke's development of the tension between Jesus and the imperial system is elucidated in terms of the "margins." The margins are described as a place of creative, critical engagement with hegemony. In Luke-Acts Jesus is characterized as one who restores marginalized people to the social order. In the trial narrative, Pilate personifies imperial power that perpetuates injustice. And Jesus' silence during the interrogation is interpreted as a refusal to acknowledge the system. Lee suggests that Jesus' silence establishes an alternative commitment to a community that is not dependent upon the dominant center.

The remaining three essays in this volume focus on Acts. In "Paul, Agrippa, and Antiochus: Two Persecutors in Acts in Light of 2 Macc 9," Kazuhiko Yamazaki-Ransom proposes that Luke was drawing upon the description of Antiochus IV Epiphanes death in 2 Macc 9 in his account of Agrippa's death in Acts 12. Antiochus IV is a persecutor of Jews, while Agrippa I is a persecutor of Christians. Luke depicts the Jewish king Agrippa playing the role usually attributed to oppressive Gentile kings in traditional Jewish literature. Yamazaki-Ransom points out that Paul in Acts is also portrayed as a former persecutor and enemy of the church in Acts; in that sense, Paul was like Agrippa I and Antiochus IV. However, Yamazaki-Ransom reads Paul's conversion in the light of 2 Macc 9 and emphasizes the similarities between Paul and Antiochus IV. At one time, both were violent persecutors. Moreover, Antiochus IV vows to visit every inhabited place to proclaim the power of God. In this respect, Paul's call to carry the Lord's "name before the Gentiles and kings and before the people of Israel" (Acts 9:15) is comparable. The difference is that Paul carries out his mission while the hope of Antiochus IV is never fulfilled, because God struck him down.

In "Trying Paul or Trying Rome? Judges and Accused in the Roman Trials of Paul in Acts," Steve Walton examines the three Roman trials of Paul in Acts and asks whether it is not really the Roman judicial system and its representatives who are on trial. He links Paul's trials before the proconsul Gallio in Corinth and before the governors Festus and Felix in Caesarea with the Roman trial of Jesus in Luke's Gospel, and underlines the rhetorical impact of the declaration of their innocence. According to Walton, Gallio is portrayed as being under the control of God and giving a ruling that benefits the renewed people of God. Walton compares Felix to Pilate inasmuch as Felix finds Paul and his gospel to be appealing but nevertheless fails to respond positively to it. He describes Paul as "turning the tables" on Felix by speaking of the values that should be guiding his judgment. Paul does not expect justice from Festus, because, like Felix, Festus was "wanting to do a favor for the Jews" (Acts 25:9). The story ends with Festus and Agrippa saying to one another, "This man is doing nothing to deserve death or imprisonment" (Acts 26:31). Nevertheless, Paul is not set free, because he appealed to Caesar. Walton observes that although the governors as representatives of Roman justice consistently find Jesus and his followers innocent, their character flaws mean that justice is delayed or denied in practice. Nonetheless, what Luke emphasizes is the triumph of God's purpose in bringing Paul to Rome.

In "Paul's Allegiance to Lord Jesus as a Chained Prisoner in Rome: Luke's Ending Is in His Beginning," Richard Cassidy reads the ending of Acts in the light of Luke's Gospel. And he finds it to be a fitting conclusion to the two-volume narrative. Cassidy takes aim at the "political apologetic" interpretation of Luke-Acts that contends that Luke is tailoring his narrative to curry favor with Roman officialdom. He calls attention to Luke's depiction of Paul in chains in the capital of the Roman Empire and to Luke's portrayal of the corruption exhibited by Antonius Felix and Porcius Festus in adjudicating Paul's case. Cassidy emphasizes Luke's consistent depiction of Paul as proclaiming the "kingdom of God" in the capital precincts of an emperor who styles himself as "lord." Pivotal to his interpretation are the last four words of Acts, "with all boldness and without hindrance." Cassidy asserts that ἀκωλύτως is the word that sounds Luke's final chord, a word that refers to the quality of Paul's witness and not to favorable conduct on the part of Roman officials. He ties the ending of Acts back to the opening chapters of Luke's Gospel in which the claims of Caesar are contrasted with the sovereign status of Jesus and God's kingdom.

The essays in *Luke-Acts and Empire* are dedicated to Robert Brawley, who has made significant contributions to scholarship on Luke-Acts. The hope is that these essays continue the conversation and offer constructive proposals in the ongoing effort to understand Luke-Acts in relation to the realities of the Roman Empire and the realities of Judaism in this period. The volume is offered in the generous and open spirit of Robert Brawley.

Singing in the Reign

Performing Luke's Songs and Negotiating the Roman Empire (Luke 1–2)

Warren Carter

IN A COLLECTION OF ESSAYS, ROBERT BRAWLEY, THE HONOREE OF THIS volume, comments: "Readers of this volume will constantly encounter the problem of ethics—the inevitable failure. But they will also constantly encounter the hope of ethics. Here it is especially the hope that interpretations of the New Testament form both communities and persons for living accomplished lives."[1]

I explore in this chapter the dynamic of failed human efforts yet the hope of transformation as a foundational interplay in the songs of Luke 1–2.

Frederick Douglass writes in his autobiography about the songs sung by African-American slaves as expressive of the "soul crushing character of slavery":

> Nowhere outside of dear old Ireland, in the days of want and famine, have I heard sounds so mournful . . . I have sometimes thought that the mere hearing of these songs would have done more to impress the good people of the north with the soul crushing character of slavery than whole volumes exposing the physical cruelties of the slave system; for the heart has no language like song . . . [The songs] breathed the prayer and complaint of souls overflowing with the bitterest anguish . . . The

---

1. Brawley, *Character Ethics and the New Testament*, xii. It is a pleasure to honor the work of Professor Robert Brawley.

songs of the slaves represented their sorrows, rather than their joys. Like tears, they were a relief to aching hearts.[2]

Yet they expressed hopefulness and expectation of change, though in self-protective, disguised, and ambiguous ways. As Douglass and others plot their escape in 1836:

> We were at times remarkably buoyant, singing hymns, and making joyous exclamations, almost as triumphant in their tone as if we had reached a land of freedom and safety. A keen observer might have detected in our repeated singing of
>
> "O Canaan, sweet Canaan,
> I am bound for the land of Canaan,"
>
> something more than a hope of reaching heaven. We meant to reach the *North*, and the North was our Canaan.
>
> "I thought I heard them say
> There were lions in the way;
> I don't expect to stay
> Much longer here.
> Run to Jesus, shun the danger,
> I don't expect to stay
> Much longer here,"
>
> was a favorite air and had a double meaning. On the lips of some it meant the expectation of a speedy summons to a world of spirits; but on the lips of our company it simply meant a speedy pilgrimage to a free State, and deliverance from all the evils and dangers of slavery.[3]

In his *The Souls of Black Folks*, W. E. B. du Bois observes the combination of sorrowful lamenting and hopeful envisioning that the songs performed. They

> tell in word and music of trouble and exile, of strife and hiding; they grope toward some unseen power and sigh for the rest in the End . . . [yet in these] Sorrow Songs there breathes a hope—a faith in the ultimate justice of things. The minor cadences of despair change often to triumph and calm confidence. Sometimes it is faith in life, sometimes a faith in death, sometimes assurance of boundless justice in some fair world beyond. But whichever it

2. Douglass, "Life and Times," 502–3.
3. Ibid., 607–8.

is, the meaning is always clear: that sometime, somewhere, men will judge men by their souls and not by their skins.[4]

Bernice Johnson Reagon, reflecting on the performative function of protest songs and Spirituals sung during the civil rights struggle of the 1960s, also emphasizes their hope-promoting power: "They could not stop our sound. They would have to kill us to stop us from singing. Sometimes the police would plead and say, "Please stop singing." and you would just know that your word was being heard, and you felt joy. There is a way in which those songs kept us from being touched by people who would want us not to be who we were becoming . . . The only way you survive the singing is to open up and let go and be moved by it to another place."[5]

Cheryl Kirk-Duggan identifies further functions: "The Spirituals challenge the repetitive, terrible plot of racism by first telling the story and then suggesting a new vision of the story . . . In the Spirituals, the language tells about the evil and suffering, describes the relationship between divine and human characters; questions or describes the related action/reaction; and champions the just and decries the unjust." To so function, they assumed and addressed a common experience of oppression. In unmasking and protesting it: "African-American Spirituals are . . . chants of collective exorcism, aural, oral, stories or narratives that recite and expose communal subjugation and hope for change. These chants celebrate the remembrance that everyone has the right to live, a gift of life . . . [T]he persons singing this song ["This Little Light of Mine"] affirm their beingness, their own importance, without ever using words of self-esteem or personal pride, and without talking about the revolutionary power of one light amid vast darkness."[6] Subsequently, Kirk-Duggan's rich "womanist musings" specify various functions that Spirituals perform; they motivate, they plead for justice, they assume God's care, they affirm identity, they give voice to pain and dreams, they empower, they bestow dignity, they create meaning and purpose, they build community, they secure communal solidarity, they revise and

---

4. Du Bois, *The Souls of Black Folks*, 202, 206.

5. Quoted in Kirk-Duggan, *Exorcizing Evils*, 263. See also Greenway, *American Folksongs of Protest*; Epstein, *Sinful Tunes and Spirituals*; for the study of Spirituals, Cruz, *Culture on the Margin*.

6. Kirk-Duggan, *Exorcizing Evil,* 59–60.

rename reality. "Spirituals are songs of motivation that champion the possibility, the process, and the product of liberation and freedom."[7]

I have two vivid memories of the struggle against Apartheid in South Africa in the 1970s and 1980s. The first concerns the fear and intimidation I experienced while participating in New Zealand in protest marches against apartheid and against New Zealand's ongoing sporting, especially rugby, contacts with South Africa. Such matters were very controversial in rugby-mad New Zealand. Not surprisingly, protest marches were often confrontational, a contested space marked by clashing worldviews, walled in by snarling police dogs and lined by police in riot gear. The heightened presence of police reflected the New Zealand government's effort to reframe the issue from one of human rights to one of "law and order." My fear and intimidation, while very real, were of course nothing compared with the terror under which millions of South Africans lived their daily lives.

My second memory concerns television coverage of the funerals of South Africans killed in their struggle against apartheid. The funerals were highly politicized and dramatized vigils, with processions, crowds, flag-draped coffins, banners, slogans, dancing, speeches from leaders, and singing, providing key aspects of "symbolic repertoire."[8] Belinda Bozzoli in her marvelous study *Theatres of Struggle and the End of Apartheid* analyzes the theatricality of funerals in the segregated and poverty-stricken township of Alexandra after a revolt in 1986. Funerals were performances or political theater that presented "townships as symbolic spaces from which an undifferentiated mass of the suffering and the helpless deserved to be liberated." Providing "the central organizing storyline for this display" was the contested and variously defined notion of nationalism, the transformative vision of "emancipation from racism and colonial oppression."[9]

> The songs sung by youths at funerals were typical of the nationalist repertoire . . . The motifs of oppression, freedom, the benign father and sometimes the mother figure of nationalism, innocent suffering, and martyrdom by the 'children' of the nation and the biblical idea of a 'way' to freedom were all themes within them . . . :

7. Ibid., 158–68.

8. Bozzoli, *Theatres of Struggle*, 206–32.

9. Ibid., 206.

We the children of Africa need Freedom (2x)
Freedom, Freedom we don't have (2x)
It doesn't matter whether we are arrested
But we need freedom
It doesn't matter whether we are shot
But we need freedom

Their leaders were benign fathers:

Our Father Mandela (2x)
We are being shot by the police (2x)
We don't know what we have done (2x)
Our Father Sisulu (2x)
We are being shot by the police
We don't know what we have done (2x)

'Freedom' was the goal:

Rolihlahla Mandela, Freedom is in your hands
Show us the way to freedom
In this land of Apartheid
Mandela, Mandela, Freedom is in your hands
Show us the way to freedom
In this land of poverty."[10]

The songs, along with other aspects of the symbolic repertoire of funerals, named the present injustice, protested its reality, emboldened engagement against it, linked the local with larger "nationalist" contexts and narratives, articulated contrapuntal themes that envisioned a different world, secured and redefined community, and thereby negotiated power. C. Michael Hawn comments that such singing functioned to "unify the prayer of the suffering community, offering healing through

10. Ibid., 224–25. See also Gilbert, "Singing against Apartheid"; Olwage, ed., *Composing Apartheid*; also, the award-winning video documentary directed by Lee Hirsch of South African freedom music, *Amandla: A Revolution in Four Part Harmony*. For discussion of other songs, Hawn, "Singing with the Faithful," 115–16 for discussion of "Siyahamba" or "We are marching in the light of God." Hawn notes South African songs in contemporary hymn books: for example *United Methodist Hymnal* #497 "Thuma Mina"; *Chalice Hymnal* (1995) #30 "Masithi"; #442 "Siyahamba"; #499 "Hallelujah! Pelo Tso Rona"; also Hawn, "Siyahamba," 23–27; for the song Thula Sizwe, "Hush Nation, Do not cry; Our God will protect us. Freedom, We will get it; Our God will protect us" (http://singAfrica.londongt.org); see also the discussion of "David Dargie and South African Liberation Song" in Hawn, *Gather into One*, 104–47, and 125–26 for discussion of "Sikhulule' ("Lord, Liberate Us").

the solidarity of singing together, and maintaining hope in the face of seemingly insurmountable odds."[11]

These African-American and South African instances of songs as performative speech—there are numerous others from Korea[12] and Ireland,[13] for example—alert us to some of the dynamics at work when songs are involved in negotiating massive power differentials. At the risk of being reductionist and of concluding more than can be drawn from limited examples, it is possible to identify at least four interweaving dynamics that are evident as songs perform the important and multi-faceted work of negotiating contexts of power.

1. *Naming Contexts of Oppressive Suffering.* Songs emerge from, name, and engage, an oppressive status quo. They are contextual in that they name and engage the suffering and evil that are perceived to be ever-present. The songs protest these supposed "life-as-normal" dominant societal structures and official versions of reality as unacceptable. The songs refuse to accept them as normative or natural. The world is not as it should be.

2. *Bestowing Dignity.* The songs oppose the dehumanizing and degrading impact of oppression. They dignify those who suffer, because they do not deserve to suffer and because the suffering is not their fault. The songs affirm the worth of those in their midst. They strengthen resolve. They build courage and determination to survive. They effect healing. They are contrapuntal, contestive, against-the-grain, even as the language and the protest are coded and self-protective.

3. *Fostering Hope for Change.* The songs link the particular and personal experiences of suffering with larger, especially biblical, narratives of transformation. They locate the individual in a greater struggle. They demand justice and freedom. They thereby envision a different and better reality, at odds with the present one. They express and create hope for change.

11. Hawn, *Gather into One*, 125; see also "What is Liberation Hymnody?" 137–47.

12. My colleague, Dr. Namsoon Kang, has referred me to a Korean hymn based on the gospel episode of Jesus calming the storm, composed during Japanese colonization of Korea. See *The United Methodist Hymnal* # 476. Written by Helen Kim, a pioneering woman leader in Korean history, the hymn was well received by political protesters in Korea under President Park's dictatorship in the 60s to 70s.

13. Zimmerman, *Songs of Irish Rebellion.*

4. *Securing Communal Solidarity.* The songs strengthen community. They name a communal experience of suffering and a communal aspiration of transformation. They affirm the identity of a people in solidarity with each other struggling against a common enemy. They secure participation in the struggle for a new future.

Luke-Acts attests some familiarity with the dynamics of these songs. Paul and Silas' earth-shattering singing in prison in Philippi strengthens their bond with each other and their faith in God. Their singing serves to secure their freedom after the city's magistrates beat and imprison them "for customs that are not lawful for us as Romans to adopt or observe" (Acts 16:16–40). Luke's Gospel is only forty verses long when the first of four songs in the Gospel's opening two chapters appears. Mary celebrates God's action known to her in both her pregnancy and that of Elizabeth (Luke 1:46–56). Zechariah celebrates God's intervention and John the Baptist's roles in God's purposes (Luke 1:67–80). The angels perform the first Christmas cantata before the shepherds, praising God for the birth of Jesus (Luke 2:14). And in the temple, the elderly Simeon takes Jesus in his arms and praises God for the salvation for Jew and Gentile manifested in Jesus (Luke 2:29–32).

Previous work has investigated the songs' form, sources, redaction, and role in Luke's larger narrative.[14] My interest here is more circumscribed. What role might these songs perform in Luke's negotiation of Roman imperial power? Perhaps the dynamics identified above from African-American and South African oppression-engaging songs provide helpful entry points to Luke's songs. What might the presence or absence of these dynamics indicate about Luke's negotiation of Roman imperial power?[15]

---

14. For discussion, Farris, *The Hymns of Luke's Infancy Narratives;* Horsley, *Liberation of Christmas,* 107–20; Johnson, *Gospel of Luke;* Brown, *Birth of the Messiah,* 346–65; 377–92; 425–27; 456–60; Hendrickx, *Third Gospel for the Third World;* Green, *Gospel of Luke.*

15. I set aside the interesting question of the possible implications of this discussion for the origins of Luke's songs in chapters 1–2. Frequently, discussion of matters of origin and sources has been conducted as though a literary model was the only one. But attention, as here, to the performative and functional dimensions of the songs might suggest we might look profitably to contexts of oral/aural performance, perhaps in the worship life of early Christians.

Luke-Acts' interaction with Roman power in general is complex and contested.[16] Does the Gospel defend the empire to the church[17] or the church to the empire[18] or is it essentially disinterested in the empire?[19] Does it assure believers that there is no incompatibility between allegiance to Jesus and allegiance to the empire?[20] Does it guide followers when they are on trial before imperial officials?[21] Does it parallel imperial cult ideology and practices so as to reintegrate Jesus-followers "into the community from which it [the Gospel] had alienated them?"[22] Does it commend a "strategy of critical distance,"[23] or does it offer other perspectives that include subversion and accommodation?[24] I am not suggesting that attending to the songs of chapters 1–2 alone (often neglected in the "Luke-and-Rome" discussions) will solve the overall problem of Luke's relation to empire. The database, so to speak, is far too limited. Nevertheless, as one act of imperial negotiation among many others, the songs provide some insight into the dynamics of imperial negotiation performed in the Gospel's opening chapters.

To structure the discussion about these four songs in Luke 1–2, I will employ the four dynamics outlined above: contexts of oppressive suffering; bestowing dignity; envisioning change; and community solidarity. This structure should highlight significant dimensions in these songs as well as indicate any neglected dimensions.

Naming Contexts of Oppressive Suffering

Mary "rejoices in God my Savior because he has looked with favor on the lowliness/humiliation/oppression of his servant" (Luke 1:47b–48a).

---

16 I am following the useful summary of Walton, "The State They Were In," 11–41.

17. Walasky, *And So We Came to Rome*; Maddox, *The Purpose of Luke-Acts*.

18. E.g., Conzelmann, *The Theology of St Luke*, 137–49.

19. Jervell, *Theology of the Acts of the Apostles*, 15–16, 86–88, 100–106, 134; Franklin, *Christ the Lord,* 134–39.

20. Esler, *Community and Gospel in Luke-Acts*, 201–19.

21. Cassidy, *Jesus, Politics, and Society*; Cassidy, *Society and Politics in the Acts*, 145–70.

22. Brent, "Luke-Acts and the Imperial Cult," esp. 437–38.

23. Walton, "The State They Were In," 35.

24. Gilbert, "Luke-Acts and Negotiations of Authority; Burrus, "The Gospel of Luke and the Acts of the Apostles.

As the multiple translations suggest, the noun "lowliness/oppression" (ταπείνωσιν) can designate a range of situations. One situation comprises the "humiliation" of childlessness,[25] but this meaning is not relevant here. Mary is betrothed, not married, and not seeking to have a child. More significantly, the same term reappears in the plural in 1:52b to denote those of low social status, powerlessness, and poverty.[26] Mary belongs to and represents this group, the non-elite. Beyond this, while the word also denotes difficult but often unspecified circumstances,[27] its dominant meaning concerns oppressive and threatening circumstances. These circumstances may be more than personal.[28] They may also be communal, especially in terms of Israel's domination by foreign powers such as Egypt, Assyria, Babylon, Persia, and Syria, among others.[29] Given Luke's context, Mary, as with many others, lives under the oppressive Roman Empire ruled by a different "savior" and "god." Zechariah's song names this situation further as one dominated by "enemies" and by "those who hate us" (1:71, 74).

James Scott identifies three spheres of oppression in situations with huge disparities of power. Roman elites and their provincial allies exercised *material domination,* exacting agricultural production through taxation, services, and labor. Land ownership, the hard manual work of non-elites, including slave labor, and coerced extractions of production sustained the elite's extravagant and elegant elite way of life. There was no middle class; most people comprised the non-elite and were involved in agricultural production or worked as artisans and traders.[30] Elite alli-

25. Leah, Gen 29:32; Hannah, 1 Kings [LXX] 1:11.

26. Also Prov 16:19; Sir 11:12; 13:20; 20:11.

27. Pss 22(LXX21):22 unspecified enemies; 25(LXX24):18 sin?; 31(LXX30):7 unspecified enemies; 119(LXX118): 50, 92, 153; Sirach 2:4–5

28. For example, the pregnant slave-girl Hagar who, unprotected by Abraham, flees into the wilderness from Sarah's harshness Abraham (Gen 16:11); Jacob's flight from Laban (Gen 31:42), Joseph captive in Egypt (Gen 41:52); David, 2 Sam [2 Kings LXX] 16:12; Josephus' difficulties (Josephus *JW* 2.255).

29. Egypt, Deut 26:7; Philistines, 1 Sam [1 Kings LXX] 9:16; Arameans, Moabites, and Ammonites, 2 Kings [4 Kings LXX] 14:26–27; Egypt, Neh 9:9; Assyria, Judith 6:19; 7:32; 13:20; Persia, Esther 4:8; Babylon, Isa 40:2; 53:8; Babylon, Jer 2:24 [LXX]; Babylon, Lam 1:3, 7, 9; Syria, the Seluecid Antiochus IV Epiphanes, 1 Macc 3:51; and unspecified enemy nations (Pss 9:13; 136[LXX]:23). Josephus (*Ant* 2.205, 234, 238, 255) denotes Moses' threat to accomplish Egypt's downfall.

30. For a description of pre-industrial, agrarian societies in which most people are involved in agricultural production or as artisans and traders, see Lenski, *Power and*

ances also enacted *status domination* damaging the personal wellbeing of the subjugated non-elites.[31] Status domination—comprising social and economic practices, rituals, social interactions, and punishments— deprived people of dignity. It ensured humiliation, indignities, insults, degradation, and forced deference. It exacted an enormous personal toll of anger, resentment, and learned inferiority. *Ideological domination* utilized a set of convictions and/or narratives that justified and expressed elite oppression, privilege, self-benefiting rule, and societal inequality. The elite's political, economic, societal, and cultural hierarchical order and exploitative practices were sanctioned as the will of the gods. This stable, "natural," and immutable societal and cosmic order awed, impressed, and cowered the subordinated, while bolstering the elite.[32] This ideological domination comprised the "Great Tradition," the official version of reality. Mary's oppressive context shaped by Roman imperial power embodies these three forms of domination. All four songs name this oppressive context.

Luke's songs elaborate four aspects of oppressive powers (1:51–54). First the context is dominated by those designated as "the proud" (1:51b ὑπερηφάνους). The proud comprise much more than arrogant individuals. Rather, drawn from scriptural tradition, this term casts the whole imperial societal system in negative theological perspective as resistant to God's purposes. Throughout the scriptural tradition, the proud are those who are enemies of God. They are ungodly (Job 38:15; 40:7), rich and powerful (Sir 13:20; 21:4), often contrasted to and in conflict with the oppressed/lowly who experience God's favor (Ps 18[LXX17]:27; Prov 3:34). Their pride does not consist of "spiritualized" dispositions, but actions against the powerless and the poor (Sir 13:19–20). They tell lies and oppress the poor.[33] They mock and abuse (Sir 27:28). They stir up strife and bloodshed (Sir 27:15). Such actions are the way of the powerful. The "proud" include local elites and the most powerful rulers and empires such as Egypt (the exodus, 3 Macc 6:4), Israel's leaders (Isa 2:12), Babylon (Isa 13:11), the Egyptian ruler Ptolemy IV Philopater (3 Macc 1:27; 5:13), Syria under Antiochus Epiphanes (2 Macc 9:11; 4 Macc 4:15; 9:30), the domestic rulers of the Hasmoneans as well

Privilege, 189–296; Carter, *Roman Empire and the New Testament*.

31. Scott, *Domination*, 111; see 198 for summary chart.
32. Ibid., 2.
33. Pss 119[LXX118]:69, 78, 122; 140(LXX139):5; Sir 25:2.

as Rome (Ps Sol 17:13, 23; cf 2:1–2, 26–32), and the emperor Nero (Josephus, *JW* 3.1). God opposes the "proud" and their hierarchical societal structure by bringing them low in judgment.[34]

A second feature of the oppressive status quo comprises "the mighty" (δυνάστας), who occupy thrones in ruling over those of low status and poverty (Luke 1:52). The term may specify a ruler,[35] denote alliances of rulers of various rank,[36] or identify powerful and wealthy ruling figures in general.[37] Often "the mighty" contrast with the poor (Lev 19:15), the weak, and the needy (Job 5:15), to whom "the mighty pose some danger (Sir 7:6; 8:1–2). God saves the poor and powerless from "the mighty" (Job 29:12) by removing the mighty from their thrones (Job 12:19; Jud 9:2), including Roman rulers (1QM 11:13; 14:10–11). The term is thus deeply embedded in and expressive of key dynamics of oppressive imperial societies: the concentration of power and wealth in the hands of a few; alliances of international and local leaders in exercising power; the importance of taxes, tribute, and military power in sustaining this hierarchical society at the expense of the poor; the antithetical yet symbiotic relationship between the mighty and the powerless, and God's use of yet disapproval of this hierarchical societal structure.[38] Zechariah names the proud and mighty as "enemies" whose basic disposition toward the subjugated is "hate" (1:71, 74).[39]

---

34. Pss 89[LXX88]:10; 94[LXX93]:2; 119[LXX118]:21; Isa 29:20; Zeph 3:6 [LXX].

35. Egypt's Pharaoh (3 Macc 6:4), Nicanor the Greek governor of Judea (2 Macc 15:5), Aristobulus, ruler of Judea (Josephus, *Ant* 14.36), Parthian rulers (Josephus, *Ant* 20.245), Herod (Josephus, *JW* 1.365), various local kings who meet with Agrippa (Josephus, *Ant* 19.338–341), or an official of the court of the queen of Ethiopia (Acts 8:27).

36. For example, Pharaoh's court officials or household (Gen 50:4), the rulers and mighty ones of David's court (1 Chr 29:24), Israel's leaders (Dan 9:6, 8), rulers of a city (Sir 10:3) to whom tribute is paid (Philo, *Spec Leg* 1.142), those in command under the Assyrian Holofernes (Jud 2:14), local rulers of other kingdoms (2 Macc 9:25), or local rulers destroyed by Antiochus Epiphanes (Dan 8:24). In Josephus, *Jewish War*, 2.301, 316, 422 leaders of the Jews and chief priests; 2.411 leaders, chief priests and notable Pharisees; 2.418 leaders ally with governor Florus and Agrippa; 4.414 leaders of Gadara send embassies to Vespasian.

37. Prov 8:15; 14:28; Wis 8:11; Sir 10:24; Josephus *Ant.* 19.291.

38. For imperial structures, Lenski, *Power and Privilege,* 189–296; for God's opposition to, use of, and punishment of Assyrian power, see, for example, Isaiah 7–9, and Carter, "Evoking Isaiah."

39. MacMullen, *Roman Social Relations.*

A third element concerns the destructive societal impact of this oppressive situation, namely economic oppression. Verse 53 juxtaposes the hungry and the rich. Imperial structures ensure that the rich exist because of the hungry poor; the latter are the price exacted by the former. "The poverty and hunger of the oppressed" are thus not "primarily spiritual," as Raymond Brown argues,[40] but are the literal consequences of empire then and now. In his study of food in the Roman empire, Peter Garnsey remarks that "for most people, life was a perpetual struggle for survival."[41] A land-based economy produced much of the empire's food. Food production, distribution, and consumption were shaped by and expressive of the fundamental values of the elite-controlled, hierarchical, exploitative political-economic system. Fine-quality, abundant food reflected elite wealth, status, and power; deprivation and frequent shortages revealed the "low entitlement" for many non-elites in accessing food resources.[42] While the "Mediterranean diet," comprised mainly of cereals, olives, vine products, and beans, was theoretically healthy,[43] its actual nutritional value was diminished by various factors that limited supply and quality. Accordingly, malnutrition, especially among non-elites, was common and widely evident in deficiency diseases (eye problems; limb deformity)[44] and contagious diseases (diarrhea; dysentery). Food availability and quality reflected power, hierarchy, and injustice.

A fourth element names Israel's need for God's "help" (Luke 1:54). The verb (ἀντιλαμβανόμαι) evokes Israel's suffering under imperial domination: Babylon (Isa 42:1 LXX; 49:26); Assyria and Babylon (Jer 12:14), and Syria under Antiochus Epiphanes (1 Macc 2:48) and under governor Nicanor (2 Macc 14:15). Zechariah's song continues to underline Israel's captivity to "enemies" and "those who hate us" (1:71, 74). "Enemies" include Pharaoh (Ps 106:10), Babylon (Isa 42:13; Jer 12:7), and Syria under Antiochus Epiphanes (1 Macc 2:7, 9). Israel needs "visiting" and "redeeming" (1:68), and a "savior" (1:69) to "save us" (1:71, 74, 77; 2:30) from such powers. Its reality is "darkness" and "the shadow of death" (1:79; 2:32), an image that evokes perhaps subjugation to Assyria

---

40. Brown, *Birth*, 363.

41. Garnsey, *Food and Society*, xi. Whittaker, "The Poor."

42. Garnsey, *Famine and Food Supply*, 218–225; Garnsey, *Food and Society*, 1–11.

43. Foxhall and Forbes, "*Sitometreia*: The Role of Grain"; Mattingly, "First Fruit? The Olive"; Purcell, "Wine and Wealth"; Garnsey, "The Bean: Substance and Symbol."

44. Garnsey, *Food and Society*, 54–61.

(Isa 9:2) and Babylon (Ps 107:10), as well as the more general reality of a world contrary to God's light-giving and life-giving commands (Gen 1). That is, while the first two songs emphasize Israel's plight, both songs in chapter 2 extend the analysis to the larger Gentile world. In the angels' song and in Simeon's song, this whole oppressed imperial world is presented as lacking "peace" (1:79; 2:14, 29), despite the claim of *Pax Romana*. Simeon declares that God's salvation is "prepared in the presence of all peoples," that it impacts both the Gentiles and Israel as "a light for revelation to the Gentiles and for glory to your people Israel" (2:31–32).[45]

Bestowing Dignity

James Scott argues that in situations of massive differentials of power, oppressed groups often develop a "little tradition" or "hidden transcript" of dissent or counter ideology that narrates an alternative way of societal being. This development is aided by certain circumstances such as growing conflict between oppressors and oppressed, a veneer of apparent public compliance, the existence of a "safe space" out of the sight and supervision of the oppressors where dissent can be expressed, and the emergence of effective leaders[46] among the oppressed. This "hidden transcript of indignation" embraces discourse and practices[47] that contest the public transcript.[48] Against dehumanizing and dignity-depriving status domination, Scott argues that the hidden transcript—comprising gossip and rumor, slander, insider gestures of defiance, coded talk, jokes, tales of revenge, rituals of aggression, and the protection of autonomous social space—asserts the dignity of the oppressed. Luke's songs, I am arguing, are performative speech, part of the dignity-bestowing, hidden transcript. In Luke's narrative, the songs are located in concealed, "private" spaces: Mary speaks in the "safe space" of a Judean, hill-country town in the privacy of a family context (1:39–45), Zechariah speaks in a family gathering (1:59–67), the angels sing in a field to lowly shepherds (2:8), and Simeon in the busy temple with a small group comprising Jesus' parents (2:27–33).

45. For an interesting analysis of Simeon, LaGrand, "Luke's Portrait of Simeon."

46. Scott, *Domination*, 118–24.

47. Ibid., 7.

48. Ibid., 3.

Several sources of dignity are evident in the songs.

One source of dignity involves the conviction that God is present to the singers. Notable are the personal pronouns that emphasize a relationship with God: "God my savior" (1:47), "for me" (1:49), "our fathers" (1:54, 72, 73), "his people" (1:68, 77), "for us" (1:69), "from our enemies" (1:71), "our God" (1:78). Confidence and security mark this relationship. In addition, the songs are quite clear about God's disposition to the singers. The anthropocentric presentation of God as "regard[ing] the low status of his handmaiden" (1:48) employs a verb that denotes God's active concern for Israel under the oppressive rule of Egypt (Exod 14:24), Assyria (Jud 6:19; 13:4), and Babylon (Lam 1:11; 2:20; 5:1). In similar spirit, God is "merciful to those who fear him" (1:50, 54), a theme that Zechariah takes up ("through the tender mercy of God," 1:78). Zechariah also emphasizes God's faithfulness in acting "as he spoke by the mouth of his holy prophets from of old" (1:70) and recalls God's oath sworn to Abraham (1:73). The angels celebrate God's "favor" (εὐδοκίας) or "grace" to human beings (2:14; cf Ps 5:12; Sir 11:17),[49] while Simeon invokes God's faithfulness in acting "according to your word" (2:29) and on behalf of Israel and the Gentile nations (2:31–32). The references in the songs are of course a selective presentation of God's disposition, an idealized picture drawn from an idealized past that conveniently overlooks displays of God's wrath and punishment. The result emphasizes that God's merciful, favorable disposition concerns a people, not just a singer (1:54, 68)—and is not just momentary but extends across the generations and "to his posterity forever" (1:50, 55). Their oppression is not presented as God's punishment, nor as that to which God is oblivious or from which God is distant or even absent. The naming of God's relationship of favor and God's abiding faithfulness recall the covenant God has made with the people. The present oppression is thus countered by God's faithful, dignity-bestowing favor for the oppressed, along with assurances of retribution and vindication whereby "enemies" are vanquished.

A further dignity-bestowing dimension has frequently been noted.[50] The songs echo other songs that affirm God's gracious "regard" for the people. Mary, Zechariah, the angels, and Simeon are located in a long line of those who have experienced God's favor and victory

49. Fitzmyer, *Luke*, 1:410–12.
50. Green, *Luke*, 101.

over national enemies, which they celebrated with songs: Moses (Exod 15:1–18), Miriam (Exod 15:19–21), Deborah (Judges 5:1–31), Hannah (1 Sam 2:1–10), Asaph (1 Chr 16:8–36), and Judith (Judith 16:1–17) along with numerous Psalms. Again the selectivity and idealization of the past are evident.

The songs function to bestow dignity in the midst of dehumanizing oppression by naming the relationship with God, celebrating the favorable divine disposition experienced in their midst, recalling benign and faithful covenant commitments, awaiting vengeance, and echoing songs of previous interventions.

Fostering Hope for Change

The songs link this experience of oppressive suffering with the larger biblical narrative of transformation that envisions a different and better reality, at considerable odds with the present structures. Whereas the songs of slavery, civil rights, and apartheid anticipate a future transformation, Luke's songs celebrate a transformation already underway though far from complete.

With a constant procession of verbs associated in Israel's traditions with God liberating the people from oppressive powers,[51] the songs celebrate God's intervention through John and Jesus to overthrow Rome's imperial system. This intervention is located within and framed by God's previous acts of salvific intervention on behalf of Israel that provide a hopeful vision of the transformation under way. Especially important are celebrations of God the divine warrior who, in events like the exodus from Egypt, delivers people from oppressive powers (Exod 15:3; Zeph 17:3).[52] That is, the songs ascribe violent intervention to God but do not permit violence by God's people.

- God has done great things (1:49), a phrase that especially denotes God delivering the people from Egyptian oppression (Deut 6:22; 10:21–22; 11:7).

- God has shown power with his arm (1:51). This anthropomorphism presents God overcoming the Egyptians (Exod 6:6; Deut 6:21), the proud and God's enemies (Ps 89[LXX 88]:10), and the

---

51. For one selection of references, Brown, *Birth*, 386–89.

52. Emphasized by Horsley, *Liberation*, 110–20.

Assyrians (Judith 13:11), and restores punished Israel exiled in Babylon (Isa 52:10; Ezek 20:33–35).

- God has scattered the proud (1:51), punishing those who live contrary to God's purposes (Deut 30:3; Ps 53[LXX 52]:5).

- God has reversed the hierarchical, elite-biased status quo by "putting down" (or better, "destroying"[53]) the powerful and by sending the rich away empty (1:52–53). The proud, the powerful, and the rich—the ruling elite of the empire—are allied as God's punished enemies. That God "overthrows the thrones of rulers" is common wisdom (Sir 10:14a; 1QM 14:10–11), as is God's judgment on the rich and on the wealth of the nations (LXX Isa 29:5, 7–9). Conversely, God vindicates the powerless and poor (non-elites) in exalting them to be free of oppressive structures. God's intervention to feed the hungry with abundant good food (and attendant good health) features in various prophetic (Isa 25:6–10) and apocalyptic scenarios (2 Bar 29:4–8; 73:1–7).

- God has visited and redeemed God's people (1:68). The first verb ἐπεσκέψατο indicates divine intervention either to judge (Exod 32:34; Lam 4:22) or to express care and blessing such as pregnancy (1 Sam 2:21), release from Egypt (Exod 4:31) and offer provision of food (Ruth 1:6).[54] The following verb specifies the intervention here as salvific (lit. "did redemption"), although judgment is not entirely absent in that God's intervention is against the "enemies" and "those who hate us" (1:71, 74). The verb "redeem" (and cognate forms) frequently denotes the exodus from Egypt[55] and liberation from Babylon (Isa 43:1, 14; 44:23). It also appears in the Jubilee year description (Lev 25) in which land and property are restored (Lev 25:29), slaves freed (Lev 25:48), and debts cancelled. God's redeeming activity means the complete transformation of the imperial world structured contrary to God's purposes. Luke uses the verb for the liberation of Jerusalem and Israel from Roman rule (Luke 2:38; 24:21; cf 2:25).

---

53. Judg 9:45; 1 Macc 1:31; 2:25.

54. Also Sir 46:14; Luke 7:16; Acts 15:14. Often it refers to 'counting" or "numbering."

55. Exod 6:6; Deut 7:8; 9:26; 15:15; 21:8; 24:18; Ps 107[LXX 106]:2.

- God has raised up a horn of salvation (1:69). Salvation language recurs in 1:71, 77, and 2:30. God's "raising up" of this horn recalls the "raising up" of deliverers to rescue Israel from "enemy" rulers (Judges 2:16, 18; 3:9, 15). The "horn of salvation," an image of God's saving power (Ps 18[LXX 17]:2), evokes memories of David (Ps 132[LXX 131]:17) to whom is promised an eternal reign representing God's life-giving purposes (2 Sam 7; Ps 72). The vision of "salvation" as liberation from imperial oppression is elaborated by the general content of Luke's songs, as well as by the intertextual echoes of the term "salvation" (salvation from Egypt, Babylon, Rome[56]). Zechariah's song names similar entities from which the people need saving: "enemies" and "those who hate us" (1:74), and in 1:77 "release/jubilee (not "forgiveness) from sins." The common language of "forgiveness," construed as "internal" and "religious," is contextually inappropriate, hence the more appropriate translation "release." The term ἀφέσει, often rendered "jubilee," occurs some 13 times[57] in Lev 25 to denote the socio-economic transformation of release from slavery, return of property, and cancellation of debt. That is, God transforms these mainstays of imperial society expressed through the practices of local elites who are allies of Rome. The synonym "deliver" (1:74), used for both the exodus from Egypt (Exod 6:6) and the return from the Babylonian exile (Isa 44:6; 47:4; 48:17, 20), continues the vision of deliverance from imperial power. This transformed life is also imaged as "giving light" to all people (1:79; 2:32). "Light" denotes God's creative (Gen 1) and saving (from Assyria, Isa 9:2; from Babylon Isa 42:6 a light for the nations) presence (Ps 27:1) that guides "our feet in the way of peace," inclusive of Jew and Gentile (1:79; 2:32).

Securing Communal Solidarity

Communal solidarity is especially necessary for engaging the imperial context of power disparities and conflict between the mighty and those

---

56. Salvation from Egyptian captivity (Deut 33:39), from Babylonian exile (Isa 43:3, 11, 12; 46:4), from Rome (*Ps Sol* 10:8; 12:6; 17:3). The Psalms depict numerous situations.

57. Lev 25:10, 11, 12, 13, 28, 30, 31, 33, 41, 50, 52, 54.

of low status, the rich and the hungry, the people and their enemies. Evident in the discussion above are several ways in which the songs reflect their origin among the community of the oppressed and contribute to building communal solidarity.

The songs define the community as one that benefits from God's intervention. Mary's "humiliation/oppression" (1:48) represents the "low status" of the poor or non-elites excluded from power and deprived of adequate food (1:52–53). God's action "for me" (1:49) is an action to help Israel (1:54). Zechariah similarly blesses "the God of Israel" who has "redeemed his people" (1:68, 77) according to God's promises "to our fathers" and "our father Abraham" (1:72–73). The angels extend this community by recognizing that God's actions bring "peace among people" (2:14). Simeon specifies that this "people" comprises Gentiles as well as Israelites (2:32). And the songs sketch this community's future as marked by abundant food (1:53), service for God in holiness and justice (1:75), release from debt and slavery (1:77), restored land (1:77), God's presence ("light,"), and peace (1:78–79; 2:32). The songs also specify who are excluded from this community: "the proud," "the mighty," "the rich" (1:51–53), "enemies and those who hate us" (1:71, 74).

This community not only comprises the present and the future, but also the past. Luke's songs continually evoke scriptural traditions. Selected key moments from the past—promises to Abraham and David, the exodus, and the return from Babylonian exile—shape the present. The songs also evoke and update previous songs that named a communal experience of suffering and a communal aspiration of transformation. Luke's songs affirm the identity of a people in solidarity with each other in their common struggle against a common enemy. They secure belongingness and participation in this people's struggle. They dignify, they embolden, they give direction.

Another intertextuality secures this communal solidarity as an alternative to imperial society, namely, imperial praise songs. Songs honoring the emperor and the empire's accomplishments were part of the imperial cult.[58] An inscription from Teos in Asia attests the use of hymns in the combined cult of Dionysus and Tiberius, as do an association of *hymnodoi* of Artemis (often linked with imperial figures[59]) at Ephesus, and the imperial choir of Asia that sang at imperial occasions

58. This approach is usefully pursued in Brent, "Luke-Acts and the Imperial Cult."

59. Price, *Rituals and Power*, 103–4.

such as birthdays of Augustus and Tiberius.[60] Suetonius narrates that a golden shield which had been voted to Gaius Caligula was carried annually to the Capitol escorted by priests and senators, "while boys and girls of noble birth sang the praises of his virtues in a choral ode" (*Gaius Caligula* 441).

What did the songs celebrate? Fishwick comments that "we have no idea of the content or wording of [these] songs."[61] We can, however, reasonably speculate about some of the content of imperial praise-songs. One source of likely content would be the common themes of imperial theology, namely that the gods had chosen Rome to manifest their sovereignty, presence, will, and blessings among humans.[62] As numerous scholars have noted, Luke's songs echo themes concerned with the gods' blessings manifested through Rome that were common motifs in the imperial cult and likely evident in its songs: victory (*victoria* or νίκη), peace (*pax* or εἰρήνη), savior (σωτήρ) and salvation (σωτηρία).[63] Another source is the hymn composed by Horace for Augustus' Saeculum games in 17 BCE. This song has survived and offers some idea of the themes appropriate for imperial celebrations. It was performed by twenty-seven boys and girls, the very personification of the domestic fertility and civic order that were to mark Augustus' golden age. Horace celebrates:

- Morality: "Rear up our youth, O goddess, and bless the Fathers' edicts concerning wedlock and the marriage-law, destined, we pray, to be prolific in new offspring" (17–20);

- Fertility: "Bountiful in crops and cattle, may Mother Earth deck Ceres [goddess of agriculture, corn, and harvest] with a crown of corn; and may Jove's wholesome rains and breezes give increase to the harvest" (29–32);

- Social Conformity and Harmony: "O gods, make teachable our youth and grant them virtuous ways; to the aged give tranquil peace" (45–46);

- Blessing on Rome: "If Rome be your handiwork . . . [give] to the race of Romulus, riches and offspring and every glory" (47–48);

60. Fishwick, *The Imperial Cult in the Latin West*, II.1.567–71; Price, *Rituals*, 105 citing IEph 7.2 3801, recognizing the choir of Asia hymning Tiberius' birthday at Pergamum.

61. Fishwick, *Imperial Cult*, 569.

62. Carter, *Matthew and Empire* 20–34.

63. E.g., Brent, "Luke-Acts and the Imperial Cult."

- Military Victory and Alliances with the Submissive: "And what [Augustus] . . . entreats of you, that may he obtain, triumphant o'er the warring foe, but generous to the fallen!" (49–52);

- Renewed Social Morality: "Now Faith and Peace and Honour and old-time Modesty and neglected Virtue have courage to come back, and blessed Plenty with her full horn is seen" (57–60);

- Eternal Empire: may Apollo "prolong the Roman power and Latium's prosperity to cycles ever new and ages ever better" (66–68).

Augustus' attempts to reformulate family values and marriage morality did not succeed. However, the remaining themes were commonplaces.

The intertextuality between Horace's *Carmen* and Luke's songs highlights some obvious differences. While Horace celebrates the elite-dominated social order maintained by the emperor, Luke's songs envision the transformation of that social order and demise effected by God. While Horace seeks social conformity, Luke's songs imagine disruption. While Horace blesses Rome, Luke's songs conceive its downfall. While Horace hymns Pax Romana, Luke proclaims the transformative peace or justice of God. While Horace looks to Rome's eternal rule, Luke's songs imagine God's faithfulness and mercy forever. Such differences contribute to the community solidarity that Luke's hymns create as a new societal order counter to the imperial agenda.

But Luke's engagement with the empire is not one-dimensional. While Luke's songs resist Roman imperial order, they also reflect aspects of that same order. James Scott's analysis, as well as postcolonial studies, alert us to the presence of imitations of imperial ways in little traditions that contest imperial structures. There are, accordingly, significant similarities between Luke's songs and Horace's imperial themes. Both employ the genre of song. Both celebrate fertility. Both recognize a central place for victories secured by force and the defeat of enemies. Both celebrate peace. Both envision eternal empires. While there are significant differences within these lexical items that cannot be elaborated here, it is important to note that mimicry or imitation along with resistance contributes to an ambivalent stance in relation to the empire. That is, the songs do not only resist, they also imitate and perpetuate the imperial structures that they oppose. This hybridity or ambivalence of interaction marks the imperial negotiation evident in Luke's songs.

I am not suggesting that the similarities are restricted to Horace's *Carmen*. Space precludes an extensive cataloguing of imitative connections with imperial themes and texts, but three examples can be noted. 1) Mary describes herself in 1:48 as a slave of God, thereby expressing her relationship to God in the language of one of the empire's most oppressive structures. While it can be argued that language thereby contestively refuses allegiance to earthly masters and ascribes it to God, it nevertheless reinscribes the relationship with God in terms of the dominant imperial structure of master and slave. A similar dynamic exists in her language of "savior." 2) While Mary's song declares God's destructive scattering of the proud (Luke 1: 51), so Virgil's Anchises declares Rome's mission to be the subduing of the proud: "you, Roman, be sure to rule the world (be these your arts), to crown peace with justice, to spare the vanquished and to crush the proud" (*Aeneid* 6.851–53). The term "the proud" has different referents in each text, yet both texts use the term to denote the destruction of those who oppose their dominant power's will and agenda. 3) Simeon's declaration of God's salvific purposes that embrace Israel and the nations (2:32) echoes Anchises' statement of Rome's purposes to rule the "world." Both texts assert universalizing purposes in which compliance with and submission to the dominant power is the only commendable option. The communal solidarity that Luke's songs reflect and seek to secure replicates the Roman imperial order even as the songs simultaneously resist and contest it.

Conclusion

Luke's songs, born from the experience of Roman imperial power, perform functions similar to the songs of African-American slavery and civil rights struggles, as well as South African resistance to apartheid. They name contexts of oppressive power, bestow dignity, envision transformation, and secure community. At the beginning of Luke's narrative, they serve an important role in formulating the Gospel's negotiation of Roman power. They frame that negotiation as contestive resistance even as they imitate and thereby replicate that which they resist. Whether this is the whole of Luke's approach, whether one element will overwhelm the other, whether both elements will be kept in tension, whether other dynamics will emerge, will only be known by reading on through the gospel. While the songs have the initial say, they do not have the final say in the narrative.

3

Women Prophets of God's Alternative Reign

Barbara E. Reid

Introduction

IT IS AN HONOR TO CONTRIBUTE TO THIS *FESTSCHRIFT* IN RECOGNI-tion of Robert Brawley. In the years that we have been colleagues in Chicago, we have shared an interest in Luke and in many other areas of New Testament study. I have especially valued Robert's insights shared in meetings of the Association of Chicago Theological Schools New Testament group, where we have both tried out works in progress and benefitted greatly from each other's wisdom.

In this essay I will first sketch the prevalence of references to Roman rulers and their collaborators in the Lucan narrative, which keeps the reality of Roman imperial rule ever before the hearers of the Gospel. I will then focus on how Luke sets the tone for his gospel with a prophetic utterance by Jesus' mother that offers a counter-ideology to Roman imperial rule. Using language that is evocative of the claims of the Roman Emperor, Mary announces an alternative realm in which God, who is the "Lord" and "Savior," mercifully dismantles structures of domination, abolishes servitude, humiliation, hunger, and powerless-ness, and empowers both women and men as prophets of this divine reign. Mary, true to Luke's overall portrait of women, speaks this chal-lenging word within the privacy of a home. In public space in Luke and Acts, it is the male disciples who make public declarations. Outwardly the women in Luke may seem to conform to Roman imperial values, but inside the home they sing subversive songs that shape the hopes and dreams of their families.

Setting the Stage: The Presence of Roman Rulers and Their Collaborators

A notable feature of Luke and Acts is that at regular intervals the narrative names Roman rulers and Jewish leaders who collaborated with them. The gospel story begins with the notice that what is about to be recounted took place in the days of King Herod of Judea (1:5).[1] The birth of Jesus is related to a decree of Emperor Augustus for a census, carried out while Quirinius was governor of Syria (Luke 2:1–2; Acts 5:37).[2] The appearance of John the Baptist and the beginning of Jesus' public ministry are set in the "fifteenth year of the reign of Emperor Tiberius, when Pontius Pilate was governor of Judea, and Herod was ruler[3] of Galilee, and his brother Philip ruler of the reign of Iturea and Trachonitis, and Lysanias ruler of Abilene, during the high priesthood of Annas and Caiaphas" (3:1–2).[4] Herod (Antipas) appears early in the narrative and is mentioned more frequently by Luke than by any other evangelist.[5]

Having noted at the outset that Pontius Pilate was governor of Judea (3:1), Luke makes mention of him again at 13:1, with a cryptic reference to Galileans whose blood Pilate "had mingled with their sacrifices." Pilate is referred to as "the governor" (ἡγεμόνος) in 20:20, where the religious leaders are looking for a way to hand Jesus over to him. The emperor is also in view in the same episode, in so far as Jesus is confronted about paying taxes "to Ceasar" (Luke 20:22–26). After Jesus is arrested he is brought before Pilate (23:1–5), who sentences him to death (23:13–25). It is to Pilate that Joseph of Arimathea must go to ask for the body of Jesus (23:52).

The chief priests appear in the gospel as opponents of Jesus and as collaborators with the Roman authorities in seeking his death.[6] With the exception of Acts 6:7, where Luke notes that many of them became

---

1. This reference is to Herod "the Great," who ruled between 37–4 BCE.

2. The problem of aligning Jesus' birth, which occurred approximately 6 BCE, with Quirinius' legateship, which began in 6–7 CE, is well known.

3. This reference is to Herod Antipas, the son of Herod the Great. The Greek τετραρχοῦντος specifies him as "tetrarch."

4. Biblical quotations are taken from the NRSV.

5. Luke 3:1, 19; 8:3; 9:7, 9; 13:31; 23:7–12, 15.

6. Luke 9:22; 19:47; 20:1, 19, 22; 22:4, 52, 54, 66; 23:4, 10, 13; 24:20.

obedient to the faith, the chief priests continue in the oppositional role toward Jesus' followers in Luke's second volume.[7] The Gospel is set during the reign of the high priests Annas and Caiaphas (Luke 3:2). Peter faces Annas the high priest along with Caiaphas, John, and Alexander, who are members of the high priestly family (Acts 4:6). Paul is brought before Ananaias (Acts 23:2).

In Acts of the Apostles, the Roman rulers are even more visible than in the Gospel. Herod (Antipas) is mentioned in 4:27 in reference to Jesus' death. Herod (Agrippa I)[8] enters the story in 12:1–12, when he imprisons Peter. His gruesome death is recounted in 12:20–23. At 23:35 Herod's praetorium is mentioned as the place where Paul is held in custody. Herod Agrippa II comes on the scene at 13:1, and, like Herod Antipas, is dubbed "Herod the tetrarch." Later, Luke will call him "King Agrippa."[9] The emperor comes into view when Paul and Silas are accused of acting "contrary to the decrees of the emperor, saying that there is another king named Jesus" (17:7). Further on, Paul insists he has committed no crime against the emperor (25:8) and appeals to Caesar (25:10–12, 21; 26:32; 27:24; 28:19). The emperor Claudius comes on stage in Acts 18:2, where his expulsion of Jews from Rome is said to be the reason for Prisca and Aquila's resettling in Corinth. Pilate is mentioned in speeches of Peter and Paul for his role in Jesus' death (3:13; 4:27; 13:28). Two other governors, Felix (23:24; 24:1–27) and Portius Festus (24:27–25:13), hear the case against Paul in Caesarea. King Agrippa and Bernice join the latter in hearing Paul before sending him to Rome because he had appealed to Caesar (25:13–26:32). Proconsuls are also in view in three episodes. In Cyprus, the proconsul Sergius Paulus is persuaded by Paul to become a believer (13:7–12). In Corinth, the proconsul Gallio is indifferent to the complaints against Paul (18:12–17). In Ephesus, the town clerk recommends that if Demetrius and the artisans have a complaint against Paul they bring it to the proconsuls (19:38).

There is also frequent mention of the Roman military in Luke's two volumes. Tribunes, χιλίαρχοι, commanders of a thousand, appear numerous times, as they maintain order, and arrest and guard Paul

7. Acts 4:6, 23; 5:17, 21, 24, 27; 7:1; 9:1, 14, 21; 19:14; 22:5, 30; 23:2, 4, 5, 14; 24:1; 25:2, 15; 26:10, 12.

8. This Herod was the grandson of Herod the Great and Mariamne, son of Aristobolus, and was appointed king of Judea 41–44 CE.

9. Acts 25:13, 24, 26; 26:2, 19, 27.

when he is imprisoned.[10] One, Claudius Lysias, is referred to by name (21:31; 23:26). Centurions and soldiers appear in both volumes. Some are portrayed very favorably, such as the soldiers who responded to John the Baptist's message (Luke 3:14), the centurion whose servant Jesus healed (Luke 7:1–10), the one who declares Jesus' righteousness at his crucifixion (23:47), and Cornelius, the first Gentile convert (Acts 10:1–48). Other soldiers mock Jesus (Luke 23:11, 36) and participate in the arrests and imprisonments of Peter and Paul (12:4, 6, 18; 22:25, 26; 23:10, 23, 31; 24:23; 27:1–43; 28:16). In one instance, soldiers save Paul from attack by Jewish opponents (21:31, 32, 35). Luke names the centurion Julius, into whose custody Paul was given when he was taken to Rome, and notes that he was of the Augustan Cohort (27:1). Finally, a centurion saves Paul from the soldiers who want to kill the prisoners en route to Rome so that they do not escape during the shipwreck (27:42–43).

The ubiquitous presence of Roman emperors, governors, tetrarchs, proconsuls, tribunes, centurions, and soldiers, along with the collaborating high priests, in Luke's narrative does not simply reflect the evangelist's interest in history.[11] It also serves as a pervasive reminder that the Roman empire and its agents dominated every aspect of the life of the people under its rule. This mirrors the historical reality of the time in which the narrative is set and the later time in which the Gospel was composed. Just as in the narrative, so also in the daily life of the empire, reminders of Roman imperial power were visible to all in the form of public monuments, temples dedicated to the emperor, coins, and military. While Luke has created ambiguity by painting some of the Roman rulers and soldiers as open to the Jesus movement, there is the constant reminder that it was the Roman governor who had Jesus executed and whose power is threatened by the message that his followers continue to spread. The good news of the inbreaking of the reign of God is not compatible with the Roman imperial rule.[12]

10. Acts 21:31, 32, 33, 37; 22:24, 26, 27, 28, 29; 23:10, 15, 17, 18, 19, 22; 24:22; 25:23.

11. On Luke's interest in history see Barrett, *Luke the Historian;* Robinson, *Luke the Historian*; Marshall, *Luke: Historian and Theologian;* Plümacher, *Lukas als hellenistischer Schriftsterrler*; Talbert, "What is Meant by the Historicity of Acts?" Dahl states that Luke "himself was a minor Hellenistic historian, albeit one who dealt with a very special subject matter" ("Purpose of Luke-Acts," 88).

12. I agree with Robbins ("Luke-Acts: A Mixed Population Seeks a Home") that Luke's purpose is neither to present an *apologia pro ecclesia* nor an *apologia pro impe-*

Responding to Roman Imperial Power

Recent studies that draw on insights from social and political history, sociology, anthropology, and political science, have opened the way for biblical scholars to consider the realities and the responses of peoples subjugated to Roman imperial power.[13] These studies have shown that the responses of dominated people are far more complex than simply choosing between passive acquiescence or open armed revolt. In between these two extremes there are multiple ways of expressing discontent and resistance. Those who live on the underside of a repressive power may not dare to "speak truth to power," for fear of brutal retaliation. Instead, they may "wear masks of obedience" externally, while "offstage" they say what they really think and "vent their feelings to each other."[14] They may sustain their hope for change by imagining the overthrow of the oppressor, as when Paul writes that Christ will destroy "every ruler and every authority and power," putting "all his enemies under his feet" (1 Cor 15:24–25).[15] Or they may express protest in disguised and ambiguous ways. Jesus' entry into Jerusalem, for example, may have appeared to the authorities to be a simple group of pilgrims coming to the holy city for the Passover feast, while Jesus and his followers were symbolically claiming the city for God's anointed, declaring messianic fulfillment of God's reign.[16] One other important strategy for resisting the ideology imposed by ruling powers is to construct a counter-ideology and develop tactics for bringing it into reality. This is what Luke does from the very outset of his Gospel. In the first two chapters the angelic and prophetic figures, Gabriel, Elizabeth, Zechariah, Mary, Simeon, and

rio. However, I disagree with his thesis that Luke shows the empire as good, working symbiotically with Christianity.

13. The studies by Scott (*Weapons of the Weak* and *Domination and the Arts of Resistance*) have been foundational for the works of Horsley (*Hidden Transcripts* and *Jesus and the Spiral of Violence*), Crossan (*Historical Jesus*), Herzog (*Jesus, Justice, and the Reign of God*), and Carter (*Roman Empire*), to name a few.

14. Horsley, *Hidden Transcripts*, 9, summarizing Scott, *Domination and the Arts of Resistance*. See also Crossan, *God and Empire*, for an analysis of Rome's social and imperial power as territorial, military, political, and ideological. Crossan contrasts the violent power of domination with nonviolent power of persuasion (11–15), illustrates how the latter is operative in biblical traditions, and gives examples of nonviolent resistance from first-century documents outside biblical traditions (88–94).

15. Carter, *Roman Empire*, 120–28.

16. Ibid., 130.

Anna, articulate God's alternative reign, which is further elaborated and enacted by Jesus in the remainder of the gospel.[17] I will focus on the prophetic call of Mary in the Annunciation scene (Luke 1:26–38), and her declaration in the Magnificat of a counter-ideology to that of the Roman empire (Luke 1:46–55).

Mary's Prophetic Call (Luke 1:26–38)

While the scene of the Annunciation has often been likened to that of other biblical annunciation-of-birth stories,[18] it also has many characteristics of a prophetic call story. Like the prophets of old, Mary's encounter with God's messenger comes in the midst of everyday life. Moses, for example, was tending his father-in-law's sheep when God's angel appeared to him in a flame of fire out of a bush (Exod 3:1–2). Amos was a herdsman and a dresser of sycamores when God took him from following the flock and asked him to prophesy to Israel (Amos 7:14–15). Likewise, Mary is presented as an ordinary Galilean girl making wedding plans when God's messenger comes to her.

An authentic prophet resists the call. Jeremiah objected that he was too young (Jer 1:6). Moses protested that he couldn't speak well (Exod 4:10). Amos insists, "I am no prophet, nor a prophet's son" (Amos 7:14). Isaiah worried that he was "a man of unclean lips," living among "a people of unclean lips" (Isa 6:5). In like manner, Mary objects that what she has heard from Gabriel is impossible (Luke 1:34). Prophets know that what God asks of them is beyond their human abilities. Their objections are always met by assurances of divine assistance. To Jeremiah, God says, "Do not be afraid . . . I am with you to deliver you" (Jer 1:8). For Moses, God provides a companion, Aaron, and guarantees that "I will be with your mouth and with his mouth, and will teach you what you shall do" (Exod 4:15). Isaiah is given a seraph who touches his lips with a live coal, declaring that his guilt had departed and his sin was blotted out, which allows him to respond to God's invitation with the words, "Here am I, send me!" (Isa 6:5–8). As with Isaiah (6:1) and Ezekiel (2:2), upon whom God's Spirit came, so Mary is given the

17. See Reid, *Taking Up the Cross*, chapter 3 "Prophetic Martyr," for a more thorough treatment of the theme of prophecy in the Gospel of Luke.

18. See Brown, *Birth of the Messiah*, 155–59, 292–96 for analysis of this scene in relation to other annunciations of birth in the Scriptures.

assurance that the Holy Spirit would come upon her and that the power of the Most High would overshadow her (1:35). Nothing, she is told, is impossible for God (1:37).

Prophets always risk rejection and suffering in the exercise of their mission. Jesus remarks in Luke 13:34 that Jerusalem always kills the prophets. While that may not always be literally true, it is certain that the ruling powers oppose the denunciations of prophets, and do whatever is necessary to silence them. Luke does not tell of Mary being silenced or killed, but we can infer her pain when her son suffers the consequences of proclaiming publicly the vision of an alternate rule, the same vision that Mary articulates in the privacy of the home of Elizabeth and Zechariah (1:46, 55, echoed in 4:18). The evangelist hints at Mary's suffering in a later scene when Simeon says to her that a "sword will pierce your own soul" (2:35).[19]

Proclamation of an Alternate Rule (Luke 1:46–55)

Mary's prophetic task involves both giving physical birth to the one who will claim the throne of his ancestor David who will rule forever (1:32–33) and singing out what this rule of God will be like (1:46–55). By voicing this counter-ideology in song, she follows in the footsteps of other female prophets—Miriam, Hannah, Judith, and Deborah—who proclaimed God's victorious power in song and dance.[20] As Wilda Gafney has shown, prophets not only declare oracles, they also engage in "intercessory prayer, dancing, drumming, singing, giving and interpreting laws, delivering oracles on behalf of YHWH (sometimes in ecstasy, sometimes demonstratively), resolving disputes, working wonders,

19. Fitzmyer (*Luke I–IX*, 430) advances the suggestion that this is an allusion to the sword of discrimination in Ezekiel 14:17, pointing toward the difficulties Mary will have as a result of her son's mission.

20. There are five women who are specifically identified as prophets in the Old Testament: Miriam (Exod 15:20), Deborah (Judg 4:4), Huldah (2 Kgs 22:14; 2 Chr 34:22), the unnamed woman with whom Isaiah fathers a child (Isa 8:3), and No'adiah (Neh 6:14). In addition, there are references in Joel (3:1–2) and Ezekiel (13:17) to daughters who prophesy. First Chronicles 25:3–5 speaks of Heman who directs his sons and daughters in musical prophecy. The Talmud adds Sarah, Hannah, Abigail, and Esther to those women recognized as prophets. In the New Testament there are: Anna (Luke 2:36–38), the four virgin daughters of Philip (Acts 21:9), and the women prophets of Corinth (1 Cor 11:5). A false woman prophet appears in Rev 2:18–28.

mustering troops and fighting battles, archiving their oracles in writing, and experiencing visions."[21]

The parallels between Mary's song and the songs of Miriam (Exod 15:1–21),[22] Judith (Jdt 16:1–16), and Deborah (Jdg 5:1–31) make it impossible to miss the subversive nature of the Magnificat.[23] Miriam, identified as a prophet in Exodus 15:20, sings and dances, with tambourine in hand, exulting in God's triumph over the Egyptians.[24] She leads the people to understand their experience of liberation as a gift from God and to further imagine—and thus be able to achieve—a new future in the land of God's promise.[25] Judith, likewise, led her people in a victory hymn after freeing them from the terror of the Assyrian general, Holofernes (Jdt 16:1–16). In similar fashion, Deborah sings of God's victorious power after she leads the successful campaign against the Canaanite King Jabin (Jdg 5:1–31). These songs are not sweet lullabies; they are militant songs that exult in the saving power of God that has brought defeat to those who have subjugated God's people. In the same vein, Mary's song declares the overthrow of Roman imperial ways and the triumph of God's reign. Familiarity with the use of the Magnificat in religious contexts as well as the tendency to interpret Mary as sweet, docile, and utterly compliant can cause contemporary believers to miss

21. Gafney, *Daughters of Miriam*, 6.

22. It is likely that originally the entire Exodus hymn was led by Miriam, not simply v. 21, which mirrors v. 1. That women were the ones who would lead victory songs and dancing is reflected in 1 Samuel 18:7. See further Brooke, "A Long-Lost Song of Miriam," 62–65. Brooke proposes that a separate Song of Miriam, partially suppressed in the book of Exodus has survived in part in a Qumran text, 4Q365. Further, he shows that Mary's Magnificat, the Song of Hannah (1 Sam 2:1–10), the victory hymn of Judith (Jdt 16:6, 7, 13), and two sections of the Qumran War Scroll (1QM 11, 14) all sing of how the powerful are brought low by God's action through those who are lowly. That this theme survives in songs associated with women reflects an effort on the part of the then-current power structure to marginalize the threat of these poems. See also Burns, *Has the Lord Indeed Spoken Only Through Moses?*; Trible, "Bringing Miriam Out of the Shadows," 14–25; Janzen, "Song of Moses, Song of Miriam," 211–20. For a more detailed analysis of parallels between the songs of Mary and Miriam see Reid, *Taking Up the Cross*, 103.

23. More frequently noted are the parallels with Hannah's song (1 Sam 2:1–10).

24. Setel, "Exodus," 36, observes that Miriam's actions and lineage are priestly and proposes that her designation as prophet may be due to male transmitters of the tradition who found this title less objectionable than "priest."

25. Nowell, *Women*, 52.

the subversive power of Mary's song.[26] The Guatemalan government, however, recognized its revolutionary potential and banned the public recitation of the Magnificat in the 1980s.

Lordship

One of the first notable features of the Magnificat concerns the titles that Mary attributes to God: κύριος, "Lord" (1:46), σωτήρ, "Savior" (1:47), and ὁ δύνατος, "the Mighty One" (1:49). Each of these titles evokes claims that were made by Caesar and counters them. There are many known instances, both literary and archaeological, where the title κύριος, "Lord," is attributed to the emperor. One notable example is found in the *Discourses* of Epictetus, where the emperor is referred to as ὁ παντῶν κύριος καῖσαρ, "Caesar, lord of all" (*Disc.* 4.1.12). Another example is where Suetonius notes that Domitian wanted to be addressed as *dominus et deus noster* "our lord and our God" (*Dom.* 13.2). The Roman epigrapher Martial also attributes to Domitian the title *omni terrarium domino deoque*, "the Lord and God for the whole world" (*Epig.* 8.2.5–6). Nero is given the title ὁ τοῦ παντὸς κόσμου κύριος, "lord of the whole world," in an inscription from Aeraephiae in Boetia.[27] Luke's awareness that the emperor had appropriated this title for himself is evident in Acts 25:26, where Festus refers to the emperor as ὁ κύριος.[28] To counter this, Luke clearly asserts in the opening line of the Magnificat that God is ὁ κύριος. He reinforces this by using κύριος, his preferred christological title,[29] some two hundred times in his two volumes in reference to God and Jesus. In Peter's speech in Acts 10:36, Luke counters Caesar's claims with the assertion that Jesus is κύριος πάντων, "lord of all." Moreover, Luke deliberately contrasts the manner in which the Gentiles exercise their lordship with that of Jesus. "The kings of the Gentiles," he says, "lord it over (κυριεύουσιν) them, and those in authority over them are called benefactors. But not so with you, rather the greatest among you

26. Davison observes that these hymns "have lost their power to stun and offend" (*Preaching the Women,* 91).

27. These examples are cited by Rowe, "Luke-Acts and the Imperial Cult," 292–93. See also examples given by Walton, "The State They Were In," 26 n. 82; and Crossan, *God and Empire,* 15–25.

28. Rowe, "Luke-Acts and the Imperial Cult," 293–94.

29. Ibid., 294.

must become like the youngest, and the leader like one who serves"
(Luke 22:25–26).

Savior

Another important designation for God in the Magnificat is σωτήρ,
"Savior," in contradistinction to Roman emperors who claimed that
title. Every emperor from Augustus to Vespasian, with the exception of
Caligula, and then Trajan and Hadrian, used the title σωτήρ.[30] Julius
Caesar was described as "the god made manifest . . . and common savior
of human life." Augustus was called "a savior who put an end to war"
and "savior of the entire world." Claudius was said to be "savior of the
world" and "god who is savior and benefactor."[31] Mary's acclamation of
God as "Lord" and "Savior" is a direct affront to imperial claims. As the
narrative progresses, these terms are also used of Jesus, God's agent of
salvation.[32]

Slavery and Servitude vs. Service

Mary also asserts that she is God's servant (literally "slave," δούλη, 1:48),
repeating what she has already said to Gabriel at the Annunciation: ἰδοὺ
ἡ δούλη κυρίου, "behold the servant of the Lord" (1:38). She is not the
servant of Caesar, only of God. She says covertly what Peter and the
apostles will say to the high priest in Acts 5:29: "We must obey God rather than any human authority." The term δούλη, "slave," also calls to mind
that enslavement would be the fate of any who dared to rebel against
Rome. Luke has noted that Mary was from Nazareth (1:26), which calls
to mind that she dwells only a few short miles from Sepphoris, whose
inhabitants revolted at the death of Herod in 4 BCE and who were enslaved in punishment (Jos., *J.W.* 2.68; *Ant.* 17.289). Others could find
themselves enslaved as victims of Roman imperial economic practices.

30. Richey, *Roman Imperial Ideology*, 85.

31. Walton, "The State They Were In," 27 n. 86.

32. Luke is unique among the Synoptic evangelists in his use of σωτήρ (Luke 1:47;
2:11; Acts 5:31; 13:23) and σωτηρία (Luke 1:69, 71, 77; 19:9; Acts 4:12; 7:25; 13:26, 47;
16:17; 27:34; 28:28). In Matthew, Joseph is told that Jesus will "save (σώσει) his people
from their sins" (1:21). In the Fourth Gospel these terms occur only in the episode with
the Samaritan woman. Jesus remarks to her that "salvation is from the Jews" (4:22), and
the Samaritans who come to Jesus acclaim him as "Savior of the world" (4:42).

Many were incapable of meeting the excessive demands of "tribute, temple taxes and offerings, tithes, and other debts" and were forced to sell lands and family members into debt slavery.[33] Mary subverts the system of enslaving subjected peoples by presenting herself as an empowered person who chooses to serve. She is not a person upon whom servitude is imposed. This ethos is further embodied in Jesus' mission, as one who serves (22:27) and as one who makes the deliberate choice to risk the consequences of imperial backlash for his liberating proclamation and actions (Luke 9:52).

Humiliation

There is another significant challenge to Roman imperial values in 1:48 and 52. In contrast to powerful elites who delight in humiliating those whom they dominate, God "looks upon," ἐπέβλεψεν, Mary's "humiliation," ταπείνωσις, with the intent of alleviating her affliction. The same combination of divine "looking upon," ἐπιβλέπω, with "humiliation," ταπείνωσις, with a merciful intent, is found three other times in the Old Testament. In 1 Samuel 1:11, Hannah prays for God to look upon (ἐπιβλέπω) the misery (ταπείνωσιν) of God's servant (δούλη) and grant her a male child (1 Sam 1:11). Likewise, in 1 Samuel 9:16, God reveals to Samuel the one whom he is to anoint to be ruler over Israel to save them from the Philistines, "for I have seen (ἐπέβλεψα) the suffering (ταπείνωσιν) of my people." Judith implores God to "have pity on our people in their humiliation (ταπείνωσιν), and look kindly (ἐπίβλεψον) today on the faces of those who are consecrated to you" (Jdt 16:19). The resonances of these texts with the Magnificat create the expectation that God delights in relieving suffering that comes through humiliation,[34] quite the opposite of the ruling powers in the imperial system who impose humiliation on their subjects. Elizabeth also voices this divine alleviation of humiliation when she exclaims "this is what the Lord has done for me when he looked favorably on me and took away the dis-

---

33. Elliott, "Temple versus Household," 235.

34. In two other instances ταπείνωσις refers to affliction suffered by barren women, which God alleviates by giving them a son. In Genesis 16:11, God heeds the affliction (ταπείνωσις) of Hagar and she conceives Ishmael. In Genesis 29:32, God sees the affliction (ταπείνωσις) of Leah, and she bears Reuben. These references shed less light on Luke 1:48, since Mary's affliction is not caused by barrenness but by her conception of a son outside the bounds of patriarchal marriage arrangements.

grace (ὄνειδος) I have endured among my people" (1:25). Mary's song declares not only that God has done this for Mary, but that God lifts up all the lowly (ταπεινούς, v. 52).

It is also important to recognize that the verb ταπεινόω is used often in the LXX to refer to the sexual humiliation of a woman, as in the case of the rape of Dinah (Gen 34:2), the abuse of the concubine of the Levite (Judges 19:24; 20:5), Amnon's rape of Tamar (2 Kgs 13:12, 14, 22, 32), and the ravishing of the wives in Zion and the maidens in the cities of Judah by the enemy (Lam 5:11).[35] The Magnificat voices the dream of having no more fear of sexual humiliation by occupying imperial forces.

The Mighty One

The Magnificat also challenges Roman imperial might by naming God "the Mighty One," ὁ δυνατός (v. 49), a title also used of YHWH in LXX Zeph 3:17; Ps 89:9. Divine might (δύναμις) is God's power that protects the most vulnerable, as Gabriel assures Mary (1:35). It is the power such as resided in Elijah and John the Baptist, "to turn the hearts of parents to their children, and the disobedient to the wisdom of the righteous, to make ready a people prepared for the Lord" (1:17). It is the power of the Spirit that impels Jesus throughout his mission (4:14) to do good and to heal (Luke 5:17; 6:19; 8:46; Acts 10:38) and to cast out unclean spirits (Luke 4:36). Jesus' "deeds of power" are meant to bring repentance (Luke 10:13) and to cause all his disciples to acclaim him as the "king who comes in the name of the Lord" as he enters Jerusalem (Luke 19:37).[36]

By naming God as ὁ δυνατός, "the Mighty One," the Magnificat sets the stage for the way in which Jesus embodies God's power, namely as a contrast to imperial power. An inclusio is formed when at the end of the gospel, δυνατός is used of Jesus by Cleopas and his companion who say that he was "a prophet mighty (δυνατός) in deed and word before God and all the people" (Luke 24:19).

---

35. Schaberg, *The Illegitimacy of Jesus,* 100, points out these references. See also Deut 21:14; 22:24; Isa 51:21, 23; Ezek 22:10–11.

36. This power is also given to Jesus' disciples: Luke 10:19; 24:49; Acts 1:8; 4:33; 6:8.

Mercy and Meals

The Magnificat then makes explicit the ways in which divine power differs from that of imperial Rome. While the empire relies on military might, fear, economic domination, and a complex system of patron-client relations, among other strategies, to maintain power,[37] the divine Mighty One exudes mercy (vv. 50, 54) by bringing down the powerful (δυνάστας) from their thrones and lifting up those humiliated (v. 52), and by filling the hungry and emptying the rich (v. 53). It is not a simple reversal of fortunes for which Mary longs, but a leveling of the distribution of goods and power. She envisions a simultaneous movement of relinquishment on the part of those who have power, privilege, and status, and an empowerment of those who have not.

Divine mercy is manifest in the birth of a son to Elizabeth (1:58), and in the promise of a savior (1:72) who will bring light to those who "sit in darkness and in the shadow of death" (1:78). Jesus embodies this divine mercy by healing people afflicted with leprosy (17:13) and blindness (18:38, 39). He teaches his disciples to be merciful by loving enemies, doing good, and giving to those who beg without expecting recompense (6:27–36). This teaching subverts imperial ways of violent retaliation and equal reciprocity. Jesus tells a lengthy story about a hated Samaritan that embodies this kind of mercy, and he exhorts his followers to "go and do likewise" (Luke 10:29–37). He tells a parable about a tax collector who went home justified after praying in the temple for mercy (18:13).

While the hope of bringing the powerful down from their thrones is clearly an affront to Roman imperial power, so too is filling up those who are hungry and emptying out the pockets of rich people. As Warren Carter has shown,

> food was about power. Its production (based in land), distribution, and consumption reflected elite control. Accordingly, the wealthy and powerful enjoyed an abundant and diverse food supply. Quality and plentiful food was a marker of status and wealth . . . that divided elites from nonelites. It established the former as privileged and powerful and the latter as inferior and of low entitlement. The latter struggled to acquire enough food as well as food of adequate nutritional value. For most, this was a constant struggle. And it was cyclic whereby most dropped

---

37 See further Carter, *Roman Empire*, 1–15.

below subsistence levels at times throughout each year. Food,
then, displayed the injustice of the empire on a daily basis.[38]

As Mary sings of filling up the hungry, she subverts the imperial system
that keeps non-elites struggling and starving while elites enjoyed the
abundance that the imperial propaganda touted as one of the gifts of
the Roman Empire to its citizens.[39] Throughout the rest of the Gospel
we see Mary's son, who is so often portrayed in meal settings, carrying
out this agenda of filling up the hungry.[40]

When Mary sings of God sending the rich away empty, she introduces a theme that runs strongly throughout the Gospel. In an
empire where two to three percent of the population possessed most
of the wealth and where the majority constantly struggled to sustain
a subsistence-level existence, Mary articulates an end to economic
structures that are exploitive and unjust. She speaks of a time when all
will enjoy the good things given by God. Throughout the Gospel, the
Lucan Jesus will frequently warn about the dangers of riches (12:16–21;
16:13, 19–23; 18:25). The ideal presented in Acts is that no one is in need
(2:42–47; 4:32–34).

Roman Imperial Values and Women

In the way Luke portrays Mary's actions and words, he also subtly challenges the portrait of the ideal woman in the Roman Imperial world. "In
principle, a Roman woman was always under some form of masculine
control."[41] Yet, when Mary is introduced in Luke 1:26, there is no mention of her father or her fiancé; rather, she is identified in relation to her
town, Nazareth. She interacts freely with God's messenger, asking questions, and answering for herself, without the control of a husband or
father. In their discussion of the household code in Eph 5:21–33, Osiek
and MacDonald describe how idealizations of marriage served the
moral and political purposes of the empire. Civic harmony was linked
with marital concord; the married couple was idealized as a microcosm

38 Ibid., 109–10.

39. Ibid., 110.

40. At times he is host (9:10–17; 22:14–20), while at other times he is a guest (5:30;
7:36; 10:38; 14:1; 19:7). At many of these meals Jesus challenges the assumptions of the
Roman imperial world and offers an alternative vision of God's reign.

41. Osiek and MacDonald, *Woman's Place,* 24, quoting Dixon, *Roman Mother,* 44.

of the society as a whole.[42] Luke's depiction of the relationship between Mary and Joseph, however, undermines these purposes of the empire. We find Mary outside the bounds of the ideal marriage. Furthermore, she articulates her submission to God, but not explicitly to her husband. We also find Mary traveling from Nazareth to Judea to visit Elizabeth (1:39), without any mention of a companion or guardian.[43]

While in some aspects Luke portrays Mary as contrary to the ideal image of a submissive woman in the empire, there are other ways in which she does conform. Like most other women in Luke and Acts, Mary speaks only within the confines of a home (1:40).[44] Public proclamation is reserved for men, so that the themes sounded in the Magnificat are brought out into the open by the prophetic announcement of Jesus in the synagogue at Nazareth (4:18–19).[45] Throughout his Gospel, Luke gives a double message with regard to women. He depicts the majority of his female characters as silent and passive, staying behind the scenes, and choosing the "better part" by listening silently, not engaged in min-

42. Ibid., 120.

43. The popular fourteenth century writer Ludolph of Saxony (*Vita Domini nostri Jesu Christi ex quatuor evangeliis*) solved what appears to be a most unorthodox situation by asserting that a train of virgins and angels accompanied her to protect her. Malina and Rohrbaugh opine: "It seems Mary considers the son she conceives as apotropaic, clearly capable of warding off evil" (*Social-Science Commentary,* 291).

44. Elizabeth conforms to the ideal for pregnant women, remaining five months in seclusion after conceiving (1:24). Her prophetic speech when naming her child and conveying God's message of grace takes place in a family gathering (1:59–66). Mary will not speak out in public, but rather "ponders" everything "in her heart" (2:19, 51). Anna is one exception, who is in a more public space in the temple. She seems at first to conform to the ideal of a pious, prayerful widow, but her speech about the child to all who were "looking for the redemption (λύτρωσιν) of Jerusalem (2:38) is quite subversive. Other women who appear to be autonomous female leaders, exercising their authority within a household (without the presence of a male *paterfamilias*), include: Martha (Luke 10:38–42); Mary (Acts 12:12), Dorcas/Tabitha (Acts 9:36–42), and Lydia (Acts 16:14–15, 40). Prisca and Aquila hear Apollos preach in a synagogue and then "take him aside" to explain the way more accurately to him (Acts 18:26). It is not clear where they took him; Luke appears to want to avoid portraying Prisca as teaching in the synagogue. One other instance where women are ministering outside the confines of their home is Luke 8:1–3, where Mary Magdalene, Joanna, Susanna, and other Galilean women are accompanying Jesus as he journeys from one town and village to another as he is proclaiming and preaching the good news. One other exception is the widow who confronts the unjust judge in public space, demanding justice (Luke 18:1–8).

45. For further elaboration on how prophetic speech is reserved to men in Luke and Acts, see D'Angelo, "Women in Luke-Acts," 441–61; Reid, *Choosing,* 30–35, 144–62, 198–204.

istries of diaconal leadership (Luke 10:38–42).[46] However, while women in Luke seem outwardly to accommodate to the empire, inside their homes they equip their children and family members with stories and songs that envision an alternative rule to that of Caesar. By telling the stories of what they do in their homes, Luke serves to bring their words into public space through the proclamation of his Gospel.

---

46. See further Reid, *Choosing*; Seim, *Double Message*; Schaberg, "Luke," 363–80.

4

Jerusalem and Rome in Luke-Acts

*Observations on the Structure and the Intended
Message*

Michael Bachmann

WITH HIS BOOK *LUKE-ACTS AND THE JEWS*,[1] PUBLISHED SOME TWENTY
years ago, Robert L. Brawley made a significant contribution that was
justifiably critical of certain influential German-language interpretations, especially that of Hans Conzelmann,[2] and in this respect the
study was stimulated not least by the work of the Norwegian scholar
Jacob Jervell.[3] Within the Anglo-American domain, then, Brawley's
book demonstrated a perspective quite distinct from that taken in *The
Jews in Luke-Acts* by Jack T. Sanders,[4] also published in 1987. Brawley
concludes his study by stating that this book has led him "to join the
company of scholars who are now resisting the standard reading of
Luke-Acts as a triumph of gentile Christianity over Judaism."[5] Since
then, and also with his aid, this "company" of those who refused to go
along with that mainstream has substantially increased, and the previous "standard reading," without actually having disappeared, has at any

1. Brawley, *Luke-Acts and the Jews*. Cf., e.g., also Brawley, "Covenant Traditions."

2. See esp. Conzelmann, *Mitte*.

3. See esp. the collection of essays: Jervell, *Luke and the People of God*. Cf. Jervell,
Apostelgeschichte, furthermore, e.g., Jervell, "Gottes Treue." Cf. Bauckham, "Restoration
of Israel," 466 n. 63. See Tyson, *Luke, Judaism and the Scholars*, esp. 127: ". . . Brawley's
work is significant."

4. Sanders, *Jews in Luke-Acts*. On Sanders (and Brawley) cf. only Tyson, *Luke,
Judaism and the Scholars*, 113–22 (and 126–27).

5. Brawley, *Luke-Acts and the Jews*, 159.

rate forfeited its dominance.[6] In Germany, I had also in my doctoral thesis, published in 1980, undertaken a critique of the view presented by Conzelmann. I was especially critical of the presumption that Luke strictly separated the Jewish Temple from its indigenous location, Jerusalem.[7] While Martin Rese completely ignored my study in his overview "'Die Juden' im lukanischen Doppelwerk" (published in a *Festschrift* for Gerhard Schneider in 1991),[8] my impetus is taken up by Brawley (whose work, in turn, was arrogantly treated by Rese[9]). Brawley maintains, for instance, that the Temple and Jerusalem "are of one piece for Luke. Luke . . . apparently associates 'holy' (ἱερός) or 'Temple' (ἱερόν) with 'Hierosolyma' (Ἱεροσόλυμα)."[10] And in the meantime, it has become obvious that Brawley is not at all alone with this view.[11]

This compatibility of our views on the topic of "Jerusalem in Luke-Acts" would alone be sufficient reason for me to contribute a paper on Jerusalem and on the capital of the Roman Empire, a city, which is also explicitly mentioned in the Lukan writings, to the book "Luke-Acts and the Empire." Yet, my indebtedness to and friendship with Robert L. Brawley[12] provide even greater motivation to make this study available here.

Luke's mention of the two cities is, moreover, of a certain statistical significance. Not only is the frequency of 'Hierosolyma' (Ἱεροσόλυμα: 27 occurrences, compared to 26 in other writings of the NT; cf. Ἱεροσολυμῖται [Mark 1:5; John 7:25]) or 'Jerusalem' (Ἱερουσαλήμ: 62 occurrences, 12 in other NT writings) remarkably high in Luke: 70% at less than 30% of the total number of words in the New Testament

6. On this see esp. Kurth, *Juden*, 19–36. Cf. Rese, "Jews."

7. Bachmann, *Jerusalem*, esp. 8.

8. Rese, "Bericht" (and, correspondingly, also: Rese, "Jews").

9. Rese, "Bericht," 68 n. 16. Critically on this Wasserberg, *Israels Mitte*, 66 n. 84 (cf. 189–90).

10. Brawley, *Luke-Acts and the Jews*, 123 (together with nn. 38–39) (cf. generally esp., 118–32). Cf. Bachmann, *Jerusalem*, 13–66, esp. 17, 63–65 (and cf. below [at] n. 17).

11. Cf., e.g., Sanders, *Jews in Luke-Acts*, 35–36 (together with n. 80); Klauck, "Jerusalem," 101 (together with n. 2) and p. 114; Ganser-Kerperin, *Zeugnis des Tempels*, esp. 308–11 (together with n. 19).

12. To mention only this: Robert did not shrink back from the effort to translate my book of essays on Galatians (Bachmann, *Antijudaismus im Galaterbrief?*); this made possible the English version (*idem, Anti-Judaism in Galatians?*). This commitment demands, I think, great respect!

(Luke-Acts: 89 occurrences, otherwise in the NT: 38).[13] Much the same applies for 'Rome' ('Ρώμη: Luke: 0 [but cf. for instance Luke 2:1: Caesar Augustus; οἰκουμένη]; Acts: 5 occurrences; cf. 'Ρωμαῖος [John 11:48; Acts: 11 occurrences]; 'Ρωμαϊστί [John 19:20]): some 62% of all the occurrences in the New Testament (the only further occurrences are: Rom 1:7.15; 2 Tim 1:17[14]). Given the high number of instances of "Jerusalem" and "Rome" in Luke-Acts compared to the rest of the New Testament, it would seem imperative to deal with the topic of Jerusalem and Rome in Luke-Acts.

Jerusalem

Turning to *Jerusalem* first, there can be no doubt about the emphasis placed on this city in Luke-Acts, as the remarks on its frequent occurrence already have demonstrated. Let us first consider the fact (touched upon above) that there are two distinct forms of the name Jerusalem in Luke-Acts and let us at least note the particular emphases involved in this distinction—with respect to, for instance, the evaluation of the Temple, and, further, with respect to the history of salvation and to integrating the city into this history, in particular into the fate of the "people of the twelve tribes." After dealing with these matters, then, we can summarize the role of this city in Luke-Acts, especially with reference to its literary functions in these writings.

The distribution of the two forms of the city name occurring in Luke-Acts appears relatively complicated, yet seems not especially difficult to delineate.[15] The non-declinable term 'Jerusalēm' ('Ιερουσαλήμ), which corresponds more closely to the Hebrew (*Jerūšālēm*, *Jerūšalājim*), is fairly common in Luke (26 occurrences) and even more so in Acts (36). The final occurrence, however, is Acts 25:3. The more Greek form

13. On this see Bachmann, *Jerusalem*, 13–66, esp. 14.19–21 (where I count [14 n. 4] Luke 13:34 ['Ιερουσαλήμ, 'Ιερουσαλήμ] only as *one* occurrence [and, correspondingly, also Matt 23:37], and where I prefer [31] 'Hierosolyma' ['Ιεροσόλυμα] for reasons of textual criticism), and see, furthermore, on the extent of the New Testament and of its individual writings Morgenthaler, *Statistik*, 164.

14. Furthermore, another word, the word 'Babylōn' (Βαβυλών), in 1 Peter 5:13 seems to be an "apocalyptic code for . . . Rome" (Strobel, "Βαβυλών," 453), correspondingly also in Rev 14:8; 16:19; 17:5; 18:2.10.21 (on this see 453).

15. On this see once again Bachmann, *Jerusalem*, 13–66, esp. 40 n. 2 (here a chart on the data).

of the name, the declinable form (τὰ Ἱεροσόλυμα), although on the whole much less common (Luke: 4 instances; Acts: 23), is used also afterwards and occurs a total of nine times from Acts 25:7 on. In nearly every case (with the single exception of Acts 25:7), the occurrences are within the context of quoted speech. Apparently, neither Hebrew nor Aramaic is presumed to have been the language used in the quoted speech, but, instead, Greek (or Latin). The occurrences are as follows: quotes from the Roman governor Festus (Acts 25:9, 15, 20, 24); Paul's words (Acts 26:4, 10, 20)[16] in his own defense before Festus, Agrippa (II) and Bernice (see, e.g., Acts 25:23–24); and later, when he addresses Roman Jews, Paul also uses 'Hierosolyma' (Acts 28:17: Ἱεροσόλυμα). Before these instances, and without exception, 'Jerusalēm' (Ἱερουσαλήμ), the form closest to the Hebrew, is used within the *oratio directa* and in all of these cases (a total of 40 occurrences) those speaking were presented as Jews who spoke Hebrew or Aramaic. Based on this analysis, it becomes apparent that Luke consistently distinguishes in his quotations the specific linguistic medium of the speakers and that he is aware that 'Jerusalēm' (Ἱερουσαλήμ) is the more appropriate form for the Semitic language. The author himself was probably more familiar with the form Ἱεροσόλυμα, that is, the term used in the very first mention of Jerusalem in Luke-Acts (Luke 2:22). Wherever in his narrative Ἱερουσαλήμ occurs, this seems to indicate the use of tradition. In any case, with this wording Luke implies that these points in his story have something to do with pre-established facts, with features of the history of salvation.

Both of these findings—one related to the *oratio directa* and the other related to Luke's narrative—are not without relevance for the message intended in Luke's work. As mentioned above, the first finding indicates in any case that Luke, who refers over 35 times to the location of the Temple in Jerusalem as τὸ ἱερόν, wants his readers to understand that Ἱεροσόλυμα is the city where this sacred site of the temple is to be found. This can hardly be doubted, as both non-Jewish and Jewish authors (e.g., Hekataios of Abdera, Eupolemos, Flavius Josephus) establish an "etymological" connection between just this name of the city

---

16. Acts 26:14(–19) specifically gives (differently from Acts 9:4–7; 22:7–10!) the hint that the exalted Jesus did address Paul "in the Hebrew language" (which is alluded to also with Σαοὺλ Σαούλ [cf. Acts 9:4; 22:7; differently, e.g., Acts 12:25; 13:9: Σαῦλος]). Paul himself, therefore, does not use here the Hebrew or the Aramaic language.

and ἱερόν.[17] But the term Ἱεροσόλυμα is also of further interest in our context. It indicates that Luke wrote as an author familiar with diction prevalent in the Roman Empire beyond Palestine. As the words of the silversmith Demetrius in Acts 19:27 (τὸ τῆς μεγάλης θεᾶς Ἀρτέμιδος ἱερόν) definitively show,[18] Luke was knowledgeable about temples at other locations (in this case: a temple with worldwide significance in Ephesus). This fact makes the references to Jerusalem as the city of the Temple even more noteworthy. They correspond to several mentions within the Lucan work that indicate that this sacred place is presumed to be central for Jews.

Perhaps it is sufficient here to refer to the scene with the twelve-year-old Jesus in the Temple, displaying this locality as a place of pilgrimage (Luke 2:41–51/52, esp. 2:41–43). We could also refer to Paul's Nazirite vow—near the end of his stay in Corinth (Acts 18:18[–22])—, which implies that, according to Luke, the Jews of the Diaspora also felt a strong bond to the Temple in Jerusalem (cf. Num 6:13–20).[19] The form of the name Ἱερουσαλήμ goes along with this train of thought well, because it furnishes what we have just noted on the level of locality with an historical dimension. As the "more Hebrew" form of the word, the name recalls the continuing history of God with his people, the Jews. The profile of this intention may become more pronounced if we recall Jesus' "presentation" in the Temple (Luke 2:22–39/40)—in particular Simeon's remarks speaking, with respect to Jesus, of God's salvation (σωτήριον) for the peoples (λαοί) and Gentiles (ἔθνη) (2:30–32), and also talking of "the fall and rising of many in Israel" (2:34). In the same section dealing with Jesus' presentation, Anna speaks of the "redemption of Jerusalem" (2:38: λύτρωσις Ἱερουσαλήμ).[20] At this point, then, salvation history and eschatology are connected with Jerusalem.

17. On this see Bachmann, *Jerusalem*, 17.63–65, and Bachmann, "Tempel III," 56 (cf. above [at] n. 10).

18. Only here Luke uses the word ἱερόν for a non-Jewish temple. This peculiarity is expressed by a genitive attribute—lacking throughout otherwise.

19. On this see Bachmann, "Tempel III," 58.

20. The version "redemption of Jerusalem" (λύτρωσιν Ἱερουσαλήμ [א B *inter alia*]) is better attested (than "redemption of Israel" [λύρωσιν Ἰσραήλ]), and there is also the fact that in the context (*i.e.*, in Luke 2:25) it is said: the "consolation of Israel" (on this see Bachmann, *Jerusalem*, 33 together with n. 86). To these phrases the wording "to redeem Israel" (Luke 24:21: λυτροῦσθαι τὸν Ἰσραήλ) could be added. These expressions correspond to the political and religious expectations of the Judaism of that time. It may

Two features of this section on the presentation of Jesus are particularly interesting for our purposes. First, the prophetess Anna is assigned (in 2:36) to the tribe of Asher (which a hundred years before had been exiled to Assyria, Media [see, e.g., 2 Kings 17:6; cf. Acts 2:9]). Second, we are told that this woman "never left the temple", but that she worshiped there, "serving night and day with fasting and prayer" (Luke 2:37). This wording, together with the similar phrase used by Paul in Acts 26:7 (of the hopeful "people of the twelve tribes" who "serve God night and day") demonstrate that the Temple—and along with it Jerusalem—is understood by Luke as a symbol of the impending restitution of the people of Israel, the "twelve tribes" (δωδεκάφυλον).[21]

Special attention should be paid to the number "twelve" in this context[22]. For with a particular eschatological nuance, the participants of the "Last Supper" (Luke 22:14–38) are told that those who have stood by Jesus in His trials will one day eat "at His table in His kingdom" and (sitting on "thrones") "judge the *twelve* tribes of Israel" (Luke 22:30; cf. Matt 19:28). In contrast to Matt 19:28, the context here has to do with concrete wrongdoing within the group of the Twelve surrounding Jesus, that is, by the "traitor" Judas and by Simon Peter (Luke 22:21–22.31–34; cf. 22:47–48.54–62). Luke's reference to the remaining "eleven" (24:9.33; cf. Matt 28:16) is to be understood as emphasizing the fact that "one of the twelve" (Luke 22:47; par. Mark 14:43; Matt 26:47), Judas, had withdrawn from the group. Only Luke, of course, accentuates the numerical factor with a replacement for the deficient group of "eleven apostles" in the person of Matthias (Acts 1:15–26; esp. 1:26), so that once again there exists a group of "twelve" (Acts 6:2; cf. 2:14). In this way, the number of the group corresponds both to the "twelve patriarchs" (Acts 7:8)

---

be remembered that during the first Jewish war (67–70/73 CE) the insurgents minted coins presenting *inter alia* the following inscriptions: "'shekel of Israel. Jerusalem (is) holy', 'shekel of Israel. Jerusalem the Holy', 'freedom of Zion', 'For the deliverance of Zion'", and in the second Jewish war (132–135 CE) correspondingly it goes, for instance: "'for the deliverance of Israel' or 'for the freedom of Israel/Jerusalem'" (see Reiser, *Numismatik*, 465–67 [with bibliographical hints; citations: 466]; cf. Bachmann, *Jerusalem*, 365–366 together with n. 596), furthermore Bauckham, "Restoration," esp. 451–52, 457–59.

21. On this see Bachmann, *Jerusalem*, 336–340 together with n. 511, Stegemann, "Licht der Völker," esp. 92, 95, and Bauckham, "Restoration," esp. 457–58 (cf. Bauckham, "Anna," esp. 166–67). Cf. below at nn. 57, 75.

22. On this see Holtz, "δώδεκα," 877–80. Cf. (once again) Bachmann, *Jerusalem*, 337–40 n. 511, furthermore Bauckham, "Restoration," 469–77.

and to the twelve tribes of Israel. This accentuation of salvation history is certainly not meant to be ignored.

In Luke-Acts, the group of twelve apostles is, in turn, brought into connection with the Temple (see Acts 2:42–47, esp. 2:46; 5:42; cf., e.g., Luke 24:44–53) and, in particular, with Jerusalem. This is especially clear in Acts 8:1,[23] which says that due to the "great persecution against the church" in the aftermath of Stephen's death, "they were all scattered throughout the regions of Judea and Samaria," all, that is, "except the apostles"! The twelve apostles remained in Jerusalem and in the Temple.

Thus, for Luke, the Temple and Jerusalem represent the "twelve tribes" that will be restored. In Luke's view, it is above all the twelve apostles who have this connection with Jerusalem and the Temple.

This connection with the twelve, then, casts a certain light on the role of Jerusalem in Luke-Acts, which can only be briefly outlined here.[24] It is no secret that the narrative of the third Gospel begins and ends at the Temple in Jerusalem; more precisely, there are two "Jerusalem-Temple sections": Luke 1:5—2:52; 19:45—24:53. Acts, of course, with its ending situated outside of Palestine, deviates from this scheme. Yet, here, too, there are two extensive "Jerusalem-Temple sections" which are quite conspicuous: Acts 1:3—8:3 and 21:15—23:32. Both Luke and Acts exhibit a similar emphasis—for instance, when they characterize the Temple as a place of teaching for Jesus or for the apostles (see esp. Luke 19:45; 20:1; 21:37; Acts 2:42; 4:2; 5:21–25.42; cf. Luke 2:46–47).[25]

23. On this cf. furthermore Fuller, *Restoration of Israel*, esp. 210.

24. In more detail: Bachmann, *Jerusalem*, esp. 137–70, Klauck, "Jerusalem," 114–28, esp. 115–26, and Ganser-Kerperin, *Zeugnis des Tempels*, esp. 318–19. Concerning the places alluded to in Acts 1:13 and in Acts 2:1–2 (on this cf. Klauck, "Jerusalem," 121 n. 63, and Ganser-Kerperin, *Zeugnis des Tempels*, 318 n. 41) I suspect that "the room upstairs" (Acts 1:13) is to be presumed "probably not in the Temple areal"—whereas the "story of Pentecost" (Acts 2:1–43) was connected with this locality at least in the tradition before Luke (Bachmann, "Tempel III," 58, with bibliographical hints and with short explanation). These problems are only of minor relevance for our present considerations (cf. Bachmann, *Jerusalem*, 157 n. 79).

25. On this see, e.g., Bachmann, *Jerusalem*, (152–70 and 261–87, esp. 279–87, Klauck, "Jerusalem," 118, 121. Cf. Brawley, *Luke-Acts and the Jews*, 123, and Ganser-Kerperin, *Zeugnis des Tempels*, esp. 178–91. On Acts 2:42 and on the localities thought of there, the chiastic structure of the verse and also the context (see esp. 2:43–47), as it seems to me (on this see Bachmann, *Jerusalem*, 356 together with nn. 564–66), present quite clear evidence (cf. also Öhler, "Jerusalemer Urgemeinde," 409). Correspondingly, teaching and prayer should belong to the Temple, community and breaking bread to private houses (or a private house).

Moreover, both works emphasize, at least in the second "Jerusalem-Temple section," some sort of juridical event: the passion of Jesus or the circumstances surrounding the arrest of Paul. Although both in Luke's Gospel and in Acts, a geographical note more or less connects the first "Jerusalem-Temple section"[26] with the second one, the impending trials are not the major focus. Instead, something like an overarching perspective becomes apparent.[27] Luke 9:51 says: "And it came about, when the days were come that He should be received up [into heaven], that He [Jesus] resolutely set His face towards Jerusalem." The earlier reference in the transfiguration story to Jesus' "exodus" (ἔξοδος), which he was "about to accomplish in Jerusalem," is, then, interpreted here as an "ascension" (Luke 9:51: ἀνάλημψις) that transcends the city of Jerusalem (see Luke 24:51; Acts 1:9–11; cf. Luke 24:26).[28] The note in the analogous place in Acts 19:21 is also a reference that points beyond Jerusalem: "Paul resolved in the spirit, when he had passed through Macedonia and Achaia, to go to Jerusalem, saying, 'After I have been there, I must also see Rome.'" Thus, the name of another city, Rome, has been mentioned (in Luke-Acts, now, after Acts 18:2, for the second time)—after the term Ἰεροσόλυμα previously had been used (*i.e.*, just in Acts 19:21) and after Ἰερουσαλήμ in Luke 9:51. Before we now turn to the topic of Rome, let us make a note of these structural observations in a tableau:[29]

26. On this (and on what has been said just before) see the (summarizing) chart at Bachmann, *Jerusalem*, 157 n. 70. In the context (see esp. 138, 142–44, 154–55) I emphasize that the expression "Jerusalem section," avoided in this essay (for reasons of the stressing of the Temple [and of the framing by it]) throughout by "Jerusalem-Temple section" (cf., e.g., VIII), does or shall not mean that the reported things are to be located *without exception* in this town (to which the story of Luke 2:1–20, for instance, clearly does not belong).

27. On this see esp. Bachmann, *Jerusalem*, 146, 158 (together with n. 181), and Klauck, "Jerusalem," 116–18, 124–25, who correctly says (124): "The closeness [of Luke 9:51 and Acts 19:21] further increases, if one compares the remark that Paul did send two of his helpers on ahead in the [on Acts 19:21] following verse Acts 19:22 with Luke 9:52: Jesus sends messengers ahead of him." Furthermore, regarding the two journeys to Jerusalem each time the danger is spoken of not without emphasis, *i.e.*, in Luke 13:33–35 and in Acts 20:22–25 (cf. 20:16).

28. On this feature specific to Luke see esp. Lohfink, *Himmelfahrt*. Cf. Bauckham, "Restoration," 468, and below (at) n. 47.

29. On this cf. once again Bachmann, *Jerusalem*, 157 n. 70.

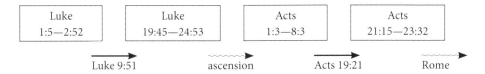

Tableau on the Relationship between the Four "Jerusalem-Temple Sections"

Rome

As mentioned above, within the context of the books of the New Testament the frequency of "*Rome*" ('Ρώμη) and "*Roman*" ('Ρωμαῖος) in Luke-Acts (5 times "Rome" and 11 times "Roman") is quite noteworthy (otherwise in the NT: 3 and 1 occurrences). One might assume, however, that this is simply due to the outline of the book, since Acts, then, finally ends in Rome (Acts 28:14–31), and this book, Acts, does contain *all* (16) of Luke's instances; not a single one is to be found in Luke's Gospel.[30] Yet, already the reference to "Roman" ('Ρωμαῖος) in Acts 2:10, which has to do with Romans who have become residents of Jerusalem,[31] calls for a more balanced judgment. Especially the use of the title 'Caesar' (Καῖσαρ) as early as Luke 2:1 and 3:1—along with the concurrent names "Augustus" and "Tiberius"—demonstrates that the Roman Empire, which dominated the Mediterranean world and, of course, Palestine, thus the οἰκουμένη, explicitly named as early as Luke 2:1 [cf. Luke 4:5; 21:26; Acts 11:28; 17:6.31; 19:27; 24:5]), is definitely being referred to in Luke-Acts, at least in the sense of a political framework. The additional mention of various specific authorities of the Roman Empire supports this interpretation.[32] The author consciously embeds his two books, in

---

30. On this cf. esp. Burfeind, "Paulus *muß* nach Rom," 76–77, and Ganser-Kerperin, *Zeugnis des Tempels*, 306–7 together with n. 8.

31. On this see Bachmann, *Jerusalem*, 301–2 together with n. 366.

32. To be taken into consideration are (P. Sulpicius) Quirinius (Luke 2:2), Pontius Pilatus (Luke 3:1 *inter alia*), Sergius Paul(l)us (Acts 13:7), (L. Iunius) Gallio (Annaeanus) (Acts 18:12 *inter alia*), Felix (Acts 23:24 *inter alia*), (Porzius) Festus (Acts 24:27 *inter alia*), a 'hekatontarchēs' in Caphernaum (Luke, 7:[1–]2 *inter alia*) and other "officers" (Luke 23:47; Acts 10:1 [*i.e.*, Cornelius]), a 'chiliarchos' named Claudius Lysias (Acts 21:31–40; the name: Acts 23:26 [and 24:22; cf. 24:7 *v.l.*]), further "military tribunes" (Acts 25:23), also "soldiers" (Luke 7:8; 23:36; Acts 21:32 *inter alia*). Cf. also Acts 16:19–24; 17:6–9; 19:31.35.38; 28:7, further see Haensch, "Prinzipat," esp. 153–54 and 162–64, and Omerzu, "Imperium," 29.

which the Jewish city Jerusalem is strongly emphasized, in a context set by Rome. This is also where the various Jewish rulers of the Herodian dynasty have their place,[33] starting from Herod the Great of Luke 1:5, until Agrippa of Acts 25:13, Agrippa II, who goes to the Roman administrative seat of 'Caesarea' (Καισάρεια) to greet the new prefect. Before Paul's journey to Rome (touched upon with the mention of Agrippa II) can be dealt with in more detail, there are two aspects that require further attention, and they are not insignificant for the apostle's journey. On the one hand, Luke is aware of more than this *one* direction of movement—towards Rome. On the other hand, it is apparent that Rome signifies for Luke something more than simply a political center, it is also a place of religious relevance.[34]

As far as the directions of movement are concerned, the idea that a prefect like Festus arrives in the Jewish 'eparcheia' (ἐπαρχεία), apparently coming from Rome, and that he then very soon goes up "to Jerusalem" from Caesarea (Acts 25:1) is not a focus here, since the term "Rome" ('Ρώμη) is not used in this context. But that such a direction of movement is assumed can hardly be contested, especially since in Acts 10:1; 27:1, for example, reference is made to Rome and to the surroundings of the city (*inter alia*) with the mention of the "Italian" and "Augustan" cohorts.[35] Even more noteworthy, as already briefly mentioned above, is the circumstance that the very first Lucan reference to "Roman" ('Ρωμαῖος), Acts 2:10, apparently designates Romans who have now become residents of Jerusalem. The corresponding first appearance of "Rome" ('Ρώμη), Acts 18:2, occurs within an account concerning a Jewish man who has come to Corinth with his wife because of an edict issued by the emperor Claudius[36] demanding that the Jews leave Rome. The characterization of this man, Aquila, as a Jew who was "a native of Pontus" refers to a major background element of such movement away from Rome and of other journeys of Jews in the Mediterranean area:

---

33. On this see particularly Horn, "Haltung des Lukas zum römischen Staat," 215–24, and Wilker, *Für Rom und Jerusalem*, esp. 471–82.

34. Similarly esp. Burfeind, "Paulus *muß* nach Rom," 91. Differently, e.g., Ganser-Kerperin, *Zeugnis des Tempels*, 306–307 (together with n. 10).

35. On this cf. Haensch, "Prinzipat," 161–64.

36. This edict is referred to by Suetonius, Claudius 25,4. On the chronological determination of this action see Riesner, "Chronologie des Neuen Testaments," 216; and Zeigan, *Aposteltreffen in Jerusalem*, 419 together with n. 12.

Luke is well aware that there is a Jewish diaspora,[37] and precisely the corresponding and comprehensive list of the diaspora in Acts 2:9–11 is introduced in 2:5 (or in 2:5–8; cf. 2:11b) by stating that these people, some of whom come from beyond the borders of the Roman Empire, are all Jews who have now become residents of Jerusalem,[38] but are originally "from every nation under heaven" (Acts 2:5).[39] To be added to these instances (for a direction towards Jerusalem) are some remarks in the Lucan works that speak of diaspora Jews having come to Jerusalem or to the Temple there, with Paul among them (Acts 6:9; 9:28; cf. 18:24), and there are references to Paul, the Christian missionary, and other

37. The noun διασπορά is, however, missing in Luke-Acts (differently to John 7:35; Jas 1:1; 1 Peter 1:1), where at any rate the corresponding verb διασπείρειν is used (Acts 8:1.4; 11:19); in the New Testament only in Acts 11:19 (cf. 11:20, furthermore 13:1) it hints clearly at the phenomenon of the diaspora (in "Phoenicia, Cyprus [cf. Acts 4:36], and Antioch"). It is referred to also in Acts 15:21 (*i.e.*, in a word of James), which applies *inter alia* to the existence of synagogues: "since old lineages in every town" (translation: Jervell, *Apostelgeschichte*, 385). Concerning the Jews of Rome, see Lichtenberger, "Organisationsformen," 15–20, 24.

38. One this see Bachmann, *Jerusalem*, 74–76 (together with n. 27) and 297–302 (together with n. 366). For two characteristics of this list one usually was ready to judge for a long time: "Completely enigmatic remain [firstly] the '*Judea*' between Mesopotamia and Cappadocia and [secondly] the '*Cretans and Arabs*' at the end" (so Hengel, "Liste," 53). But particularly Eissfeldt had made suggestions (to solve these problems) worth thinking about (Eissfeldt, "Kreter und Araber"; Eissfeldt, "Apostelgeschichte 2,9"; and Eisfeldt, "Bezeichnung nordsyrischer Bereiche"). At the word 'Judea' he thought of the territory J'dj (in the north of Syria), attested for the ninth/eighth century BCE by inscriptions found near Sendschirli and reflected probably by "Judah" in 2 Kings 14:28 (also: in the Septuagint), and "Cretans and Arabs" he interpreted as inhabitants of the islands and of the mainland (cf., e.g., Ps 71[72]:10; Isa 42:10–12; Philo *Praem* 165; *Flacc* 45–46; *LegGai* 282 [where, by the way, "Crete" is named specifically, as are the "Arabs" in the mentioned verse of the Psalter]). Whereas I have followed these proposals (see once again Bachmann, *Jerusalem*, 74–76 together with n. 27), Hengel, "Liste," esp. 55, 59–60, 67, rejects them. According to him the list has a messianic horizon and therefore thinks of a "Great-Judea", reflecting "probably expectations concerning the extent of Eretz Israel in the messianic future" (66); he thinks that the end of the list alludes to "the 'pilgrimage of the nations' to mount Zion" (67; cf. Scott, "Luke's Geographical Horizon," esp. 529–30). The curve of the diaspora, starting from the Parthians in the east (indeed, beyond the border of the Roman empire!) and stretching to the Romans in the west, and also the connection of this line with Jerusalem deserves attention in the context of Luke-Acts. But to link the "Cretans and Arabs" with the "nations" seems to me questionable because Acts 2:5 just at the beginning speaks about Ἰουδαῖοι. And, by the way, Luke knows how to use the word Συρία (see esp. Acts 15:41).

39. This is the paraphrasing given by Hengel, "Liste," 56. Similarly Bachmann, *Jerusalem*, 298–300. Cf. Bauckham, "Restoration," esp. 471–72.

Christians traveling to Jerusalem, whether because of a Nazirite vow[40] or for comparable reasons (Acts 11:29–30 [cf. 12:25]; 15:3; 18:22; 19:21; 20:4–6.22–23; 21:12.15–17.26; 22:5.17; 24:11.17–19; cf. 21:28–29; 25:2–3.9; 26:4).

To put it briefly: Despite the imperial political center designated by the term "Rome" ('Ρώμη), for Luke there remains another city that is important, at least for Jews and for Christians who are connected with Jews, namely Jerusalem. For such people, Jerusalem has a function similar to that designated by Philo (see, e.g., the passage *LegGai* 278–283; cf. Isaiah 1:26LXX) with such words as: ἱερόπολις, πατρίς, and μητρόπολις.[41] Not least does this explain the direction of movement counter to the impulse in the direction towards Rome. Even when Paul finally is in Rome, there is still the issue of what those in Judea (and Jerusalem) might think of him (see Acts 28:21; cf. 28:17), i.e., Jerusalem remains important also here.

These considerations have at least touched upon a second aspect that is often not perceived clearly enough[42]—that Rome, or the Roman Empire, is most definitely also to be seen as a phenomenon that is of religious relevance. It should be added that the author of Luke-Acts places an emphasis on decidedly critical features in this context. Thus, Acts 18:2 clearly illustrates with the edict from Claudius that this emperor has caused problems for Jews. After all, they (and perhaps a number of early Jewish Christians [cf. Acts 18:2–3]) had to leave Rome. Moreover, *all* of the Lucan references to 'Roman' ('Ρωμαῖος) or 'Romans' ('Ρωμαῖοι) exhibit a contrast with 'Jews' (Ιουδαῖοι), and the situation is similar for 'Rome' ('Ρώμη).[43] Both theological and Christological details—and this is of course of special significance—point in the same direction.

40. On this see Bachmann, "Tempel III," 58; Omerzu, *Prozeß des Paulus*, 298–308; and Zeigan, *Aposteltreffen*, 473–75 together with n. 241 (and the bibliographical hints given there).

41. On this see Klauck "Jerusalem," 103–11 (together with n. 25) and 129, furthermore Scott, "Horizon," esp. 495–99.

42. Differently, e.g., Burfeind, "Paulus *muß* nach Rom," esp. 88–91 (cf. also Klein, "Bild des Augustus," 206–9). Cf. below (at) nn. 69–72, 80.

43. 'Roman' ('Ρωμαῖος): On Acts 2:10c cf. 2:5, 10d; on 16:21, 37, 38 cf. 16:20; on 22:25, 26, 27, 29 cf. 22:30; on 23:27 cf. 23:27a (and 26:28–29); on 25:16 cf. 25:15; on 28:17c cf. 28:17b. 'Rome' ('Ρώμη): On 18:2c cf. (along with 18:2c) also 18:2a, 4–5; on 23:11 cf. 23:12; on 28:14, 17c cf. (along with 28:17c) also 28:17a. I did not mention so far 19:21; but though "the Jews" here are not named in the immediate connection with Rome (cf. at any rate 19:17, 33–34), the tension in the juxtaposition with "Jerusalem"—the city of the "twelve tribes" due for restitution—hints just towards this direction.

It may be sufficient to demonstrate the religious relevance of Rome with respect to important formulations involving "king" (βασιλεύς) and "lord" (κύριος). The scene depicted in Acts 17:5–9 is in and of itself quite instructive in this regard. In Thessalonica, the accusations made against "Jason and some brethren" (17:6), claiming that "they act contrary to the decrees of Caesar, saying that there is *another* 'king' (βασιλεύς), Jesus" (17:7), are not called "false witnesses" (in contrast to, in particular, Acts 6:13)—even though "some wicked men" (17:5) form part of the mob before the city authorities. If Jesus is thus referred to with the term "king" (βασιλεύς) as something similar to an emperor (cf., for example, 1 Tim 2:2; 1 Peter 2:13.17; Rev 17:9–11), as some sort of counter-emperor (cf. Rev 17:14), then it is likely that Luke 23:2 is to be understood in an analogous way. There, the Jews gathered before Pilate claim that the person they have accused has forbidden the people "to give tribute to Caesar . . . saying that he himself is Christ, the 'king' (βασιλεύς)." The severity of this reproach diminishes somewhat with Pilate's question of Jesus, as in the parallels (Matt 27:11; Mark 15:2; cf. John 18:33), whether he is "the king *of the Jews*" (Luke 23:3). But the explosive force of the charge of Luke 23:2 is still, especially in light of Acts 17:7, distinctly discernible (cf. John 18:[36–]37).[44]

In my opinion, the final verse of the Lucan writings is also characterized by a certain tension between the Roman emperor and the topics about which Paul, as a prisoner, is able to speak "unhindered." For at the words "preaching the kingdom of God and teaching the [things] about the 'lord' [κύριος] Jesus Christ," the attentive listener and reader of the book will remember (much like in Acts 26:15 [cf. also esp. Acts 2:36; 10:36; 23:11]) that earlier, in Acts 25:21–26, *Caesar* was called "lord" (κύριος).[45] Thus, the two spheres, Rome and the Roman Empire on the one hand, the Jewish center of Jerusalem where a King and Master, Jesus, died (see, for example, Luke 13:33; 23:7; Acts 4:27) on the other, are not at all in peaceful juxtaposition in Luke. How moderate the writer's tone may be, the explosive nature of these matters is nevertheless apparent.

---

44. Similarly Burfeind, "Paulus *muß* nach Rom," 84–85, furthermore Stegemann, *Synagoge und Obrigkeit*, 149–50 and 232–33 (where the tension spoken of seems to be eased too much [but see 232]). Cf. Karrer, *Der Gesalbte*, 319–20, 409–10 (cf. 141–47), furthermore Wolter, *Lukasevangelium*, 738–39.

45. Correspondingly already Burfeind, "Paulus *muß* nach Rom," 89 together with n. 65. Cf. Omerzu, "Imperium," 32.

This feature of the Lucan writings, the interplay (and tension) between "Jerusalem" and "Rome," is also discernible in Paul's journey to Rome, even up to the point of his "unhindered" preaching and teaching in Acts 28:31. The man who finally and interestingly enough arrives at exactly the place from which Jews, including Aquila and Priscilla, had been forced to withdraw (see again Acts 18:2) during the reign of Claudius (41–54 CE), makes his initial appearance in Acts in Jerusalem as a very agreeable witness to the stoning of Stephen (Acts 7:58; 8:1; cf. 22:20). At later points in the narrative the author explains that Paul, a diaspora Jew born in Tarsus, Cilicia, had come to Jerusalem at an early age and had undergone rather strict religious instruction there (see 21:39; 22:3–4). According to Luke, then, after experiencing his calling at Damascus (see, for instance, 9:3–4), Paul soon returns to Jerusalem (9:26–29), is threatened by Hellenistic Jews and retreats to Tarsus (9:30). Over time, he then becomes an important representative and propagandist of Christian teachings in the eastern Mediterranean, in Asia Minor, and in Greece (11:25—19:20); nevertheless, he also remains in contact with Jerusalem (see esp. 11:29–30; 12:25; 15:1–33; 18:18–22). On the occasion of a further visit to Jerusalem, Paul becomes subject to suspicions arising from rumors of his disloyalty to Judaism and, then, becomes captured in the Temple district and imprisoned by Roman officials (see 20:1—26:32, esp. 21:17–33). But before that Acts 19:21 mentions, as noted, Rome as Paul's destination—after the planned visit to Jerusalem. A considerable number of aspects could be discussed with regard to this gradual movement towards the Roman destination, which is not least facilitated by Paul's appeal to his rights as a Roman citizen (see esp. Acts 22:25, 27; cf. 23:27; 25:10–11; also 26:32).

For this essay, it may suffice to focus on three such aspects. First, a certain parallelism to Jesus' journey to Jerusalem is established especially by means of something like predictions of Paul's passion (see esp. 20:20–25; 21:10–11; cf. 22:18b–20, also 9:16),[46] while here, as 21:13 indicates, the idea is connected with a willingness to be bound and perhaps to die "for the name of the 'kyrios' (κύριος) Jesus." Second, in contrast to the third Gospel (see Luke 13:33), the divine imperative, the Greek δεῖ, now refers to the destination of Rome (see 19:21; 23:11;

46. On this cf. Stolle, *Zeuge*, 215–20; furthermore, Dunn, "ΚΥΡΙΟΣ in Acts," (368–72). But cf. Omerzu, "Imperium," 33.

cf. 25:10; 27:24),[1] even though this destination seems to be approach-able only via Jerusalem (see again 19:21; 20:22; 21:11; cf. 21:4, 12)—and Jerusalem remains topical in other ways as well (see [again] 28:17–21). Third, it is especially notable that the journey to Rome (much like Jesus' 'exodus' [ἔξοδος] in Jerusalem [see Luke 9:31]) is legitimized by some-thing like a paranormal proclamation, even several proclamations:[2] Whereas the ecstatic experience sending Paul *away* from Jerusalem (22:17–21) does not explicitly mention the city of Rome—and, instead, uses the more general wording: "far away to Gentiles" (22:21: εἰς ἔθνη μακράν; cf. 1:8)—verse 23:11 is more specific: "to/in Rome" (εἰς Ῥώμην). The destination outside of Jerusalem[3] in 22:17–21 becomes especially conspicuous, since in comparison to chapter 9 (but cf. there 9:13–14, 29–30, also the "I will appear" [ὀφθήσομαι] in 26:16) these verses are a later supplement that has apparently been consciously added to the closer context of 19:21. Moreover, it is notable that the journey away from Jerusalem, away to nations far away—to Rome—is initially related and proclaimed in a scene that takes place in the *Temple* at Jerusalem, during a prayer, 22:17–21.[4]

Heavenly Sanctuary

All of this brings us to an element of the Lucan imagination that is only rarely perceived or conceded, but which seems to allow Luke to describe the journey to Rome in such a way that the focus on Jerusalem noted above is not and need not be abandoned: namely, the conviction that there is a *heavenly place* or *residence of God*, a *heavenly Temple*. If this thesis can be made plausible—as will, of course, immediately be

1. On this see Burfeind, "Paulus *muß* nach Rom," 77–78. A certain parallel to the 'dei' (δεῖ) hinting to Rome seems to be (cf. above at. n. 28), however, the ἔδει of Luke 24:26, concerning not only the passion of Jesus, but also his "entering into the glory" (cf. Luke 9:31, 51).

2. By the way: Harnack, *Apostelgeschichte*, 111–30, esp. 116 (together with n. 1) and 118–19 (together with n. 1), had already dealt with this feature of Acts.

3. The compound 'exapostellein' (ἐξαποστέλλειν), used in Acts 22:21, emphasizes in Luke-Acts the trait (cf. esp. Luke 24:49; Acts 7:12; 13:26, furthermore, e.g., Ps 109[110]:2) that a "leaving of a certain area" is intended, and as "this [area] remarkably for the most part Palestine or Jerusalem is to be imagined" (Bachmann, *Jerusalem*, 231–32, 254–55, together with nn. 162–63 [citations: 231]).

4. On this see Bachmann, *Jerusalem*, 332–69, esp. 363–67, where particularly Luke 1:10–22 and 2:22–39 are compared with Acts 22:17–21.

attempted—then we could superimpose a further zone on the tableau designed above, a zone that also has to do with a "locally" conceived area, but one that, in principle, can constantly and at every turn be connected with the events recounted.[5] Then, the arrow connected to the word ἀνάλημψις or to the ascension, the arrow which up to this point had been arranged horizontally (just like the final one connected to Rome), would probably better serve its purpose if it were pointed upwards:

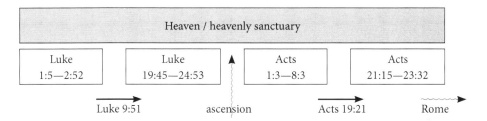

Tableau: Structure of Luke-Acts with Reference to "Jerusalem / the Temple"

With the "receiving up" of Jesus into heaven, Jerusalem and the Temple are, on the one hand, decidedly not renounced (see, e.g., Luke 24:50–53); on the other hand, the worldwide, universal preaching of the Gospel, which not least takes place "with power from on high" (Luke 24:49), is facilitated (see, e.g., Luke 24:46–49).

That the heavenly "locale" mentioned, which is also, then, of particular importance in Acts,[6] is not lacking in Temple connotations becomes apparent as early as Luke 24:26–27, where reference is made to Jesus' "entering into his glory" (εἰσελθεῖν εἰς τὴν δόξαν αὐτοῦ). For in the Old Testament writings to which this "entering into" is supposed to correspond according to 24:27, "glory" (*kābōd*, δόξα) is known to be connected with the tabernacle and with the Temple (of Jerusalem) (see, e.g., Exod 40:34–35; 1 Kgs 8:10–11). Moreover, *kābōd* is also perceived there in visions as the "glory of the Lord" or "of God" (see, e.g., Ezekiel

---

5. Particularly the wordings of Acts 2:5(–11); 4:11–12; 14:14–18; 17:24–29 are demonstrating that a concept like this suits very well other motifs of salvation history and theology.

6. On this heavenly "locale" see Acts 1:10–12; 2:2–4, 32–36; 7:55–56; 9:3–5; 10:11–16; 11:5–10; 17:24–25; 22:6–11, 17–21; 26:13–18 (cf. also, e.g., 4:31; 8:26; 21:11). Cf., furthermore, once again Harnack, *Apostelgeschichte*, 111–30.

1:28; cf. 43:2).[7] As expressed in a preceding occurrence, namely in Luke 19:38 (cf. Luke 2:14, also 9:31–32), Luke connects "glory" ($\delta \acute{o} \xi \alpha$) with "in the highest" ($\dot{\epsilon} \nu$ ὑψίστοις)[8] (cf. again Luke 24:49). This interpretation is supported by the Stephen episode (Acts 6:1–8:3). Also the passage on "ecstasy" (see Acts 22:17; cf. 10:10; 11:5) situated in the Temple at Jerusalem, Acts 22:17–21, relates to this episode. It is this later passage, as noted, that legitimizes Paul's journey "away from Jerusalem" (22:18), "far away" (22:21). Shortly before, in Acts 22:11, reference has been made to Paul's having seen the "glory" ($\delta \acute{o} \xi \alpha$) at his conversion.

About a decade ago I argued, that the Stephen episode allows the idea of a "heavenly sanctuary" to gain a rather clear profile (and my thesis has been picked up since then several times).[9] This is of some import for our present context, as this scene—with its assurance of the ubiquity of the Temple, so to speak—marks the beginning of the spread of the Christian Gospel beyond Jerusalem and, thus, also inaugurates the journey towards Rome (see, e.g., 8:2, 4; 11:19, 25).

At any rate, a few significant reasons for my interpretation of Acts 7:55–56 should be briefly recapitulated here.[10] On the synchronic level we can, first, observe that Stephen's speech in Acts 7:2–53 is primarily concerned with the issue of where to worship God, which is prepared for in particular by verses 7:6 and 7:7β (here [in contrast to Exod 3:12]: τόπος [not: ὄρος]) and finally realized through 7:45–50. In this latter passage (see esp. 7:46), Solomon's Temple is characterized as "dwelling place for the house of Jacob" (σκήνωμα τῷ οἴκῳ Ἰακώβ, that is, in contrast to Ps 131[132]:5, where it says τῷ θεῷ Ἰακώβ). The Temple, then, is there for the "people of the twelve tribes" (cf. once again Acts 26:7)[11] and is

7. On this see Rad, "*kābōd* im AT."

8. Schweizer, *Evangelium nach Lukas*, 246, says in view of Luke 24:26: the "glory . . . , which prevails according to 19:38 'in the highest.'"

9. Bachmann, "Stephanusepisode," 545–62 (cf. Bachmann, "Tempel III," 61). This case (which has been made already earlier by Nestle, "Vision of Stephen") has been picked up in the main by Ganser-Kerperin, *Zeugnis des Tempels*, 252–59, by Kurth, *Juden*, 157–77, by Heckel, *Segen*, 90–92, and by Wilk, "Geschichte des Gottesvolkes," 255 (cf. furthermore Backhaus, "Mose," 417 together with n. 53)—other than, e.g., by Jeska, *Geschichte Israels*, 142–44 together with n. 105, and Lang, *Studien zum lukanischen Paulusbild*, 208–9 together with nn. 23–24. Chibici-Revneanu, "Stephanusvision," does not mention the dialogue.

10. Additional meticulous evidence (and further arguments) at Bachmann, "Stephanusepisode."

11. On this cf. above (at) n. 21.

presented in a decidedly positive way (see esp. 7:46–47), even though the status of being a place of residence for God is denied (see esp. 7:48–49). Second, it is noteworthy that, of the two charges made against Stephen (Acts 6:11, 13, 14 [cf. 7:44, 53]), only the one referring to the Mosaic Law is answered with a countercharge (i.e., in 7:51–53). The assumption presents itself forcefully that the alleged agitation against the Temple (see esp. 6:13–14) is finally repudiated only in Stephen's visionary experience in Acts 7:55–60 and, at the same time, is then returned to the accusers (see esp. 7:58). Third, according to Stephen's speech, Moses had already seen in a vision the heavenly "pattern" (τύπος) of the earthly sanctuary (see esp. 7:44 [cf. 7:30–35, 38]; cf., for example, Exod 25:40), moreover, "the God of glory" (ὁ θεὸς τῆς δόξης) had already appeared to Abraham (Acts 7:2). This strongly suggests that the vision of the "glory" (7:55: δόξα), displaying also Jesus or the Son of Man (cf. Luke 12:8)—as something of an intercessor (7:59–60), "standing at the right hand of God" (7:55–56)—has to be interpreted as referring definitely to God's heavenly realm. On the diachronic level, the rare expression (of 7:2) just cited,[12] used also in reference to the Temple in Ps 28(29):3 and *1 Enoch* 25:(3–)7, attracts attention. In addition, the motifs of heavenly intercession (see again Acts 7:59–60) and of "standing at the right hand of God" (as befitting a priest) (7:55–56) can both be understood (on the synchronic level [cf. Luke 1:11; Acts 5:31] as well as) on the tradition-historical level as related to the idea of a heavenly temple (see e.g., Zech 6:13; 2 Macc 15:12; *Testament of Abraham* A 12:8, 12; *Testament of Levi* 2–5; Rev 5:6–7; 8:2–3; cf. also Heb 10:11).[13]

Thus, it is certainly possible to speak of a heavenly sanctuary as a conception shared by Luke. According to him, there is to a certain extent, and especially for the "house of Jacob", a correspondence to this realm in the earthly Temple at Jerusalem. The celestial sphere, to which Jesus Christ is linked because of his ἀνάλημψις (Luke 9:51), is an idea that was also readily comprehensible for Gentiles during the principate of the first century.[14] For Luke, it is an especially important condition

12. On this see Bachmann, "Stephanusepisode," 556 (together with) n. 41.

13. Cf. the "parallels" at Bachmann, "Stephanusepisode," 554–59, and, furthermore, at Hannah, "Throne of His Glory," esp. 87–91.

14. On this see Lohfink, *Himmelfahrt*, 76–77, who (at 77) says: "Apparently most of the early Christian authors simply could not make a clear distinction between the Ascension of Jesus in Luke-Acts and the raptures of antiquity . . . formally." Cf., e.g., Kollmann, *Neutestamentliche Zeitgeschichte*, 152–53.

for what we have observed with reference to Jerusalem and Rome. The
journey to the main city of the empire is legitimized "from above", but
without abandoning the connection to Jerusalem in terms of salvation
history.[15]

In the light of these findings, we will need to examine briefly
two text segments that have to do with the juxtaposition of Jews and
Gentiles, *i.e.*, non-Jews. First, we should deal with the closing scene of
Luke's works, the end of Acts in Rome. Then, a further topic will be the
passage referring to Jerusalem in Luke 21:20–24, in particular 21:24.

Naturally, the section at the conclusion of Luke's work, Acts
28:16/17–31, deserves increased attention simply because of its
prominent position in the framework of the Lucan writings. Yet, with
reference to its significance in determining the intended message
of Luke, it is anything but uncontroversial.[16] But with a view to the
data and findings we have compiled above, we can reasonably assume
that important aspects related to our topic can be found here with
relative ease. First, it is notable that, if we ignore the soldier guard-
ing Paul (mentioned in 28:16), only Jews—leaders of the Jews (28:17;
cf. 28:23)—are explicitly mentioned among those who come to Paul's
rented quarters (28:30). Including Gentiles in the phrase "all who came
in" (28:30: πάντες οἱ εἰσπορευόμενοι), especially in light of the preceding references to the "Gentiles" (ἔθνη) and their "listening" (28:28),
is not at all inconceivable, but certainly not an absolute necessity.
Conversely, excluding Jews from this group of "all" (πάντες)[17] would

---

15. It may be hinted on an important collection of essays: Ego *et al.*, *Gemeinde
ohne Tempel* (see Bachmann, Review of *Gemeinde ohne Tempel*). Some of the papers
present "spiritual conceptions" of the Temple in Early Judaism and analogously also in
Rabbinic Judaism. (On this cf., furthermore, e.g., Ego, *Im Himmel wie auf Erden.*) Of
course I am skeptical of the opinion of Klauck ("Jerusalem," 129), "that Luke never felt
the temptation, which Philo has succumbed at least partially, to spiritualize Jerusalem
into a heavenly entity." For the *Temple* of Jerusalem—other than for the town itself—
this seems to be not correct. The destruction of this building in the year 70 CE lies
behind at the time, when Luke-Acts was written (on this see Bachmann, "Tempel III,"
60; cf. below [at] n. 78). And so a "spiritual conception" of the Temple may suggest itself
(just as in Early and Rabbinic Judaism).

16. On this see particularly Koet, "Paul in Rome," esp. 119–20. Cf. esp. Lehnert,
"Verstockung Israels," and Eisen, *Poetik der Apostelgeschichte*, furthermore Neubrand,
Israel, die Völker und die Kirche, 40–50, 218–19, 252–53.

17. So, e.g., Haenchen, *Apostelgeschichte*, 648–49: "That Paul 'welcomed all who
came to him' does not mean . . . 'Jews and Greeks', but . . . the unhindered access of all

turn the findings just summarized on their head. Since Paul is able to preach and teach "unhindered" (28:31) in Rome (see 28:16), he is still able to communicate his message to Jews. Some of them, indeed, those mentioned first, are convinced by his teachings about Jesus and the kingdom of God, according to 28:(23–)24. This means that Paul's quote (see 28:26–27) from the prophet Isaiah, Isa 6:9–10, does justify and emphasize directing the gospel to the "Gentiles" (ἔθνη; 28:28), but it does not at all involve an ultimate rejection of "the Jews."[18]

Three additional circumstances make an interpretation stressing criticism of Jews implausible. First, the quote from Isaiah contains at the end—just as before in the Septuagint (cf. 4Q 177 IX:3)—a positive statement about the future: "and I [that is: God] will heal them [*i.e.*, members of the Jewish people]."[19] Second, the teachings to be directed towards the "Gentiles", which, not least, are teachings about Jesus, are characterized in 28:20 in terms of the "hope *of Israel*"—in terms of the hope that, according to Acts 26:6–7, is precisely expressed by the service of the "people of the twelve tribes" at the Temple in Jerusalem.[20] Third, the wording "the salvation of God" (τὸ σωτήριον τοῦ θεοῦ) of 28:28 re-calls in the context of Luke-Acts also the theme "Israel" (expressed just at the Temple),[21] however little this "salvation" (σωτήριον) excludes in Simeon's *Nunc dimittis* (Luke 2:27–32) the view to the "Gentiles" (see esp. Luke 2:32: ἔθνη; cf. Luke 3:6 [cf. 3:8–9, 18]: πᾶσα σάρξ).

visitors, who now are to be thought of as Gentiles." Differently, e.g., Brawley, *Luke-Acts and the Jews*, 77, 143; and Koet, "Paul in Rome," 139.

18. However, very often interpretations were just like this (on this see Koet, "Paul in Rome," 119, 137 [together with nn. 2, 82]), and also the textual history of Acts 28:19, 25 (and, furthermore, of 28:29) displays traces of an understanding somewhat critical of Jews (on this see Metzger, "Zeitspiegel," 257–59). Differently, for instance, Bauckham, "Restoration," 484–85, and Wilk, "Geschichte des Gottesvolkes," 256 together with n. 47 (cf. 259).

19. On this see Bachmann, "Entstehung," 47–48 together with n. 31 and the bib-liographical hints given there. Cf. also Koet, "Paul in Rome," 129–30, Brawley, "God of Promises," esp. 294–96 (cf. Brawley, "Ethical Borderlines," esp. 420–21), Metzger, "Zeitspiegel," esp. 245–50 (and 257–61), and Eisen, *Poetik der Apostelgeschichte*, 212–13 (cf. Lehnert, "Verstockung Israels," esp. 14–15). Cf. Lang, *Studien zum lukanischen Paulusbild*, 424(–426) together with n. 71.

20. On this see Haacker, "Hoffung Israels" (now also in: *idem, Versöhnung,* 77–94), furthermore, for instance, once again Metzger, "Zeitspiegel," 243–50. Cf. Lehnert, "Verstockung Israels," 17–18, and Eisen, *Poetik der Apostelgeschichte,* 212–15.

21. On the expression "the salvation of God" (τὸ σωτήριον τοῦ θεοῦ) see particularly Hoffmann, "Heil Israels," esp. 130–33.

Correspondingly, the final scene of Luke-Acts in Rome involves a Jewish hope not abandoned, a hope connected with Jerusalem and the Temple, a hope that Gentiles now undoubtedly share in some way (cf. esp. Acts 26:16–18, also, e.g., Luke 10:1 in reference to 9:1).[22] Rome (and the Roman Empire) does not, then, replace Jerusalem and the world-wide Judaism. But after Paul has been handed over to the Romans by Jews (Acts 28:17) and has appealed "to the emperor" (Acts 28:19), this empire allows this Jewish Christian to speak of the "kingdom of God" (βασιλεία τοῦ θεοῦ) and of Jesus as the "lord" (κύριος)[23] even in the capital of the Roman Empire—and to do this "unhindered" (Acts 28:31).[24] This is certainly of special significance for the Christian Gospel, which was, as is said in Acts 1:8 (cf. Luke 24:46–49), originally to be preached in Jerusalem and from there, eventually, to the rest of the world.[25] In this sense, then, Acts 28:16/17–31 is a very appropriate and impressive conclusion to the Lucan writings. The passage is also significant insofar as this testimony, according to Acts 1:6 (cf. Acts 3:19–26, also esp. Luke 2:34), is concerned with the eschatological issue of the "kingdom to Israel" (βασιλεία τῷ Ἰσραήλ).

Of course, something like eschatology is also the topic of Luke 21:24 and of the broader context of this verse, not least of Luke 21:20–24. Here, too, the issue at hand is the Jewish hope of salvation.[26] Even before, in Luke 19:41–44, there is mention of the destruction of Jerusalem, and it is expressed here in a sympathetic way that this destruction will mean the terrible death of children. Prophesying this, Jesus "wept over it," over the city (19:41). It will be its "enemies" (ἐχθροί [cf. esp. Ezek 39:23;

22. Similarly, e.g., Koet, "Paul in Rome," esp. 133–37. Cf., for instance, Ganser-Kerperin, *Zeugnis des Tempels*, 373–74, and Fuller, *Restoration of Israel*, 268–69, furthermore Bauckham, "Restoration," 485–59.

23. Cf. above nn. 42–45.

24. Because, as we saw (above at n. 36), the first instance of 'Rome' (Ῥώμη) in Luke-Acts hints at the expulsion of Jews from the town Rome, there should be considerable emphasis just at the characteristic that Roman authorities do not hinder the message of Paul. For this reason I am not really convinced by Wolter ("Juden," 401), who says, one should "apply the last word of Acts . . . [only] to the Jews" (similarly: Bendemann, "Paulus und Israel," 301). However, this aspect seems to be not completely irrelevant (cf., e.g., Acts 25:1–12, furthermore 28:19, 21–22, 24): Now it is guaranteed in Rome, that Paul is not hindered by Jews in his message.

25. On this cf. Bachmann, *Jerusalem*, 86–92, furthermore Eisen, *Poetik der Apostelgeschichte*, 216.

26. On this see Bachmann, "Tempel III," (59–)60.

Ps Sol 17:45]: 19:43) who take action against this 'polis' (πόλις: 19:41). In a similar way—after the remarks of Luke 21:5–6 on the destruction of the Temple at Jerusalem—Luke 21:20–24 again takes up the topic of the end of Jerusalem itself, and again not at all in a spiteful, but in a sympathetic manner: "Woe to those who are with child and who nurse babes in those days," which will bring "great distress" (21:23)! Insofar as the fulfillment of "all things which are written" (in the Jewish Scriptures) is announced (21:22), there is again (as in Luke 19:41–44) no lack of language characterized by traditional ideas and expressions.[27] This is especially true for the concluding section of the passage, which speaks of Jerusalem being "trampled under foot by the Gentiles" (cf., e.g., Zech 12:3; *Ps Sol* 17:22) and of the inhabitants of Jerusalem being "led captive into all the nations" (cf., e.g., Ezek 39:23; Tob 14:4 [especially: Codex Sinaiticus version]). For these reasons alone, the final words "until the times of the Gentiles are fulfilled" (ἄχρι οὗ πληρωθῶσιν καιροὶ ἐθνῶν) would seem to demand attention sensitive to the nuances expressed. A conceivable interpretation—for which not least Robert L. Brawley has argued[28]—is that this phrase not only hints at a limited phase of non-Jewish domination, but that, in addition, God's renewed turn to and care for Jerusalem and "the people of the twelve tribes" is implied.[29] Tradition-historical considerations point exactly in this direction, since "in the Old Testament and postbiblical Judaism the desolation of Jerusalem and/or the temple was consistently followed by the promise of the restoration of the precincts."[30] In *2 Bar* 6:9, for example, (after

27. It has been and will be hinted at this with some comments added in parantheses. Cf., furthermore, below n. 76.

28. Brawley, *Luke-Acts and the Jews*, 125 (cf. Brawley, "God of Promises," 286). Similarly, e.g., Chance, *Jerusalem*, 133–35, Hoffmann, "Heil Israels," 164–65, Bachmann, "Stephanusepisode," 562 (together with n. 64), Ganser-Kerperin, *Zeugnis des Tempels*, 191–94, and Wolter, *Lukasevangelium*, 678–79 (cf. Wolter, "Israels Zukunft," esp. 314–15). Though Flusser, *Entdeckungen im Neuen Testament 2*, 158–62, with regard to Luke 21:(20–)24 assumes a "Jewish-national tendency" (162), he denies it—which according to him leads back to Jesus himself—for the author of the third gospel ("Luke, that Gentile Christian") (161); the "prophetic word" probably should come "in its present form" from "Jewish Christian groups".

29. On this cf. above nn. 21–23, 57.

30. Chance, *Jerusalem*, 135, who supports this by (successively) naming the following passages: Zech 12:4.9; Ps 79:8–13; 2 Macc 10:1–5; Isa 65:17–25; *2 Bar* 67:6–8; Dan 8:13–14; 1 Macc 4:36–60; *Ps Sol* 17:23–27. Supplementing this list and also the comments added above in parentheses (on this cf. above n. 73) some further references may be added: Isa 64:10–11; Ezek 39:25–29; Dan 7:25–27; 9:24–27; 1 Macc 3:45–60; 2 Macc

previous references in 6:8 to "strangers" and to waiting "until the last times") the author says that "the time has arrived when Jerusalem will also be delivered up for a time, until the moment that it will be said that it will be restored forever."[31] The Lucan wording "until the times of the Gentiles are fulfilled" most probably implies such a renewal. Otherwise this phrase would be totally unnecessary! Of course, this expression of Luke 21:24, which alludes *de facto* to the Roman Empire,[32] is a tentative formulation. But when Luke chooses to take it up at this eschatological outlook, Luke 21, this would seem to be the maximum risk a Christian writer during the principate could take in view of the difficult relationship between Judaism and the empire (cf. once again Acts 18:2)[33] in a book that was, at least ultimately, available to the public (cf. Luke 1:3–4; Acts 1:1: Theophilus). The events related to in Luke-Acts actually belong precisely to this scenario.

If we combine these remarks with the similarly tentative ones on Jesus as "king" (βασιλεύς) and "lord" (κύριος) and if we recall how Luke speaks of the apostles "judging the twelve tribes of Israel" and speaks of the "kingdom to Israel" (βασιλεία τῷ Ἰσραήλ),[34] we can conclude the following: Giving witness to Jesus in Luke-Acts does, in fact, lead geographically to the center of the Roman Empire, but this is not at all a qualification of the perspective of salvation history established by the Jewish roots of the Jesus movement. As emphatic as that final word of Acts, "unhindered," is, just as little is Luke willing to simply applaud the Roman Empire. In his view, the religious elements of the empire—in light of the testimony to Christ being so unmistakably embedded in salvation history—require a certain skepticism towards Rome, especially

6:12–16; 8:5; Tob 13:2–3, 16–18; 14:5–7; *Ps Sol* 17:28–46; *2 Bar* 4:1–6:9; *SibOr* 3:657–808, furthermore Rev 11:2 (cf. 11:8, 10–13), finally Josephus, Bell 5:19 (where this author [switched over to the Romans], quite remarkably, carefully takes into consideration a positive perspective for the city Jerusalem destroyed at the time of writing).

31. *OTP* 2:673 (translation: A. F. J. Klijn).

32. The destruction of Jerusalem by the Romans in the year 70 CE probably belongs, as has been said already in n. 61 above, at the time when Luke-Acts was written, to the past—to an important past.

33. Similarly tentative remarks (as those of Luke 21:24) are made in this period in Rev 17:10–11 and in *Lib Ant* 51:5, possibly also in 2 Thess 2:6–7 (on this see Metzger, *Katechon*, esp. 283–84). Cf., furthermore, above all Stegemann, *Synagoge und Obrigkeit*, esp. 268(–80) and Omerzu, "Imperium," esp. 30–34.

34. Cf. above (at) nn. 69–72, furthermore once again above nn. 42–45.

since it is not the emperor, but the (heavenly) "Father", as Acts 1:7 maintains, who "has fixed times and epochs (καιροί) by his own authority."

(Translation by Thomas La Presti)

5

Pilate and the Crucifixion of Jesus in Luke-Acts

Jae Won Lee

MY INITIAL READINGS OF PILATE'S ROLE IN JESUS' DEATH IN LUKE LED me to think with many others that Luke exonerates Pilate,[1] portraying him as speaking for Jesus' innocence and as offering resistance to attempts by Jesus' adversaries to put him to death.[2] In contrast to some Judeans who seek Jesus' death (Luke 22:2, 47–54; 23:2), Pilate states three times that Jesus is not guilty (23:4, 14, 22). In addition, Pilate claims Herod Antipas's support by default; that is, Pilate concludes from the fact that Herod sent Jesus back to him that he also found nothing to warrant a death sentence (23:15). Indeed, Pilate's conclusion fits evidence about Antipas earlier in Luke. In connection with John the Baptist, Luke characterizes Antipas as an "evil doer" (3:19) who not only arrests John but also beheads him. Further, Luke also records Antipas's desire to kill Jesus (13:31). It is appropriate to bring to mind these earlier references, because 23:8 recalls the statement in 9:9 that Antipas wanted to see Jesus.[3] So if Antipas sent Jesus back, he must have found nothing to justify his desire to kill him; otherwise, he would have executed him.

---

1. E.g., Conzelmann, *Acts*, 35; Walaskay, *We Came to Rome*. Plümacher speaks of "a rare unanimity" for the period covered by his article that a political apology was one of Luke's purposes in composing Luke-Acts ("Acta Forschung," 1–56, 51).

2. Though it finds little favor today, a long line of interpretation has understood Pilate as part of a positive presentation of Roman officials in an attempt to show that belief in Jesus does not conflict with the duties of imperial authorities. For an account of these views and opposition to them, see Maddox, *Purpose*, 93–97; Stegemann, *Zwischen Synagoge und Obrigkeit*, 30–32.

3. The present participle and complementary infinitive θέλω ἰδεῖν with the imperfect ἦν in Luke 23:8 emphasize Herod's desire to see Jesus over the period from 9:9 to 23:8.

In addition, in response to Pilate's proposal to release Jesus, some Judeans suggest releasing Barabbas. This also has been interpreted as Luke's attempt to exonerate Pilate. The request involves not only the high priestly party and elite rulers but some new characters who appear suddenly—the people (ὁ λαός, 23:13; crowds [ὄχλοι] are present in 23:4). In Mark the crowd is under the sway of the high priestly party (15:11), but Luke gives no such direct information. Rather, the people are associated with the high priests and rulers simply because Pilate calls them all together (Luke 23:13–16). Whereas in Mark the high priests urge the crowd to ask for Barabbas, in Luke when Pilate proposes to release Jesus, the high priests, rulers, and people all together introduce Barabbas into the scene and request his release (23:18). Pilate complies.

Further, the supposedly benign behavior of Pilate in Luke 23 stands in contrast to what we know of him from the few sources we have outside the New Testament. Warren Carter advises putting extra biblical sources aside in order to deal with Pilate as a character in each Gospel.[4] He correctly focuses on the internal context of the Gospels. However, cultural commonplaces that readers might presume as part of understanding the narrative are pertinent. References to Pilate in external sources help interpreters recognize cultural presumptions ancient readers were likely to have. Carter actually follows this method much of the time: "[Pilate's] role as governor in a trial *assumes* imperial dynamics of power, elite alliances, and legal privilege"[5]

Josephus relates an incident in which Pilate brought military standards bearing the image of Tiberius into Jerusalem—an act asserting the emperor's dominance over Judean religious values.[6] When Judean masses demonstrated against this, Pilate had soldiers surround them and threaten them with death. According to Josephus, the demonstrators bared their throats and declared their willingness to die rather than accept the violation of their law. Pilate relented and removed the standards (*J. W.* 2.169–74; *Ant.* 18.55–59).

---

4. Carter, *Pontius Pilate*, 20–23.

5. Ibid., 33–54, citation 54 (my emphasis).

6. McGing argues that the introduction of standards was tactless but not intentionally provocative ("Pontius Pilate and the Sources," 416–38, 434–35). If not intentionally provocative in terms of Judean sensitivities to images, from a postcolonial perspective it asserts the dominance of the Empire.

In another case, Pilate appropriated money from the temple treasury in order to build an aqueduct.[7] When there another mass protest followed, Pilate sent some soldiers dressed like Judeans with daggers under their robes, and they slaughtered a number of the demonstrators (*Ant.* 18.60–62; in *J.W.* 2.175–77 the soldiers beat the demonstrators with wooden clubs).

Josephus also relates a brutal incident in which Pilate ordered troops to stop a gathering of Samaritans at the foot of Mt. Gerazim. The Samaritans assembled at the invitation of a man who promised to show them Moses' sacred vessels. The military strike against the Samaritans was massive. Many were killed, others captured. Some who fled were later captured, and Pilate ordered them to be executed (*Ant.* 18.85–87).

Against this type of characterization, does Luke present Pilate in such a way as to paint a favorable picture of the Roman governor and of the Roman Empire that he represents? A number of scholars have answered this question in the affirmative, assuming either Luke's "political apologetic" or "ecclesial apologetic."[8] In other words, they have asserted that Luke presents the Roman Empire as posing no political threat to Christianity or vice versa. In what follows I revisit this question by calling attention to some aspects of postcolonial theory in order to shed further light on the experience of Roman imperialism in Judea and to provide a hermeneutical perspective for Pilate's role in the trial of Jesus in Luke-Acts. I will focus on issues of imperial dynamics such as indirect experiences of imperialism, assimilation, collaboration, and resistance among colonized people, as means to reassess the role of Pilate in the trial and crucifixion of Jesus in Luke-Acts. I will argue that rather than exonerate Pilate in the trial of Jesus, Luke portrays Pilate as part of a system that makes a travesty of Roman (in)justice.

7. Uncertainty surrounds how Pilate acquired the funds, but because Josephus mentions no forceful act by Pilate, Helen Bond suggests that the high priestly party collaborated and placed the funds at Pilate's disposal (*Pilate*, 86); so also McGing, "Pontius," 429.

8. For the summary and critique of the traditional views on Luke's stance toward Pilate see Cassidy, *Society and Politics*, esp., 145–70; also see Carter, *Pontius Pilate*, 101–25.

Postcolonialism and Experiences of Imperialism

In general, postcolonial theory accepts the postmodern disruption of the alleged norm of *objectivity* that has been dominant in Western academic environments. Postmodernism not only accepts "earlier historicist claims about the inevitable 'situatedness' of human thought within culture" and the value-laden aspect of any theoretical inquiry of interpretation, but also focuses on "the very criteria by which claims to knowledge are legitimized."[9] Postmodernism undermines the notion that universal truth is available if observers adopt a perspective of impartial detachment from particular contexts. By contrast, postmodernism insists on a different relationship with reality, a relationship that Elizabeth Berg calls "partiality" (as the opposite of impartiality).[10] Such partiality expresses preference in relationships. It also implies "changing the subject,"[11] a move in which colonized people who have been objects of the discourse of the dominant culture become subjects producing their own discourse. The dominant discourse that produces the colonized as "the other" is subverted when "the other" attains the subject position. The outcome of "partiality" and the move to the subject position constitute an ideological stance, if you will, that stops short of making universal claims for truth but nevertheless creates a position from which to make assertions in relation to specific contexts. Postcolonialism also profits from postmodernism's challenge to foundationalism and essentialism, which reveals that they represent ideologies of the dominant culture.

On the one hand, postcolonialism largely parts company with some forms of postmodernism, namely, those forms that lack support for political agendas.[12] This is partially due to postmodernism's assertion that the rejection of foundationalism should lead to modesty in making truth claims, such that commitments may become tenuous. Against such fragile commitments, postcolonialists assert political obligations from their distinct socio-historical locations. In other words,

9. Nicholson, "Introduction," 3.

10. Berg, "Iconoclastic Moments," 213.

11. This phrase plays on Fulkerson, *Changing the Subject.*

12. See During, "Postmodernism or Postcolonialism?" 366–80; Gallagher, "Introduction"; Tiffin, "Post-Colonialism," 161–81; Mishra and Hodge, "What Is Post(-)colonialism?" 276–90.

in spite of the postmodern tendencies of some postcolonialists, others hold that deconstruction as such cannot be the goal of their discursive practice. Rather, they wish to maintain a place from which they can make claims for their own distinctive re-formation of reality.[13] As a case in point, Susan Gallagher contends that for postcolonialists "the unmasking and dismantling of authority is merely a strategy, a means of fulfilling a political agenda to retrieve identity in the face of cultural imperialism. By questioning colonial authority, post-colonial writers do not necessarily question *all* authority. Rather, they set out to dismantle a specific historically grounded discourse in the hopes of demonstrating that an alternative discourse is possible."[14]

On the other hand, other postmodernists defend their political awareness. In fact, to read Derrida's opposition to certainty and decidability as leaving feminists and citizens of the Third World no place from which to act is at best a partial reading. Because of the inability to make final determinations, action can only come from a position of undecidability. Undecidability exposes the risks involved in action, which is true for all action, though modernity's positivism supported an illusion of certainty that eliminates the risks. Derrida exposes all action as risky business. But this does not eliminate what he also spoke of as absolute responsibility for the other.[15] Furthermore, Derrida himself has responded to his critics by arguing that issues like undecidability are not excuses for avoiding struggles for justice.[16]

In the move to the subject position, postcolonialsm resists the idea of determining one's identity by assimilation to hegemonic powers. In the assimilationist strategy, "privileged groups implicitly define the standards according to which all will be measured . . . The strategy of assimilation aims to bring formerly excluded groups into the mainstream.

---

13. Postmodernism has a place for the situatedness of truth claims, all of which are tropological. That is, against essentialism, all truth claims are figural interpretations of reality. In a discussion of Rousseau's defense of natural religion in which he elaborates on the distinction between sensation and perception, Paul de Man notes that reference in language is figural and this figural language can be put in question by means of the very language that produces the figural reference (*Allegories of Reading*, 234–36); see Spivak, *Critique*, 147.

14. Gallagher, "Introduction," 14 (her emphasis).

15. See Caputo, *Radical Hermeneutics*, 131.

16. For example, see Derrida's interpretation of Abraham's willingness to act in face of the dilemma of giving up the life of his beloved son (*Gift of Death*, 94–97).

So assimilation always implies coming into the game after it is already begun, after the rules and standards have already been set, and having to prove oneself according to those rules and standards."[17]

Western hegemony presumes that those who are different will assimilate toward its center where they meld into sameness. Indeed, Western culture entices them to emulate the center, luring them by possibilities of gaining power and privilege. And if they do not flow toward the center, it is taken for granted that they will remain powerless and dispossessed. Politically they can even be designated "aliens"—if not "illegal aliens," then "resident aliens." The rejection of assimilation, however, turns this table upside down. The margin is no longer defined by the dominant center but is a place from which to engage hegemony with a distinctive way of construing reality. The margin no longer encounters hegemony from a position of submission and weakness as the objectified other, but maintains its own integrity from a position of creative critical action.[18] The margin is not a place of deficiency but teams with possibilities of re-forming life no longer as determined by the alleged unified center. Rather, the margin espouses values that differ from hegemonic norms. Further, the margin often seeks to rehabilitate its own long-established norms, which the dominant center judges deficient.[19] This is not a call to separate from a so-called center, which would mean that the margin would still be defined by the hegemonic center from which it takes its orientation, even if in opposition. Gayatri Spivak even calls such polarization between the West and the rest "a legitimation-by-reversal of the colonial attitude itself."[20] Rather the margin is a place of creative, critical engagement with hegemony.[21] I indicate below how this is Jesus' position when in Luke 22:25 and in his trial he marks out a subject position that is distinct from the assimilation of the high priestly party and from the opposition of political resistance.

An emphatic "but" is now appropriate. *But* it is hardly possible for colonized people to avoid complicity with imperial powers. So, for example, when Paul appeals to Caesar in Acts—quite distinct from Jesus' reluctance in Luke 23 to cooperate with his own hearings before Pilate

17. Young, *Justice and the Politics*, 164.

18. See Spivak, *Post-Colonial Critic*, 156.

19. See Judith Butler in Butler and Spivak, *Who Sings?*, 31.

20. Spivak, *Critique*, 39.

21. See Sugirtharajah, "Introduction," 2.

and Antipas—he is complicit in collaborating with the imperial system. It is even possible for me to make this personal. In our own language Koreans refer to the pigment of our skin as "flesh." So if I refer to myself as "a woman of color," I am participating in categorizing difference in a way that is decidedly Western. Further, as a South Korean who supports the exit of U.S. troops from my country, I am nevertheless complicit when as a seminary teacher in the U.S., I pay taxes to the United States. My very ability to write these words depends on my complicity. Not to be legitimized, complicity is not altogether negative, as we shall see in the case of the Judean high priestly party. Further, complicity is necessary if people such as elite Judeans are to play any role in maintaining aspects of Judean (albeit limited) autonomy and identity. Complicity may also be prudent in that perspectives and resources of the dominant culture may be selectively appropriated to the advantage of the colonized. In any case, acknowledging complicity is an important part of overcoming binary dichotomies (such as male/female) including colonizer/colonized.[22]

Colonization contributes to the production of complex configurations of power that impinge upon colonized people.[23] For the Judean world of the first century, among the obvious contributors to configurations of power are many factors: village mores competing with imperial ideology, cultural traditions confronted with a new reality, gender, class, subdued local Aramaic language up against dominant global Greek and hegemonic Latin, synagogue discipline, Roman military, temple police, Sanhedrin rule, client kings, and governors—not to mention the "state of mind" of "dispossessed" Judeans who, as N. T. Wright suggests, may have had the psychological mindset that their subjugation was the consequence of the sins of their people.[24] In light of these complex configurations of power, it is significant that Luke-Acts often deals with the reintegration of marginalized people to the social order (e.g., in healing stories), which is a restoration of Israel's social order. Further, Luke also

22. Spivak, *Other Asias*, 63–64, and passim.

23. See Butler, *Who Sings?* 1–6, and passim.

24. N. T. Wright makes the case for such an interpretation of Deuteronomy 27–30 in Paul's letters (*Climax,* 140–42). Josephus also interprets the Roman conquest as God's verdict of judgment against Judeans (e.g. *J.W.* 5.368, 396, 408; 6.250–52; 7.331–32, 359). On the state of mind of dispossession see Butler, *Who Sings?*, 15–16.

envisions an inversion of the marginalized and the elite (e.g., in Mary's song in Luke 1:51–55).

Pilate in Luke-Acts

Earlier I mentioned a common argument that Luke-Acts presents a favorable picture of Pilate in Jesus' trial in contrast to portraits drawn of Pilate by Philo and Josephus.[25] But Luke also is aware of Pilate's treachery. In 13:1–3, anonymous people tell Jesus about some Galileans whose blood Pilate mingled with their sacrifices. Wolfgang Stegemann has suggested that the relevant texts for understanding Roman authorities in Luke-Acts involve a triangle among Roman authorities, Jews, and people of the Jesus movement.[26] As we shall see, this is an important insight. However, by this criterion Stegemann must regard this text as irrelevant, because at this stage in the story Pilate acts only in relation to Galilean Jews. Jesus takes the report to mean that these people understand Pilate's act to be divine judgment against these Galileans. Jesus' response first resists singling out the victims as worse sinners than other Galileans, but then he warns of a similar destiny for his interlocutors as well. The strong implication is that Pilate's treachery is understood in Deuteronomistic terms as a consequence of the unfaithfulness of the people[27] as long as the playing field is leveled to include everyone ("all of you," Luke 13:3; cf. "all of you," Deut 29:9 LXX, "Moses finished speaking to all Israel," Deut 32:45). Similarly, Josephus blames Jewish revolutionaries who transgressed the law for their defeat in the War with Rome (*J.W.* 2.454–56; 4.314–18, 383–88; 5.19; 6.99–102).

In summarizing the views of a number of scholars, I noted that in Luke the people who participate in requesting Barabbas's release are not explicitly under the sway of the high priests as are the crowds in Mark. A couple of factors, however, imply that the people do come under the influence of the high priests and rulers. (1) Elsewhere, the people (ὁ λαός) disagree with the high priestly party (20:6, 19; 22:2) and

---

25. For example, McGing speaks of the Gospels as "comparatively friendly" ("Pontius Pilate," 417). Philo's characterization of Pilate (*Legatio* 302) is generally taken as greatly exaggerated in the negative. See Reinbold, *Prozess*, 75–78.

26. Stegemann focuses especially on parts of Acts dealing with Paul. Stegemann, *Zwischen Synagoge und Obrigkeit*, 35–36.

27. See n. 24 above.

(2) Acts 4:25–28 summarizes Jesus' crucifixion interpreted through Ps 2:1–2 (to which I return below). According to Acts 4:25–28, the crucifixion involves an alliance of non-Judeans and Israelites (λαοί), and Pilate and Herod Antipas. Further, among the collaborators with the people (λαοί) Acts 4:26 names rulers (ἄρχοντες). This is significant in that with the exception of Luke 23:13, the antagonists in the trial are chief priests and scribes. But in this exception, the people (λαοί) appear alongside the rulers (ἄρχοντες), and both are associated with the high priestly party. In other words, these λαοί have come under the influence of the chief priests. Hans Conzelmann considers the interpretation of the crucifixion in Acts 4 in terms of Psalm 2 to be pre-Lukan, and if so, it is possible that this interpretation influenced Luke's account of Jesus before Pilate.[28]

Acts 4:25–27 sheds further light on Luke's portrayal of Jesus' trial. After citing Ps 2:1–2 LXX, Acts portrays Jesus' crucifixion as playing out the plot of the psalm. In the psalm, the nations (ἔθνη) and the peoples (λαοί) are in synonymous parallelism and designate non-Israelites who oppose Israel's king. However, in Acts 4:27, the terms are not synonymous but designate non-Judeans and Judeans. Further, in Ps 2:2 the kings of the earth are in synonymous parallelism with the rulers who stand against the Lord and the Lord's anointed. But Acts 4:27 understands this as a coalition between Pilate and Herod Antipas. Further, as indicated above because Judean rulers (ἄρχοντες) are mentioned in Luke 23:13, they may be implicated in the rulers (ἄρχοντες) of Acts 4:26. This text depicts an alliance of non-Judeans, Judeans, Pilate, and Herod.[29] My point is this: However this passage is construed, Pilate is portrayed as one of the opponents of God (κατὰ τοῦ κυρίου, "against the Lord," 4:26)—hardly compatible with exonerating him.

---

28. Conzelmann, *Acts*, 35. Soards understands Acts 4:25–27 to be *contrary* to Luke 23, because in Luke Herod supports Jesus' innocence whereas Acts 4 makes him a collaborator ("Tradition, Composition," 344–64, 349, 360, 362). But here Soards overlooks Herod's despising and mocking Jesus, though he discusses it elsewhere (355). Furthermore, sending an innocent Galilean over whom he has jurisdiction *back* to Pilate rather than releasing him makes Antipas complicit.

29. See Brawley, *Text to Text*, 102–3.

Indirect Experiences of Imperial Power

Nevertheless, to speak of an alliance of non-Judeans, Judeans, Pilate, and Herod on the occasion of Jesus' death is not going far enough, because even though largely unexpressed, the picture includes how people in the first century experienced the Roman Empire.[30] Convincing cases have been made for the indirect experience of the Empire by people in Galilee and Judea.[31] Roman soldiers did not stand at every corner. Pilate had only small auxiliary forces recruited locally, estimated as no more than three thousand, who functioned more like police than soldiers.[32] Roman legionary forces were stationed in Syria and intervened in Palestine only when necessary under the command of the legate of Syria. Pilate and his forces resided in Caesarea, which was the location of his headquarters. He and some of his soldiers would likely be in Jerusalem at the time of Passover when the population swelled with pilgrims, but even then they probably tried to remain inconspicuous. Villages would rarely see Roman soldiers unless there was a disturbance.[33]

Judeans seldom experienced the Empire directly, because it was hidden behind governors, client kings, and local elite Judeans,[34] the last group of whom both resisted and supported the Empire.[35] A part of this chain of command is evident from a damaged inscription that was unearthed in Caesarea in 1961. The inscription names Pilate as the prefect of Judea and associates him with a Tiberium, presumably a building (a temple?) dedicated to Tiberius.[36] This indirect experience of imperial power through a governor is reflected also in Tacitus's brief com-

---

30. See Carter, *Pontius Pilate*, 5.

31. Sanders, *Historical Figure*, 18–32; Horsley, *Jesus and Empire*, 20–34; Fredriksen, *Jesus of Nazareth*, 169–84.

32. Schwartz, "Pontius Pilate," 397; Bond, *Pontius Pilate*, 5, 13–14.

33. John the Baptist encounters soldiers in Luke 3:14, and Jesus has an indirect interchange with a centurion in Capernaum (7:3–9).

34. Peter Brunt calls prefects "agents of the emperor" and documents a move toward greater responsibilities for the Empire ("Procuratorial Jurisdiction," 163–87).

35. E. Mary Smallwood contests the collaboration for the period before the revolt against Rome arguing that Ananus was opposed to Rome and that Ananias sympathized with anti-Roman groups like the Sicarii ("High Priests," 14–34, esp. 28–30). So also Theissen, 70. This partly affirms my observation that elite local rulers both resist and support the Empire.

36. The spelling in the inscription is *TIBERIEUM*. Demandt, *Hände in Unschuld*, 72–74; Bond, *Pontius Pilate*, 11–12.

ment about the death of Christus who was executed under the reign of Tiberius by a regional procurator (*sic*)[37] Pontius Pilate (*Ann.* 15.44).

The indirect experience of the Empire is clearly reflected in Luke. In 2:1–3, for example, Joseph and Mary are displaced from Nazareth to Bethlehem by Augustus Caesar's decree, which filters down through Quirinius the governor of Syria and is carried out on a local level in Bethlehem.[38] Also, Luke's so-called great synchronization in 3:1–2 not only sets the stage chronologically for John the Baptist (and consequently for Jesus), but also for how Judeans experienced imperial power. Luke follows a chain from emperor to governor, client kings, and Judean elites rather clearly—Tiberius Caesar, when Pontius Pilate was ruling Judea, and Herod the tetrarch of Galilee at the time of the high priesthood of Annas and Caiaphas. Furthermore, as has been mentioned, Luke 23:7, 12 and Acts 4:27 associate the prefect with the tetrarch Herod Antipas, who as the son of the Idumean Herod the Great occupies a kind of intermediate position between Roman foreigners and the Judean elite. Finally, this imperial system may be reflected from the bottom up, that is, from synagogues to rulers and authorities, as indicated in Luke 12:11.

The Judean indirect experience of the imperial system through governors, client kings, and local elites is also evident in Josephus. For example, he narrates an incident in which a slave of the emperor was attacked on a public road close to Bethoron and his baggage stolen. The Roman prefect Cumanus (48–52 CE) sent troops to bring their elite leaders to him in chains so that he could rebuke them for not arresting the attackers (*J. W.* 2.228–29; *Ant.* 20.113–14). That is, the imperial system held local elites responsible for maintaining order and enforcing policies of the empire (see *J. W.* 2.236–40).[39] The same collaborative pattern is evident when Josephus attributes the execution of John the Baptist at the hands of Antipas to the typical role of client rulers in the Empire: Antipas wished to avert any possibility of rebellion and to

37. Apparently "prefect" is correct, but Tacitus used "procurator." The terms may be interchangeable. See Reinbold, *Prozess*, 73; Bond, *Pontius Pilate*, 12.

38. The registration implies other dimensions of imperial rule, such as restrictions concerning residence (residents of Galilee must travel to Bethlehem in Judea) and possessions, because the registration involves taxation. See Wolter, *Lukasevangelium*, 122.

39. For ten examples see Egger, "*Crucifixus sub Pontio Pilato*," 100–121. Ann Laura Stoler documents similar expectations of Dutch administrators that local leaders keep peace and order in the Netherlands Indies around 1875 (*Archival Grain*, 222).

maintain order (*Ant.* 18.118–19). Josephus also refers to elite Judean collaborators, especially the high priests as people who were entrusted with internal order (*Ant.* 20.251: τὴν προστασίαν τοῦ ἔθνους οἱ ἀρχιερεῖς ἐπεπίστευντο, "The high priests were entrusted with the leadership of the people"). Collaboration of the high priest with representatives of Rome was virtually guaranteed by the fact that the high priest served at the pleasure of the governor.

Collaboration with Rome among the Colonized People

Although Luke-Acts associates Pilate and Antipas in Jesus' crucifixion with some purposes that exceed a historical description of imperial collaborative systems, the association of the two still reflects that system. In Luke-Acts the local elites correspond closely with the high priestly party and the council, who in turn collaborate to a certain degree with the governor and client tetrarch.[40] According to Josephus, after the Romans deposed Archelaus as the Judean king succeeding Herod the Great, "the high priests were entrusted with the leadership of the nation" (*Ant.* 20.251). Inevitably, they would have been collaborators.

Richard Horsley gives evidence for collaboration of the high priestly elite by reading primary sources, especially Josephus, not merely at face value but in light of the the imperial system. He concludes that the high priestly party was in the position of representing the people at the same time that they maintained the imperial system. In that tension, they acted in their own interests to maintain their status, including their local rule.[41] Notably, the Pharisees in Luke, Jesus' frequent interlocutors in controversies, do not appear in the crucifixion of Jesus.[42] Instead, the high priestly group is prominent, anticipated in 20:1 and in the parable of the wicked tenants (see 20:19). This corresponds with the role of the high priestly party as collaborators with the Roman Empire.

Collaboration is a matter both of resisting and supporting colonizers. It is a matter of resisting in that local elites such as the high priestly party hold on to what remains of national identity and autonomy. But in

40. A distinction between high priestly elites and common priests is evident at several places in Luke-Acts (Luke 1:23, 39; Acts 6:7).

41 Horsley, "High Priests," 24.

42. This is true in Luke and also historically probable. See Reinbold, *Prozess*, 54, 107.

order for a Judean council to exist, some elite Judeans have to back the colonizers. Otherwise there would be no Judean council at all.[43] Such a state of resistance and support is rather explicit in the Gospel of John. Caiaphas's discussion with the council in John 11:48 reflects resistance to Rome in his desire to maintain some autonomy of the "people" at the same time that he wishes to ward off any action of Rome to destroy the temple and the nation—the kind of action the elite might expect if they could not control local upstarts.[44] Significantly, Caiaphas's advice is addressed to the members of the *council*, rather than to the Jewish people. When he says, "It is better for you to have one man die," the "you" designates the council: "It is better for you [members of the council] to have one man die." His advice means that a popular movement could trigger Roman intervention, in which case the members of the council might lose their status and no longer be in a position to maintain the same degree of national autonomy and identity.[45] Even though the present form of the so-called *Testimonium Flavium* in Josephus involves Christian redaction, it likely was not created whole cloth. Significantly, it may well preserve the picture of the collaboration of the Judean elite with Rome: "When Pilate, upon hearing him accused by men of the highest standing amongst us, had condemned him [Jesus] to be crucified . . ." (*Ant.* 18.64; see 20.200).[46] If Luke holds the same kind of cultural presumptions, elite Judeans in his Gospel also act in the interest of maintaining their status.[47] But maintaining their status is also the way to maintain a semblance of national autonomy and identity.

From this perspective, the attempts of the high priestly party and the council to restrain Jesus' followers early in Acts can be seen not only as an ideological conflict but also as an attempt to maintain order. The new movement generates large crowds, from which at first three thousand join, then the number swells to five thousand and continues to grow. Significantly, in Acts 5:36–39 Gamaliel compares the believ-

43. See Horsley, "High Priests," 28–29.

44. E.g., elite Judeans opposed revolt against Rome because Rome guaranteed social order (including their own status), property rights, and local power (see e.g. Josephus, *J.W.* 2:236–40). See Brunt, "Romanization," 272–73.

45. Egger, *"Crucifixus sub Pontio Pilato,"* 148–59, also argues for the accurate reflection in this incident of the responsibility imposed by Rome on the elite to maintain order.

46. For a simple evaluation of the *Testimonium* see Reinbold, *Prozess*, 36.

47. So also Carter, *Pontius Pilate*, 124.

ers with the followers of Theudas and Judas, which for Rome had the character of uprisings. Although Gamaliel argues that there is no need to keep order, the implicit argument among his interlocutors involves the kind of crowd control that the Empire expected from local elites.[48]

Earlier I mentioned Stegemann's observation that encounters of people in the Jesus movement with Roman authorities involve a triangle that includes other Judeans.[49] His observation coincides with the way in which people in Luke's time experienced the Empire—through governors, client kings, and elite collaborators. Whether it is a matter of Judean elites seeking to keep order and enforce imperial policies, or Roman officials seeking to resolve conflicts between the Jesus' movement and other Judeans, Stegemann's triangle is to be expected. A prominent case of the latter is the claim Jesus makes on the temple.

Often called the cleansing of the temple, the incident is much more strongly characterized by Jesus' citation from Isa 56:7, "My house shall be a house of prayer." Rather than oppose the temple itself, the incident makes a claim on its proper function. Jesus himself, however, also makes it a place of teaching and proclamation (Luke 19:47; 21:37; 22:53). In addition his followers make it a place of prayer and proclamation (Luke 24:53; Acts 2:46; 3:1, 12; 5:21).[50] The encounter of Jesus or his disciples with the high priestly party over the proper function of the temple is the kind of conflict between Jesus and other Judeans that fits Stegemann's triangle, which is also evident in Jesus' appearance before Pilate (e.g., 23:5).

Further, the plot of Luke develops tensions between Jesus and the imperial system long before his trial. To illustrate with only two instances, (1) Mary's song characterizes God's actions as an inversion of the elite and the lowly (1:51–63), which is reinforced by Zechariah's reference to being saved from enemies (1:71), and (2) tensions with the imperial system come to a peak when Jesus offers his disciples an alternative to the kings of the nations who "lord it over them" (22:25).

What is more, the Empire advertised itself as divinely destined not merely to rule the world but to bring to the people it conquered the blessings of its supposedly superior culture. The conquerors "blessed" the conquered with peace, justice, and well-being, and saved them

---

48. See Egger, *"Crucifixus sub Pontio Pilato,"* 123–28.

49. See above n. 26.

50. See Brawley, *Luke-Acts*, 120, 122–23.

where they could not save themselves. Seneca addresses his essay *On Mercy* to none other than Nero in order to reveal Nero to Nero himself so that he would "serve on earth as vicar of the gods . . . the arbiter of life and death for the nations . . . without [whose] favor and grace no part of the wide world can prosper" (1.1–3). In the *Aeneid*, Virgil has Jupiter declare: "I am imposing no bounds on his realm, no temporal limits. Empire that has no end is my gift" (1.277–78). Further Virgil calls the Romans "that people in togas, the masters of all in existence" (1.282). Paulo Freire generalizes this phenomenon from a modern perspective as the invasion of oppressors with their values, standards, and goals to convince those they conquer of their cultural inferiority and to arouse them to emulate their invaders.[51]

When conquered Judeans saw the results of Roman public works (e.g., roads, bridges, buildings, aqueducts), monuments, sports facilities, theaters, and arts, it is no stretch of imagination to suppose that many of them concurred that their civilization was inferior to that of their conquerors. Indeed, civil celebrations (inevitably religious) in honor of the emperor often demonstrated imperial benevolence with provisions of food for entire populations of cities. Some imperial coins associated the emperor with the harvest goddess Ceres, as if the emperor was the agent of the divine to guarantee provisions of food.[52] The proconsul (ἀνθύπατος) and the Greeks of Asia even authorized an inscription on a white stone that represented Augustus as the benevolent father of the population who exceeded all previous benefactors.[53] It is less than subtle that the association of the emperor with the gods (Jupiter, Ceres, Neptune, Victoria, Italia) situates imperial benevolence in a divinely legitimated paternalistic hierarchy in which the imperial and elite benefactors are superior to their beneficiaries. Differences in culture come across as differences in class.[54] In Luke 22:25–26 Jesus makes a direct reference to elite so-called benefactors with whom he contrasts his fol-

51. Freire, *Pedagogy*, 134. Josephus gives God's judgment for Israel's infidelity as the reason for the fall of Jerusalem and the destruction of the temple, and supports Roman rule as a manifestation of God's will (*J.W.* passim). The evidence is discussed in Egger, "*Crucifixus sub Pontio Pilato*," 60–72.

52. Rome imported and distributed huge amounts of grain and other foods, especially from Northern Africa, but primarily for Roman citizens, not for subjected populations (Horsley, *Jesus and Empire*, 23).

53. Dittenberger, *Orientis graeci inscriptiones selectae*, 50–59.

54. See Spivak, *Other Asias*, 58.

lowers: ". . . those who exercise power over them are called benefactors (εὐεργέται). But not so with you." Rather, Jesus inverts hierarchy into mutuality: "But let the one who is greater among you become as the younger, and the one who leads as one who serves" (22:26).

The Roman imperial system assumed patron/client relationships as a normal if not natural way of experiencing benefaction. If from time to time the Judean populace and the Judean elite experienced benefaction from the imperial system and if they also practiced paternalistic benefaction at their level, then a certain kind of collaboration "appears" to be normal and natural. Such collaboration turns out to be a pernicious *legitimation* of the imperial system of benefaction, which fits what Paulo Freire describes as internalizing the value system of the oppressors.[55] This means that both ordinary people and the elite, like both rich and poor Americans who believe in "trickle down economics," may genuinely believe that the imperial system is beneficial to them. I am aware of similar attitudes among many of my Korean compatriots who think that the domination of Korea by outsiders, especially the United States, is beneficial for them.

Thus, not only do rulers promote themselves as benefactors; so also do the ruled. If those who are ruled perceive the actors in the chain of command to be accommodating, they may view benefits from the Empire positively, even if they must cope with the flow of goods from themselves toward Rome. Paternalistic benefactions, as Paulo Freire puts it, perpetuate the myth that the elite are generous[56] (compare Jesus' contrast of a poor widow's gift with large gifts of the wealthy in Luke 21:1–4). But again, Jesus exhorts his followers not to call those who exercise power "benefactors" when he says, ". . . not so with you."

Nevertheless, Roman imperial self-presentation claimed benevolence with effective results. Philo, for example, extols Augustus as one "who in all the virtues transcended human nature" and calls him "such a [great] benefactor" (τοσοῦτον εὐεργέτην, *Embassy* 143, 148). Similarly, Josephus contrasts Pilate with two procuratorial successors, Florus and Albinus, and portrays him more positively. Unlike them, in Josephus' portrayals, Pilate did little to contribute to the outbreak of the Jewish war with Rome (*J.W.* 2.169–77).

55. *Pedagogy*, 45.
56. Lankshear, "Functional Literacy," 102.

The war with Rome, however, would raise suspicions for Luke's readers after 70 CE. What happens when maintaining the *pax Romana* and providing for the well-being of Rome's clients means devastation and destruction? For readers who know about the fall of Jerusalem and the destruction of the temple, "benevolences" of the Empire toward the Judeans in Luke-Acts would be understood as subversive irony.

Back to Pilate and Jesus

There are also traces of collaboration from Pilate's side. For one thing, the same high priest was in office for Pilate's entire term.[57] This enabled the high priest to maintain his status and (conditional) power. Indeed, the effectiveness of the collaboration of Caiaphas and Pilate may be judged by the fact that when Pilate was recalled from Judea, Caiaphas's long term of office came to an end. Vitellius removed him *circa* 36–37 (Josephus *Ant.* 18.95).[58] This indicates from Pilate's side that the collaboration involved enough indigenous cooperation to sustain the dominance of the Empire. Thus, as the term itself implies, collaboration also involves reciprocity. At times Pilate needed to accommodate toward elite Judeans in order to be perceived as benevolent. Indeed, Carter suggests that Luke's Pilate failed to collaborate adequately with Judean elites.[59]

Carter concludes that Luke characterizes Pilate as arrogant and capricious.[60] But I suggest that against the Roman ideology of justice, Pilate epitomizes imperial (in)justice.[61] The backbone of imperial propaganda was the claim that Rome had established justice, idealized in the statue of the deity *Iusticia*, a beautiful woman whose eyes are covered with a blindfold and who holds a set of balances in one hand and a sword in the other—the power to enforce justice by violence.[62] As prefect, Pilate headed the judicial system in Judea, and thus represented the justice of

---

57. Josephus *Ant.* 18:35, 95; Schwartz, "Pontius Pilate," 398.

58. See Sandmel, "Caiaphas," 481.

59. Carter, *Pontius Pilate*, 37.

60. *Pontius Pilate*, 119.

61. Josef Blinzler judges Pilate *guilty* of recognizing Jesus' innocence but nevertheless ordering his execution (*Der Prozess Jesu*, 449).

62. See Elliott, *Arrogance*, esp. 59–85.

the entire Empire. What does Pilate's portrait in Luke look like against the background of the imperial propaganda of its justice?

First, in the interrogation before Pilate the charges are political in the narrow sense of the word: Jesus causes disorder in the nation, forbids paying taxes to the emperor, and proclaims himself Messiah, a king (Luke 23:2). Likewise, the title on the cross representing the cause of Jesus' crucifixion is political: "This is the king of the Jews" (23:38). In fact, it is typical in Luke-Acts that when Jesus or his followers are accused before Roman authorities, the focus is political (including disorder among the citizenry). Otherwise, imperial authorities take complaints about customs or religion with a grain of salt (see Acts 25:19).[63]

In the face of these political charges, Pilate declares Jesus innocent three times before his crucifixion (Luke 23:22). Does this mean that for Luke, Jesus (and his followers) are innocuous to the Empire? Jesus' negative evaluation of the kings of the Gentiles who lord it over the people (22:25), and his declaration that such is not the way of his followers (22:26) clearly indicate that Jesus resists imperial domination and *calls his disciples to an alternative community*: "But not so with you." From the point of view of the high priestly party and the assembly (23:1), Jesus' alternative community is a threat to order among the people, the very type of order for which they are responsible as collaborating elites. But Pilate does not share their perception of the problem. Luke's emphasis on Pilate's three declarations of innocence can only mean that Jesus (and his followers) are not leading the people astray in terms of violent insurrection.

Three affirmations of innocence after Jesus is hung on the cross correspond to Pilate's three declarations. The first affirmation of Jesus' innocence occurs when one of the brigands crucified with Jesus declares that he and his cohort are getting the sentence of justice that they deserve, but Jesus has done nothing wrong (23:40–41). Again this helps to clarify the sense in which Jesus is innocent. Unlike the brigands, he does not advocate violent resistance against imperial power. But this means that Jesus resists by advocating an alternative community that does not assimilate to Roman imperialism.

---

63. On imperial interpretations of prophets and their followers in political terms and Roman military responses in both Luke-Acts and Josephus, see Egger, *"Crucifixus sub Pontio Pilato,"* 82–100.

I digress for a moment to note that when the brigand declares Jesus innocent he evaluates his own sentence as justice (δικαίως, "justly"). Given the role of crucifixion in the empire as a tool of terror reserved almost exclusively for seditious slaves and subversive foreigners, the brigand wrongly asserts that he and his companion had received a sentence of justice. Crucifixion was manifestly unjust in its particular application against non-Roman slaves and foreigners who refused to be submissive to the empire.[64] But like many colonized people, the brigand knows the kind of punishment he is likely to incur for his rebellion and may even internalize the value system of the colonizer enough to declare that his execution is just.[65]

The second affirmation of Jesus' innocence after the crucifixion is the declaration of the centurion who praised God and said: "Certainly this man was innocent (δίκαιος)" (23:47). The third case is not so conspicuous, because it is expressed as a gesture and not in words. The crowds (ὄχλοι) return from the place of crucifixion beating on their breasts.

Herod Antipas remains relatively passive in Jesus' crucifixion. In 13:31, some Pharisees warn Jesus that Herod Antipas wants to kill him. But when Pilate sends Jesus to him, he is glad because he anticipates seeing some "sign" (23:8). In this regard, Jesus proves to be a disappointment. Herod Antipas cannot even engage him as someone who is accused, because Jesus remains silent before him in spite of the fact that Herod Antipas interrogated him "at length" (ἐν λόγοις ἱκανοῖς, 23:9). Little wonder then that Herod Antipas finds no confirmation of the charges against Jesus (23:15). Nevertheless Herod Antipas and his soldiers treat Jesus with contempt and mock him—typical treatment for non-Roman citizens in Roman courts. They might be beaten and mocked even if they were ultimately declared innocent. This corresponds to Pilate's suggestion to flog Jesus and then release him: "I have found no cause of the things for which you have accused him . . . *therefore* after I have

64. Jennings, *Reading Derrida*, 2, 46, 55–77. See Hengel, *Crucifixion*, 13–14, 34; Scaer, *Lukan Passion*, 1. J. Marcus demonstrates the relationship between crucifixion and resistance to imperial powers for the sake of improving society ("Crucifixion," 73–87, esp. 78–79, 86–87).

65. Luke's mind is unavailable, but has he also internalized presumptions of the justice of crucifixion for brigands? Helen Bond claims that Luke affirms Roman law, but is selectively critical of governors and other agents who are charged with implementing the law (*Pontius Pilate*, 142, 206).

flogged him, I will release him" (23:14–16, my emphasis; see 23:22).[66] This parallels further Pilate's ultimate decision. He essentially says, "Jesus is innocent, therefore go ahead and execute him" (see 23:24). In any case, as already suggested, Pilate takes Herod Antipas's decision to send Jesus back to him as indicating that Jesus is innocent of charges of inciting the people to violent resistance (23:15). Further, Luke makes the puzzling comment that Herod Antipas and Pilate became friends that day (23:12). Whatever else this means,[67] Luke associates them in an alliance that perpetuates injustice.

Further evidence of the injustice of the Roman system is Jesus' refusal to play the role of an accused prisoner. When Pilate asks him, "Are you the king of the Jews?"[68] Jesus is not silent. Rather, he responds in an enigmatic way, "Σὺ λέγεις" (23:3). Even though nothing else in Luke supports identifying Jesus as king of the Jews, the dominant interpretation takes this as an affirmative declaration that what Pilate says is accurate. Because Pilate does not take Jesus' answer as treason but pronounces Jesus innocent, it is more probable that Jesus responds with a question: "Do you say [this]?" or "[What] are you saying?"[69] But if he responds with a question, he is not playing the role of someone under accusation. Such a role continues before Herod Antipas in that Jesus is completely silent. He refuses to participate in a trial before the client king (tetrarch) who has judicial jurisdiction over him (vv. 6–11). Indeed, silence before interrogation in a judicial case may be a refusal to acknowledge the system.[70] Silence establishes a subject position of an alternative commitment to a community that is not dependent upon the dominant center: "I refuse to play the game."

66. Garnsey, *Social Status*, 128–41. Pilate proposes to "discipline" Jesus. Flogging was reserved primarily for slaves, not for Roman citizens, and as such it was an act of degradation.

67. Soards makes the astute observation that in the parable of the unjust steward, friendship is associated with the conspiracy of the "sons of this age" ("Tradition, Composition," 357).

68. Surprisingly, the accusation in 23:2 is that Jesus says he is a "king," not king "of the Jews."

69. So Wolter, *Lukasevangelium*, 740, and Nolland, *Luke*, 1118. The difference between affirmative and interrogative is a matter of intonation.

70. Carter reads Pilate stories in the Gospels as resistance. God's way, which Jesus follows, is an alternative to Caesar's (*Pontius Pilate*, 32–34). In addition, God's commonwealth leaves no place for an elite overclass (see 62).

John Nolland offers cautious support for a "Passover pardon" that would fit Pilate's attempt to release Jesus and the request of some Judeans to release Barabbas instead.[71] Nolland cites an article by Robert Merritt in support of his claim.[72] But the cases that Merritt adduces reflect *temporary* social inversions associated with carnival, such as the Saturnalia. Moreover, Merritt uses the practices only to support a background for Mark's creation of the release of Barabbas, not as a basis for the historicity of the release of Barabbas.

There is also some evidence against the practice of clemency in response to the pleas of the people. Suetonius *Tiberius* 37:2, reports that Tiberius could not be moved to rescind punishment by requests of the people. Josephus *Ant.* 20:215 decries the action of Albinus to release prisoners who clearly deserved to be put to death and to execute those who were imprisoned for trifling and commonplace offenses. But in a certain sense, there is little need for this kind of argumentation in relation to Luke, because, contrary to Mark and Matthew, Luke does not associate the release of Barabbas with a "customary" act of Pilate or expectation of Judeans.[73] Further, the ambiguity of the evidence makes it unlikely that Luke's hearers would expect the prefect to release a prisoner at Passover as an act of clemency. But whether there was such a custom or not, the release of Barabbas is a further travesty of justice.[74]

Conclusion

It is conventional to assign guilt for the death of Jesus. Regrettably, for most of Christian history, Judeans/Jews have been blamed. It is somewhat in vogue today to shift the blame to Rome. But assigning blame either to Judean elites or Pilate overlooks that in the crucifixion, they collaborate with one another.[75] Contrary to conventional interpretations that assign guilt to one side or the other, I present a picture that

---

71. Nolland, *Luke*, 1130.

72. Merritt, "Jesus, Barabbas," 58–66.

73. A variant reading in Luke 23:17 supports the practice as customary, but the entire verse is secondary. See the Nestle-Aland 27th edition.

74. So also Stegemann, *Zwischen Synagoge und Obrigkeit*, 32.

75. So also Carter, *Pontius Pilate*, 158. Egger cautions that tendentious sources do not allow conclusions that attribute blame (*"Crucifixus sub Pontio Pilato,"* 5).

is complex and to a certain degree empathetic with both the ordinary people and the elite.

Maintaining dominance indirectly through indigenous collabo-rators has been a strategy of imperialism since at least Alexander the Great,[76] who after his conquests reinstated local rulers, trained soldiers from local populations, and sent his own troops back home. The same pattern of collaboration, especially with the elite in colonized popula-tions, is evident in the British Empire and in the former Soviet block as well as in present-day Afghanistan and Iraq.[77] When Ban Ki-Moon became Secretary General of the United Nations, many South Koreans experienced immense pride, but many also had apprehensions because we understood that this was possible only because he was in some sense a collaborator with the dominant global powers, especially the United States.[78] I have demonstrated a similar picture for the role of the high priestly party in relation to Pilate from the perspective of how Judeans experienced the Roman Empire.

In an attempt to explain Jesus' trial in the context of representations of Rome elsewhere in Luke-Acts, Helen Bond concludes that "Luke's narrative shows that the state was on Jesus' side."[79] Rome, however, is much more problematic in Luke-Acts. For Pilate to collaborate in the crucifixion of Jesus cannot mean that the state was on Jesus' side. To repeat, Acts 4:26–27 includes Pilate with the rulers who acted *against* (κατά + genitive) the Lord and *against* the Lord's messiah.

Against Roman imperial propaganda that the Empire had estab-lished justice, Luke, rather than exonerating Pilate, portrays Pilate as part of a system that makes a travesty of justice. For Luke, some Judeans support the case against Jesus. Still the high priestly party functions as collaborators in the imperial *system*. In this system, Pilate holds power

76. For Judea in the Roman system, see Horsley, "High Priests," 23–55, 27–28.

77. A short exposé novel *Max Havelaar* (1860) by Eduard Douwes Dekker, a Dutch colonial administrator in the Netherlands Indies, describes collusion of Dutch officials with indigenous rulers (Stoler, *Along the Archival Grain*, 199–200). Some indigenous uprisings were also understood to be directed against the Europeans *and* their indig-enous collaborators. See e.g., 218–19.

78. Is it mere coincidence that his election can be correlated with the sending of Korean troops to Iraq?

79. *Pontius Pilate*, 162. Against this view, Stegemann, *Zwischen Synagoge und Obrigkeit*, 32–33. Bond claims support from Goulder, *Luke*, 761, and Conzelmann, *Theology*, 140. As I understand Goulder, he actually indicates Pilate's injustice.

for justice but executes injustice. He is hardly exonerated. Rather, he personifies imperial power that perpetuates injustice. God's commonwealth in Luke-Acts is a dramatic alternative, reflected quite clearly in Jesus' saying (Luke 22:25–26): "The kings of the nations lord it over them, and those who exercise power over them are called benefactors (εὐεργέται). But not so with you."

6

Paul, Agrippa I, and Antiochus IV

Two Persecutors in Acts in Light of 2 Maccabees 9

Kazuhiko Yamazaki-Ransom

Introduction

THE JEWISH LITERARY BACKGROUND OF LUKE-ACTS HAS BEEN A MUCH-examined topic in recent scholarly discussions. However, most of these studies are quite limited in scope, dealing only with (1) Luke's use of the Jewish Scriptures, (2) his explicit quotations and clear allusions to the Jewish Scriptures, and (3) the Christological implications thereof. Without denying the importance of these studies, one needs to go beyond these boundaries and expand the scope of research so as to include such issues as (1) Luke's use of Second Temple Jewish literature, (2) allusions to broad narrative patterns as a basis for establishing parallels, and (3) the ecclesiological implications thereof.[1] What will follow is a case study of this expanded approach to Luke's use of the portrayal of Antiochus IV in 2 Maccabees in his portrayals of two persecutors of the early church in his Acts narrative: Agrippa I and the Apostle Paul. This study attempts to shed some new light on the understanding of God's dealing with the earthly empires antagonistic to his kingdom through the narrative portrayals of Antiochus (ruler of the Seleucid Empire), Agrippa I (client king of the Roman Empire), and Paul (converted to become an agent of God's "empire").

---

1. For a review of literature on this topic, see Yamazaki-Ransom, "God, People, and Empire," 28–37.

Agrippa I (Acts 12)

Agrippa I was the son of Aristobulus and grandson of Herod the Great.[2] In Luke's narrative Agrippa I appears in Acts 12. It is important to note that Agrippa I is the only ruler in Luke-Acts who explicitly persecutes Christians, and he is also the only ruler whom Luke explicitly describes as being punished by God. The two episodes in chapter 12 illuminate Agrippa's relationship both with the people of God and with God, respectively. The first section (12:1–19) describes him as a persecutor of the people of God, while the second section (12:20–23) portrays him as a blasphemer against God. It is God himself who rescues the faithful (12:6–11) and punishes the persecutor (12:20–23).

Agrippa's Persecution of the Church

Luke introduces Agrippa I as "King Herod" (Ἡρῴδης ὁ βασιλεὺς) (12:1).[3] He was raised in Rome and made important connections with the members of the imperial court. When Gaius Caligula became emperor in 37 CE, he made Agrippa king (βασιλεύς) over the former tetrarchy of Philip (*Ant.* 18.236– 237), and also over the former tetrarchy of Antipas in 39 (18.250–252). When Gaius was assassinated in 41, Claudius, his successor, added Judea and Samaria to Agrippa's kingdom (19.274–275). This made him capable of persecuting Christians in Jerusalem. Agrippa killed James the brother of John with the sword (12:1b–2). This was "pleasing to the Jews," so Agrippa proceeded to arrest Peter, too (12:3). Peter was kept in prison, but the church was praying for him (12:5). The night before Agrippa was going to bring him out, presumably for public trial and execution, Peter was miraculously rescued by an angel (12:7).[4]

---

2. For the historical background, see Schürer, *History of the Jewish People*, 1:442–54; Perowne, *Later Herods*, 58–83; Jones, *Herods of Judaea*, 184–216; Stern, "Reign of Herod," 288–300; Smallwood, *Jews under Roman Rule*, 187–200; Schwartz, *Agrippa I*.

3. All Scriptural citations in English are taken from the NRSV unless otherwise indicated.

4. The "angel of the Lord" (ἄγγελος κυρίου) frequently appears in the LXX, corresponding to the Hebrew מלאך יהוה. E.g., Gen 16:7; 22:11, 15; Exod 3:2; Judg 6:11–12; 2 Sam 24:16; Isa 37:36; Zech 1:12. Luke also uses the phrase in Luke 1:11; 2:9; Acts 5:19 and 8:26.

Peter's rescue from the hand (ἐκ χειρὸς) of Agrippa (12:11) reminds the readers of Zechariah, who sang of "salvation from our enemies, and from the hand (ἐκ χειρὸς) of all who hate us" (Luke 1:71 NASB) and of the rescue from the hand (ἐκ χειρὸς) of enemies (1:74). In Luke-Acts, the phrase ἐκ χειρὸς occurs only in Luke 1:71, 74, and Acts 12:11. Therefore, there can be no doubt that for Luke, Agrippa I represents an enemy of the people of God. One must also not forget that Agrippa I's kingdom was part of the Roman Empire. Indeed, Agrippa's actions – killing (i.e., beheading) with a sword (Acts 12:2), imprisonment with four squads of guards (12:4), his plan for a public trial followed by an execution (12:4), and the execution of the guards who let the prisoner escape (12:18)—are all done in a *Roman* fashion.[5]

The Death of Agrippa

Agrippa reacted to Peter's escape by executing the prison guards, after which he went down to Caesarea (12:18–20).[6] Luke describes Agrippa's death as follows (12:21–23): "On an appointed day Herod put on his royal robes, took his seat on the platform, and delivered a public address to them. The people kept shouting, 'The voice of a god, and not of a mortal!' And immediately, because he had not given the glory to God, an angel of the Lord (ἄγγελος κυρίου) struck him down, and he was eaten by worms (γενόμενος σκωληκόβρωτος) and died."[7]

12:23 is clearly the climax of the section, a heavenly blow to Agrippa. Luke's reference to the angel of the Lord in 12:23 seems to correspond to the angel of the Lord in 12:7 who rescued Peter from prison. This ties the two episodes about Agrippa together: his plan against Peter is thwarted by an angel, and he is punished by an angel for blasphemy.[8]

The adjective σκωληκόβρωτος is a composite word from σκώληξ (worm) and βιβρώσκω (to eat up).[9] Although the adjective appears

5. See Witherington, *Acts*, 385, 389; Bock, *Acts*, 425–26. See also Cassidy, *Acts*, 50.

6. Agrippa's move from Judea to Caesarea, the Roman provincial capital of Palestine, indicates a shift from a Jewish to a strongly Roman environment.

7. Josephus also reports Agrippa I's death in Caesarea (*Ant.* 19.343–51), but does not refer to worms.

8. It is also notable that while in 12:7 an angel struck (πατάξας) Peter to save him, in 12:23 an angel struck (ἐπάταξεν) Agrippa to kill him.

9. See BDAG, 933.

only in Acts 12:23 in the entire Greek Bible, the image of humans being eaten by worms appears in ancient literature as a way to depict horrible torment and death.[10] Worms often appear as instruments of divine punishment for sinners.[11] Sometimes worms are specifically associated with the punishment of evil rulers.[12] But probably the most important referent can be found in 2 Macc 9, which describes the death of Antiochus IV Epiphanes. This account is significant because it has a narrative structure that is notably similar to that of Luke's account of Agrippa's death.[13]

Agrippa and Antiochus: The Persecutor Dies from Worms

The Seleucid king Antiochus IV (175–164 BCE), son of Antiochus III, acceded to the throne after his brother, Seleucus IV. The Seleucid dynasty was founded by Seleucus I, one of the generals of Alexander the Great. The Seleucids ruled the vast eastern territories of Alexander's empire as well as Syria and part of Asia Minor. In 198 BCE Antiochus III defeated the Egyptian army at the battle of Panias, thus gaining control over Judea. Antiochus IV was determined to spread Hellenism throughout his empire, including Jewish Palestine. His persecution of the Jews culminated in the forced cessation of the Yahwistic cult and the introduction of the worship of the Olympian Zeus in the Jerusalem temple (1 Macc 1:54; 2 Macc 6:2; *Ant.* 12.248–254). This event triggered the Maccabean revolt. In Jewish literature, Antiochus IV is the archenemy of the people, and the crisis he caused produced a series of literary

10. See Job 7:5; cf. *T. Job* 20:8.

11. Isa 66:24; Sir 7:17; 19:3; Mark 9:48 (an allusion to Isa 66:24).

12. See Isa 14:11 LXX; Sir 10:10–11. Jdt 16:17 and 1 Macc 2:62 may also be included in this category. Cf. the death of Herod the Great in Josephus *Ant.* 17.169. For more references including non-Judeo-Christian sources, see Nestle, "Tod der Gottesverächter," 246–69; Africa, "Worms and the Death of Kings," 1–17.

13. So Clarke, "Use of the Septuagint," 2:75–76; Roloff, *Apostelgeschichte*, 191; Pesch, *Apostelgeschichte*, 2:368. Allen (*Death of Herod*, 29–74) states that Luke's account of Agrippa's death belongs to a literary convention of "Death of Tyrant type-scenes," the central feature of which is retribution: the tyrant's offense to a deity and his punishment.

responses.[14] Second Maccabees is one of these.[15] The king is described as arrogant and bloodthirsty, traits that are most evident in the martyrdom of the mother and her seven sons (ch. 7). The book explicitly states several times that Antiochus's death was due to divine punishment (2 Macc 1:11–12, 17; 9:4–6, 11, 18; cf. 7:31–36).[16]

The account of Antiochus's death in chapter 9 is a carefully crafted literary piece. Employing both biblical and Greek literary conventions, the author describes how Antiochus's death is the result of divine punishment for his godless behavior.[17]

The Jews, led by Judas Maccabaeus, defeated the Syrian army led by Nicanor (2 Macc 8). Upon hearing the news, Antiochus became enraged (ἐπαρθεὶς δὲ τῷ θυμῷ) and was determined to destroy Jerusalem (9:4).[18] On Antiochus' way to the city, God struck him with a severe pain in his intestines (9:5). His agony is described as follows (9:9): "so that *worms broke out* (σκώληκας ἀναζεῖν) of the unbeliever's eyes, and while he was still living in anguish and pain, his flesh rotted away, and because of his stench the whole army felt revulsion at the decay."[19]

The most striking feature of the description of Antiochus in Second Maccabees is found in 9:11–17. Struck by a sickness sent from God, Antiochus pleads with God: ". . . and in addition to all this he also would become a Jew and would visit every inhabited place to proclaim the power of God" (2 Macc 9:17). However, his prayer was not heard, because the Lord "would no longer have mercy on him" (9:13). What is remarkable here is that this is a rare instance of a Gentile ruler's wishing to become a Jew, although his request is rejected by God.[20] Thus

14. For various responses in apocalyptic literature, see Nickelsburg, *Jewish Literature*, 67–88.

15. Second Maccabees is an abridgment of the five-volume history of the Maccabean Revolt written by Jason of Cyrene (2 Macc 2:19, 23, 26, 28). Jason's original work was written after 161 BCE, and his abridger completed his work before 124 BCE. See deSilva, *Introducing the Apocrypha*, 269–70.

16. Gauger classifies the account of Antiochus in Maccabean literature in the category of the cruel death of θεομάχος (including the persecutor of God's people) as divine punishment. See Gauger, "'Tod des Verfolgers,'" 47.

17. See Goldstein, *II Maccabees*, 353.

18. Antiochus's rage can be compared with that of Agrippa (Acts 12:20 ἦν δὲ θυμομαχῶν). See Clarke, "Use of the Septuagint," 2:75.

19. Translation by *A New English Translation of the Septuagint* (NETS). For the textual problem contained in this verse, see below, n. 41.

20. It is debatable whether Antiochus's repentance was rejected because it was too late or because it was not genuine. Based on his literary analysis of 2 Macc 9, Nicklas

Antiochus died, tormented by worms, just as Agrippa I later would (Acts 12:23).[21] His death is described as follows: "So the murderer and blasphemer, having endured the more intense suffering, such as he had inflicted on others, came to the end of his life by a most pitiable fate, among the mountains in a strange land (2 Macc 9:28)."

Jörg-Dieter Gauger classifies the death of Antiochus IV as the death of the persecutor: "an especially atrocious manner of death as punishment by the gods or God for the θεομάχος, for the unbeliever, the blasphemer or the persecutor of the people of God."[22] In Second Maccabees, Antiochus is portrayed as a murderer of Jews.[23] Furthermore, he is repeatedly characterized by his arrogance.[24] The worm-ridden death of a "murderer and blasphemer" (ἀνδροφόνος καὶ βλάσφημος) also perfectly fits the overall description of Agrippa I in Acts 12. Not only did he die, eaten by worms (12:23), but he is also described as a murderer (12:2) and a blasphemer (12:23). Furthermore, just as God struck (ἐπάταξεν) Antiochus (2 Macc 9:5), so an angel of the Lord struck (ἐπάταξεν) Agrippa (Acts 12:23).

These parallel motifs as well as the overall structure of the death of the persecutor suggest that Luke is alluding to 2 Macc 9 in his description of Agrippa I's death. One should not read Luke's account of Agrippa's death (Acts 12:20–23) separately from the preceding section in 12:1–19. Agrippa I as the main character, the smooth transition in 12:19, and the reference to an angel in both accounts (12:7, 23) all indicate that chapter 12 as a whole is a literary unit. Therefore, while the direct cause of Agrippa's death is his blasphemy (12:23 "because he had not given the glory to God"), his death must also be seen in light of the

---

concludes that the latter is the case. See "Historiker als Erzähler," 90–91. In any case, it is striking that the motif of a Gentile ruler's conversion appears in an account of the archenemy of the Jews.

21. In Acts 12:23, D has the phrase ἔτι ζῶν (still alive), probably a later addition in order to emphasize the gruesome nature of Agrippa's death. It is notable that 2 Macc 9 also has ζῶντος ([still] living), although it is not certain if the addition in D is derived from this passage.

22. Gauger, "'Tod des Verfolgers,'" 47; my translation.

23. See the martyrdom of Eleazar and the seven brothers in 6:18–7:42.

24. Note the use of such terms as ὑπερηφάνως (arrogantly) (9:4); ὑπερηφανία (arrogance) (9:7, 9); ἀγερωχία (insolence) (9:7); ἀλαζονεία (pretension) (9:8). Clarke ("Use of the Septuagint," 2:75) compares the hubris of Antiochus (9:10 τῶν οὐρανίων ἄστρων ἅπτεσθαι δοκοῦντα) with that of Agrippa (Acts 12:22 θεοῦ φωνὴ).

episode of his persecution of the church.[25] In other words, Agrippa's death is to be seen as a punishment for his persecution of Christians.[26] Thus in both Acts 12 and 2 Macc 9, the subject matter is the death of an imperial ruler who persecuted the people of God.

The differences between the death accounts of Agrippa and Antiochus are also significant. While Antiochus is a *Gentile* persecutor of the *Jews*, Agrippa I is a *Jewish* persecutor of the *Christians*.[27] Thus in Luke's narrative a Jewish king is playing the role played by the oppressive Gentile kings in the traditional Jewish narratives. Furthermore, Antiochus expressed his remorse at his own arrogance and even wanted to become a Jew (2 Macc 9:17). However, his repentance was too late. By contrast, nothing in Luke's narrative indicates Agrippa's repentance or remorse. The implication may be that Agrippa was worse than Antiochus, the archenemy of Israel, for even Antiochus repented before his death but Agrippa did not. Considered in the larger political context of the Roman Empire, Luke's portrayal of Agrippa I—the *Jewish* client king of *Rome* persecuting the people of God—gives an insight into his worldview: non-Christian Jewish rulers belong to the worldly empire, an empire that is antagonistic to God's kingdom.[28]

Luke concludes the chapter with a summary statement, "But the word of God continued to advance and gain adherents" (12:24). The word of God cannot be hindered by persecution. On the contrary, Agrippa the persecutor invites divine punishment upon himself. Thus in Acts 12 Agrippa I is portrayed as God's enemy, one who persecutes the faithful but cannot hinder God's work in history.[29]

25. Contra Jervell, *Apostelgeschichte*, 337.

26. For a more detailed argument for the unity of Acts 12, see Allen, *Death of Herod*, 75–92. Contra Gauger, "'Tod des Verfolgers,'" 52.

27. Although Agrippa was not a genuine Jew, he tried to present himself as a pious Jewish king (*Ant.* 19.292–299). At the very least he was on the side of the (non-Christian) Jews (Acts 12:3).

28. For Luke those anti-Christian political powers (both Jewish and Roman) ultimately derive their authority from Satan (Luke 4:5–7). For a more detailed discussion of Luke's holistic worldview, see Yamazaki-Ransom, *Roman Empire*, ch. 3.

29. See also Kratz, *Rettungswunder*, 472–73.

Paul (Acts 9)

The above analysis clearly shows that there is a strong probability that Luke intentionally drew upon the death account of Antiochus IV Epiphanes in 2 Macc 9 in his portrayal of Agrippa I in Acts 12. However, one question remains unanswered. At the end of Antiochus's plea (2 Macc 9:13–17) comes a most remarkable statement: "and in addition to all this he also would become a Jew and would visit every inhabited place to proclaim the power of God" (9:17). This is one of the major differences between the portrayal of Antiochus in 2 Macc 9 and that of Agrippa in Acts 12. In Luke's narrative, Agrippa shows no sign of repentance when he is struck by God. Indeed, Luke does not report any response by Agrippa whatsoever. For the rest of this article, I will argue that Luke reserved the theme of Antiochus's desire to convert for another character in his narrative: the Apostle Paul.

Paul and Antiochus: The Persecutor Overthrown

In her study of the account of Paul's conversion in Acts 9, Beverly Roberts Gaventa states, "With the exception of Herod's death (12:20–23), the conversion of Saul is the most dramatic example of the defeat of the church's enemies" in Acts.[30] Gaventa also argues that throughout Luke's narrative, Paul remains the church's enemy, although he is an enemy who has been overthrown.[31] Although Gaventa's work on Paul as the overthrown enemy does not seem to have attracted much scholarly agreement, she correctly observes the importance of Paul's characterization as an enemy of the church as well as the similarity between the accounts of Paul and Agrippa I in Acts. However, she does not seem to notice the link between these two defeated-enemy stories, nor does she probe the possible intertextuality between these two accounts and the account of Antiochus in 2 Macc 9. Gaventa is aware of the potential problem with her thesis, namely the fact that as the reader moves from Acts 9 to the later retellings of Paul's conversion story, more emphasis is placed on his call to Gentile missions. She tries to argue that the theme of "overthrown enemy" has not faded

---

30. Gaventa, "Overthrown Enemy," 445. For a more detailed analysis of the accounts of Paul's conversion in Acts, see Gaventa, *From Darkness to Light*, 52–95.

31. "Overthrown Enemy," 448.

from the later chapters, thus "Paul remains the overthrown enemy."[32] However, it would be possible to reconcile the themes of persecution and mission in Paul if one reads Paul's conversion in light of 2 Macc 9, where these themes can both be found.[33]

At first glance it may seem odd to compare Luke's hero, Paul, with Antiochus Epiphanes, the archenemy of the people of God in Jewish tradition. However, a close reading of Acts and Second Maccabees reveals striking similarities between these two figures.

First of all, both Paul—or Saul, as Luke calls him in the earlier chapters of Acts—and Antiochus are characterized as violent persecutors of the people of God. As noted above, Antiochus IV is described primarily as an atrocious persecutor of the Jews in Second Maccabees. In Luke's narrative, Paul first appears as a young man called Saul, watching Stephen being stoned to death by the Jews (Acts 7:58).[34] As the narrative develops, the reader is informed that not only did Saul approve of the murder of Stephen (8:1), he was actively persecuting Christians (8:3). Thus, like Antiochus in Second Maccabees, Saul emerges as a violent persecutor of the people of God in Luke's narrative. When he next appears in the narrative in 9:1, Luke states that Saul was "still breathing threats and murder against the disciples of the Lord." The word "still" (ἔτι) refers back to 8:3, indicating the continuity of his characterization as a persecutor. Luke strengthens Saul's identity as persecutor by introducing the viewpoints of other characters in the narrative. The hesitation of Ananias (9:13–14), the amazement of the Jews in Damascus (9:21), and the fear of the Christians in Jerusalem (9:26–27) all point to the fact that Saul is a persecutor of the church. This characterization of Paul as one who had persecuted the church continues in the later chapters of Acts. In the two retellings of the so-called "Damascus event" in Acts,

32. Ibid., 448–49; *From Darkness to Light*, 92.

33. Scholars have proposed other possible literary links with Paul's conversion narrative in Acts 9. These include Aseneth (*Jos. Asen.* 14:6–8), Heliodorus (2 Macc 3), and Apollonius (4 Macc 4:1–14). See Johnson, *Acts*, 162–63, 167–68; cf. Bock, *Acts*, 353, 357; Marshall, *Acts*, 167. The argument that follows does not necessarily exclude the possibility of Luke's use of literary traditions other than that of Antiochus in 2 Macc 9, but it seems central in light of his use of the same account for the death of Agrippa, as discussed above.

34. Just as Antiochus watches the murder of the seven sons of a woman (2 Macc 7), so Paul watches the murder of Stephen.

Paul mentions his past as a persecutor of the church (22:4–5; 26:9–11).[35] As Gaventa states, "Paul remains the converted persecutor."[36] For Paul, his past as a persecutor of the church before his conversion apparently had great significance (cf. 1 Cor 15:9). Furthermore, Paul's persecution of the church had an imperial dimension. He attacked Christians under the authority (ἐξουσία) of the chief priests (Acts 9:14; 26:10, 12; cf. 9:1–2). The latter were not merely religious, apolitical figures, but under Rome's political control.[37] In a sense, then, Paul's persecution of the church was ultimately a manifestation of Roman imperial power.

Not only are both Paul and Antiochus characterized as persecutors, the overall structures of their accounts are remarkably similar. In both Acts 9 and 2 Macc 9, the persecutor rushes to a location in order to harm the people of God (Acts 9:1–2; 2 Macc 9:1–4). On his way, he is struck by divine intervention and falls to the ground (Acts 9:3–9; 2 Macc 9:5–10). In both accounts, the persecutor prays (Acts 9:11–12; 2 Macc 9:13–17). In both accounts, there is a reference to conversion and mission (Acts 9:15–16; 2 Macc 9:17).

Furthermore, there are some detailed linguistic similarities between the descriptions of Saul and Antiochus. In Acts 9:1, Saul appears "breathing (ἐμπνέων) threats and murder against the disciples of the Lord." In 2 Macc 9:7, Antiochus is described as "breathing (πνέων) fire in his rage against the Jews."[38] Antiochus is called "the murderer and

35. The alleged discrepancies between the three accounts of Paul's conversion have generated much scholarly discussion. Earlier scholarship's source-critical approach proved futile, but the more recent narratological approach convincingly supports Luke's strategic use of the three variations of the same event for rhetorical purposes. See Witherup, "Functional Redundancy," 67–86; Marguerat, *First Christian Historian*, 179–204. Considering the fact that Luke changes the way he presents the "Damascus event" according to the different settings and purposes of each account, it is remarkable that Paul's identity as the persecutor is preserved in all three accounts.

36. *From Darkness to Light*, 92.

37. From 6 to 41 CE the high priests were appointed by the Roman governors (either by the legate of Syria or the prefect of Judea). See Schürer, *History of the Jewish People*, 1:377.

38. In their commentary on Acts, Lake and Cadbury state, "The emotion of anger was in Semitic physiology connected with breath." *Commentary*, 4:99. Horst ("Drohung und Mord," 264–65) rejects their thesis, arguing that, in contrast to the abundance of parallels in Greek literature, he knows *only one possible Semitic parallel to Acts 9:1, namely 2 Macc 9:7*. However, one may argue that in light of the importance of 2 Macc 9 as the literary background for Acts 12, the parallel between 2 Macc 9:7 and Acts 9:1 indicates that Luke deliberately alludes to the anger of Antiochus.

blasphemer" (ἀνδροφόνος καὶ βλάσφημος) (2 Macc 9:28). Saul breathes "murder" (φόνος) (Acts 9:1) and tries to force Christians to "blaspheme" (βλασφημεῖν) (26:11).[39] Saul acquired his authority (ἐξουσία) from the high priest to persecute Christians in Damascus (Acts 9:14; 26:10, 12). Antiochus has "authority (ἐξουσία) among mortals" to persecute the Jews (2 Macc 7:16).[40] Scales fall from Saul's eyes (ἀπὸ τῶν ὀφθαλμῶν) (Acts 9:18); worms swarm out of Antiochus's eyes (ἐκ τῶν ὀφθαλμῶν).[41]

Similarities exist not only in the portrayals of the persecutors but also in the depictions of those who are persecuted. Ananias tells the risen Lord that Saul has the authority to bind "all who invoke (ἐπικαλουμένους) your name" (Acts 9:14). The verb ἐπικαλέω appears 14 times in Second Maccabees, mostly in the context of the Jews calling upon the God of Israel in their conflicts with Gentiles. Of special importance is 2 Macc 7:37, where the youngest of the seven brothers martyred under Antiochus calls upon God. He defies the king, even as he addresses him, saying, "I, like my brothers, give up body and life for the laws of our ancestors, appealing to God (ἐπικαλούμενος τὸν θεὸν) to show mercy soon to our nation and by trials and plagues *to make you confess that he alone is God.*"

39. In Acts 5:39, Gamaliel advises the Jews not to persecute the Christians, lest they should find themselves θεομάχοι (those who fight against God). At this point, the Jews take heed of Gamaliel's counsel, but eventually they resume their persecution against the church. The implication is that they became θεομάχοι. Saul, Gamaliel's disciple (22:3), plays the leading role in the persecution; thus he also became a preeminent θεομάχος. Johnson (*Acts*, 166) states that "Saul's conversion, after all, is the paradigmatic expression of the ironic truth spoken by Gamaliel (5:38–39)." Antiochus is also said to fight against God (θεομαχεῖν) in persecuting the Jews (2 Macc 7:19). These are the only two instances of the appearance of the θεομαχ- word group in the entire Greek Bible, so it is possible also in this passage to hear the echo of Antiochus in Luke's description of Paul.

40. Note also Antiochus's connection with the corrupt Jewish high priesthood in 2 Macc 4:7–50.

41. There is a textual problem in 2 Macc 9:9. Most MSS have the reading τοῦ σώματος as in the Rahlfs-Hanhart edition of the LXX, which is also reflected in the NRSV. However, Old Latin has τῶν ὀφθαλμῶν, while Venetus has τῶν τοῦ σώματος ὀφθαλμῶν, which most likely is a conflation of the two shorter readings. The Göttingen edition adopts the reading τῶν ὀφθαλμῶν, as in the translations by Goldstein (*II Maccabees*, 343) and NETS. The references to "bowels" (9:5, 6) and "body" (σῶμα) (9:7) as the loci of Antiochus's pain in the immediate context make the reading τῶν ὀφθαλμῶν rather unexpected, and therefore the more difficult. As such, it seems to be the original.

His prayer is heard: in 9:12, Antiochus finally acknowledges that Yahweh is God. Likewise, Saul also acknowledges that the Jesus he had been persecuting is indeed Lord and Christ (Acts 9:5, 20).

Paul and Antiochus: Persecutor Becoming "Missionary"

Thus far many similarities between the portrayals of Antiochus and Paul have been noted. But the most important one comes in Antiochus's final plea with God: "and in addition to all this he also would become a Jew and would visit every inhabited place to proclaim the power of God" (πρὸς δὲ τούτοις καὶ Ιουδαῖον ἔσεσθαι καὶ πάντα τόπον οἰκητὸν ἐπελεύσεσθαι καταγγέλλοντα τὸ τοῦ θεοῦ κράτος) (2 Macc 9:17).

First, Antiochus expresses his wish to become a Jew, to become a member of the people he previously persecuted. Likewise Saul becomes one of the Christians whom he was persecuting, which is already indicated when Ananias addresses him as "brother" (Acts 9:17).[42]

Second, Antiochus vows to visit every inhabited place to proclaim the power of God. In the narrative of Acts, Paul travels extensively to proclaim the gospel. The comprehensiveness of his mission is expressed in the Lord's words to Ananias: "he is an instrument whom I have chosen to bring my name before Gentiles and kings and before the people of Israel" (Acts 9:15). The verb "proclaim" (καταγγέλλω) is a rare word in the LXX, appearing only in 2 Macc 8:36 and 9:17. The word appears 18 times in the New Testament, eleven of which are in Acts. In Acts, the verb is almost always used to refer to the Christian proclamation of the gospel, nine times in the context of Paul's activity (Acts 13:5, 38; 15:36; 16:17, 21; 17:3, 13, 23; 26:23). Thus it seems that the verb is characteristic of Paul's proclamation of the gospel, which Luke intended as an allusion to Antiochus's vow to proclaim the power of the God of the Jews.[43]

Finally, Antiochus promises to proclaim the "power" (κράτος) of God. The word κράτος is used only twice in Luke-Acts. In Luke 1:51, Mary praises the power (κράτος) of the God who "has scattered the proud in

---

42. This does not mean that Paul ceased being a Jew. On the contrary, he stresses his identity as a loyal Jew in his retelling of his conversion in Acts 22. See Marguerat, *First Christian Historian*, 197. Paul is a *true Jew* who brings the salvation of the God of the Jews to all nations.

43. The verb has the implication of "broad dissemination" of a message (BDAG, 515), thus corresponding to the idea of proclaiming God's power in "every inhabited place" (2 Macc 9:17).

the thoughts of their hearts" and "has brought down the powerful from their thrones" (1:52). Here the power of God is related to God's activity in overthrowing the powerful and proud, which may allude to the fate of some of the characters in Luke-Acts, including Agrippa I and Saul. In Acts 19:20, Luke speaks of how the word of the Lord spread mightily (κατὰ κράτος). This statement summarizes Paul's missionary activity. To be sure, Paul is not explicitly said to proclaim the "power" of God, but his message was proclaimed with "power."

So far I have shown that there are extensive parallels between the portrayals of Paul in Acts and that of Antiochus IV in Second Maccabees. But there are also notable differences between the two figures. First, while Second Maccabees narrates the account of the *Gentile* persecutor (Antiochus) persecuting the *Jews*, the Acts narrative has the *non-Christian Jewish* persecutor (Saul) persecuting the Jewish *Christians*. Second, while Antiochus rushes *toward* Jerusalem (2 Macc 9:4), Saul rushes *from* Jerusalem, the locus of Jewish authority (see Acts 9:1–3, 13, 21). Third, while Antiochus is struck by the Lord (κύριος), the God of Israel (2 Macc 9:5), Paul is struck by the Lord (κύριος), the risen Jesus (Acts 9:5, 17).

All these differences point in the same direction: while Luke uses the literary pattern of Second Maccabees, he gives it a crucial twist so he can redefine the idea of "the people of God" with a Christological focus. The enemies of the people of God are now defined as not simply Gentiles but all who are against Christ, Jews or Gentiles, because the lordship of the God of the Jews is now manifested through his Christ. On the other hand, the "people of God" is now defined not in terms of the Jews as an ethnic group, but in terms of those who follow Jesus Christ as their Lord.[44]

The most important difference in the two accounts lies in the development of the themes of conversion and mission. Although Antiochus pleads with God to become a Jewish "missionary," his hope is never fulfilled.[45] On the other hand, Paul is called by the Lord to become a Christian "missionary," a proclaimer of the kingdom of God manifested

---

44. For Luke's systematic use of the Jewish literary tradition for this purpose, see Yamazaki-Ransom, *Roman Empire*, chapters 4–5.

45. The author of Second Maccabees makes this point clear by commenting, "Then the abominable fellow made a vow to the Lord, *who would no longer have mercy on him*, . . ." (2 Macc 9:13).

in Christ, and the narrative of Acts reveals how this calling is fulfilled. It seems that Luke, while narrating Paul's conversion in the pattern of the "overthrown enemy" in 2 Macc 9, takes up the motif of conversion and mission in Antiochus's plea and develops this unfulfilled desire into the extensive missionary work of the hero of his narrative.

Conclusion: The Significance of Luke's Use of the Antiochus Narrative for Paul and Agrippa I

This study has shown that the portrayals of Agrippa I and Paul in Acts present similar images derived from the character of Antiochus IV as described in Second Maccabees. Luke used the motif of the "divine punishment of the persecutor of the people of God" in 2 Macc 9 for his descriptions of Agrippa and Paul. However, in doing so, Luke used the negative elements of Antiochus's story (especially his worm-ridden death) for his portrayal of Agrippa, and developed its positive elements of desire for conversion and mission for the figure of Paul.

The way Luke uses the literary figure of Antiochus in Acts in his portrayals of Agrippa and Paul has significant Christological and ecclesiological implications. In both cases, Luke radically redefines the concept of the "people of God." For Luke the true people of God are those who follow Jesus Christ as their Lord, whether Jewish or Gentile. On the other hand, even the Jews can be enemies of God if they do not acknowledge the lordship of Christ. Thus Luke is undermining the traditional dichotomy between Jews and Gentiles.

One may also note Luke's strategic placement of these accounts in his narrative of Acts. In Acts 9:1–31, Saul, the prominent enemy of the church, is overthrown, converted, and given a mission to proclaim the gospel to all people. The road to Gentile missions is prepared by Peter (9:32—11:18) and by the church in Antioch (11:19–30). Chapter 12 features the last appearance of Peter as a prominent figure in the narrative of Acts, except for his brief reappearance in 15:7–11. Hereafter Luke's narrative shifts its focus to Paul. The account of Agrippa I is placed within the continuous narrative of the church in Antioch and right before Paul's extensive Gentile mission begins from there (13:1).[46]

46. This may be a coincidence, but it is interesting to note that the city of Syrian Antioch was built c. 300 BCE and was named after Antiochus, father of Seleucus I Nicator, who was an ancestor of Antiochus IV.

One may ask why Luke places the episode about Agrippa at this point in the narrative. It is noteworthy that the episode is framed by Paul and Barnabas's travels to and from Jerusalem (11:30; 12:25).[47] The reader is not told what they were doing during the incident in Judaea narrated in chapter 12, but one may speculate that Luke is trying somehow to present Agrippa as Paul's doppelgänger: Agrippa is Antiochus whose wish is not fulfilled; Paul is Antiochus who is called to proclaim the power of God. Agrippa's fate represents what might have happened to Paul if it were not for the grace of God.

Luke's two-fold use of the portrayal of Antiochus in Second Maccabees indicates God's sovereign power and mercy. God overthrows his enemies, but God deals with enemies differently. Sometimes God severely punishes them with death, as in the case of Antiochus and Agrippa. However, as in the case of the Apostle Paul, God can also convert his worst enemies into chosen vessels for his glory. It is also noteworthy that when Anitochus wished to become a Jew, he was rejected. By contrast, Saul, who did not make any explicit wish to become a Christian, was called by God for his mission. In either case, the efforts of earthly kingdoms to control the future, including those of the Seleucid Empire (Antiochus) and of the Roman Empire (Agrippa and, less directly, Paul), are overthrown by God's larger sovereign purpose for *his* kingdom.

47. For the textual problem in 12:25 and a convincing solution thereof, see Bruce, *Acts*, 290–91.

7

Trying Paul or Trying Rome?

Judges and Accused in the Roman Trials of Paul in Acts

Steve Walton

It has frequently been remarked that the trial(s) of Jesus in the Fourth Gospel "turn the tables" on Jesus' judges: rather than Jesus himself being on trial, it turns out to be others who are on trial. Thus, Pilate, the Jewish leadership, and even the world, stand under the judgment of God in the trial of Jesus.[1] Andrew Lincoln observes: "In his witness to the truth, Jesus becomes the judge and both 'the Jews' and Pilate are judged by their response to Jesus. Thus the Roman trial becomes the vehicle for the irony that the apparent judge and the apparent accusers are in reality being judged by the apparent accused. Indeed, one could just as easily entitle the episode 'The Trial of the Jews before Jesus' as 'The Trial of Jesus before Pilate.'"[2]

This paper seeks to ask whether a similar turning of the tables is taking place in the three Roman trials of Paul in Acts; that is, we shall consider Luke's narrative to see how the Roman empire and its official representatives appear in their handling of Paul. In light of the widely-recognized parallelism of Jesus and Paul in Luke and Acts,[3] our approach will be to look first at the Roman trial of Jesus in Luke's Gospel, to see whether features there might suggest a similar trial of the empire

---

1. See Lincoln, *Truth*, 123–38 with further references. More broadly, Harvey and Trites see the whole of the Fourth Gospel as presenting a "cosmic trial" scene, an insight developed in Lincoln's work; Harvey, *Jesus on Trial*; Trites, *New Testament Concept of Witness*, 78–124.

2. Lincoln, *Truth*, 137.

3. See Walton, *Leadership and Lifestyle*, 34–37, and literature cited there.

and its agents. We shall then turn to consider the three trials of Paul—one before the proconsul Gallio in Corinth and two others before the governors Festus and Felix in Caesarea—before closing with some brief reflections on how the presentation of the empire in these three trials relates to Luke's wider engagement with imperial ideology and issues.

Our approach will be to focus on the narrative presentation of the empire and its representatives.[4] To take such an approach is not in conflict with careful consideration of the historical context: rather, it necessitates placing the text in its proper historical context, so that (as far as possible) we are seeing features that a first-century reader might see.[5]

The Trial of Jesus in Luke (Luke 23)

A number of features of the Roman trial of Jesus are pertinent to our theme.

First, Luke's portrays Jesus throughout his arrest and trial as is in sublime control of events and of himself,[6] stemming from his commitment in Gethsemane to do the Father's will (22:42). Indeed, Jesus heals one man who comes to arrest him after his disciple has cut off the man's ear (22:50–51). The same sense of control is evident in the trial before Pilate. Jesus answers Pilate almost monosyllabically (23:3), and gives no answer at all to Herod, from whom Pilate has sought advice (23:9). When Jesus does speak, *after* the trial, it is to bring words of judgment on Jerusalem (23:28–31) and words of assurance to the penitent thief (23:43).[7]

Luke has prepared for this portrait of control by assuring his readers that Jesus' suffering and death are the Father's will, announced in

4. This emphasis is in tune with the fine narrative-critical work of our honoree, Robert Brawley.

5. Powell, *What is Narrative Criticism?*, 96–98.

6. Moberly, "Proclaiming Christ Crucified," esp. 36–39.

7. According to some manuscripts, Jesus also speaks in 23:34a to ask God's forgiveness on those crucifying him, and if these words were original they would add to the sense of Jesus' control. However, an impressive array of our most ancient manuscripts including p75 ℵ[1] B D* W Θ omits the words. NA[27] includes the passage in its main text, albeit in double square brackets, on the rather romantic basis that the phrase "bears self-evident tokens of its dominical origin" (Metzger, *Textual Commentary*, 154). Johnson, *Luke*, 376 argues for its inclusion on thematic grounds. More fully in defense of inclusion, see Green, *Death of Jesus*, 91–92; Brown, *Death of the Messiah*, 2:975–81.

advance by Jesus (13:33–35; 18:31–33) and in Scripture (e.g., 24:27, 44), thus redefining messianic expectation ironically to include suffering.[8]

Second, the three accusations against Jesus (23:2) are false. By handing Jesus over to the Gentile Pilate to deal with, the chief priests are admitting that they cannot deal with him as they would like to do. As such, it is they who are "perverting the nation" by implicitly accepting pagan rule.[9] Further, in a brilliantly ambiguous answer, Jesus earlier refused the dilemma offered to him as to whether the Jews should pay taxes to Caesar or not (20:25). Most ironic of all, in Luke's Gospel up to now Jesus never himself explicitly claims to be Messiah. When others offer him the title of Messiah, he offers an alternative title or deflects the question (9:20–21; 22:67–69). Of course, Luke wants his readers to believe that Jesus is Messiah, for it is announced by the angels to the shepherds (2:11). Indeed, Jesus' *deeds* imply messianic claims.[10] However, Luke does not present Jesus *speaking* of himself as Messiah before his resurrection (note Acts 2:36).[11]

Third, Jesus is declared innocent at least six times[12] in the trial and crucifixion narrative. Three times Pilate asserts Jesus' innocence (23:4, 14, 22), and Herod agrees (23:15). The penitent thief recognizes Jesus has "done nothing wrong" (23:41) and the centurion declares him innocent (23:47). And yet Jesus is condemned by Pilate to crucifixion. Strikingly, Luke is the only evangelist to record Pilate giving sentence (23:24; the verb ἐπέκρινεν is here a technical word for giving a formal judgment).[13]

Pilate appears to want to dismiss the case against Jesus quickly. As a result, his first verdict of Jesus' innocence follows the most cursory of interrogations (23:3–4).[14] Walaskay justly observes that a Roman reader

---

8. Brawley, *Centering on God*, 51.

9. The point is made more sharply in John 19:15, where the chief priests claim to have "no king but Caesar."

10. e.g. Luke 7:18–23; 19:37–38, 45–46.

11. See the judicious discussion of Longenecker, *Christology*, 72–74.

12. Perhaps eight if the women's mourning (23:27) is an implicit recognition that Jesus does not deserve to die, and the people's mourning following Jesus' death (23:48) are included—the former may anticipate the latter (Green, *Luke*, 815).

13. An NT *hapax legomenon*; see 2 Macc 4:47; 3 Macc 4:2; MM 240; LSJ 641; Bond, *Pontius Pilate*, 158. Luke's use of this term suggests that Walaskay is mistaken in thinking that Luke presents the Roman trial as incomplete (Walaskay, *Rome*, 44).

14. By contrast with 22:70 (see below), Jesus' answer "You say so" (σὺ λέγεις, 23:3), is

would have been very surprised at such a hasty ruling without due process.[15] Pilate seeks advice from Herod on learning that Jesus is a Galilean (23:6–7). He further attempts to give a ruling, but is shouted down (23:13–18).[16] He twice proposes a beating (23:16, 22), presumably the lighter beating which functioned as an informal warning (*fustigatio*).[17] However, he cannot persuade the Jewish leaders to accept his proposal. As events develop, he finally accedes to persistent pressure from the chief priests, other leaders and the people (23:1–2, 5, 10, 18, 21, 23) and hands over an innocent man to death. Not only that, but Pilate also hands over a recognized insurrectionist and murderer, Barabbas, to the people in response to their demands (23:18, 25). The irony of this exchange is underlined for those in the know by the meaning of Barabbas' name, "son of the father," for Jesus has been recognized as God's son at key points in Luke's narrative (1:32, 35; 3:22; 4:41; 8:28; 9:35) and on two occasions even identifies himself this way (10:22; 22:70).[18]

Thus, Pilate faces the test of trying an innocent Jesus and fails, for he finds himself agreeing to carry out his execution and releasing a convicted criminal and violent political activist in order to pacify the Jewish crowd outside his home early in the morning. Bond observes, "The weak Pilate has let down first himself and Herod, second the Roman administration he represents."[19] Pilate's actions form a fascinating contrast with Jesus' response to testing in Luke 4:1–11, where Jesus resists the temptation to deny his destined path. By contrast, Pilate faces the temptation to allow an innocent man to be condemned—a denial of the highest ideals of Roman justice—and gives way to pressure to permit a gross injustice to happen.

---

understood by Pilate to be a denial, as his response shows (23:4) (Bond, *Pontius Pilate*, 152).

15. Walaskay, *Rome*, 40–41.

16. "for he had to release one [prisoner] to them at passover" (ἀνάγκην δὲ εἶχεν ἀπολύειν αὐτοῖς κατὰ ἑορτὴν ἕνα) is found as 23:17 or 23:19 in various manuscripts (notably the uncials א D W Θ Ψ), but is clearly a scribal addition based on Matt 27:15; Mark 15:6 (Metzger, *Textual Commentary*, 153; Johnson, *Luke*, 371).

17. Sherwin-White, *Society*, 27.

18. By contrast with 23:3 (see above) "You say that I am" (ὑμεῖς λέγετε ὅτι ἐγώ εἰμι) is presented as an affirmative answer, albeit ironic, since condemnation immediately follows (22:71) (cf. Tannehill, *Luke*, 330).

19. Bond, *Pontius Pilate*, 159.

Luke does not regard Pilate as solely responsible for the death of Jesus—far from it. Acts 4:27 makes clear that Pilate is simply one of an array of enemies gathered against Jesus, along with Herod, the Gentiles (i.e., the Romans) and the Jews of Jerusalem (as "in this city" [ἐν τῇ πόλει ταύτῃ] implies; cf. Acts 13:28).[20] But Pilate is culpable for his part in this opposition to God's way and is thus adjudged by the divine court to have failed as a man and as a Roman administrator. If Pilate's action is representative of the empire, then the whole empire stands condemned. Thus, when God acts to raise Jesus from the dead, part of the vindication of Jesus is a vindication against the verdict on him by the Roman Empire (note the link in Acts 13:28, 30). More than that, God's hand was in control of events so that God's purpose was carried out in spite of human opposition to Jesus (Acts 4:28).

Paul before Gallio in Corinth (Acts 18:12–17)

Scholarship is divided over the proconsul Gallio. For some, he is the archetypal Roman ruler, dispensing justice fairly and acting properly.[21] For others, he is a weakling and a coward, biased and antisemitic to the extent that he is ready to turn a blind eye to Sosthenes the Jew being beaten up.[22] Our assessment of Luke's portrait of the Roman empire and its servants is affected by how we assess this debate. Several critical exegetical decisions are determinative for this.

First, there is the nature of the charge brought by "the Jews" (18:12) to Gallio against Paul. Luke portrays a united (ὁμοθυμαδόν, 18:12) attack, presumably of those unpersuaded by Paul, for some of the Jewish community have become believers (18:8). There may be a certain opportunism in coming to Gallio early in his one-year proconsulship, seeking to influence him before he knew better. The charge they bring

---

20. Sanders, *Jews, passim*, but esp. ch. 3 wrongly understands Luke to regard the entire Jewish people to be responsible for the death of Jesus, but misses key phrases such as this, and he fails to observe that the Gentiles referred to here cannot be *all* Gentiles (so rightly, Brawley, *Luke-Acts*, 146–47). For cogent critique of Sanders' overall position, see Weatherly, *Jewish Responsibility*, esp. chapters 2–3.

21. e.g., Ramsay, *St Paul*, 258–59; Winter, "Rehabilitating Gallio," 291–308.

22. e.g., Cassidy, *Society*, 91–93; Tajra, *Trial*, 56, 59, 61; Carter, *Roman Empire*, 40; Murphy-O'Connor, *St Paul's Corinth*, 168–69.

is centered on Paul acting "against the law" (παρὰ τὸν νόμον, fronted for emphasis in their speech,[23] 18:13)—but which law?

One possibility is that they are appealing to an edict such as that of Claudius concerning Egypt, which permitted Jews to practice their faith without harrassment.[24] Tajra takes the issue to be that they were seeking specifically to assert that Paul's messianic gathering should be seen as outside the bounds of Judaism, and therefore not entitled to the protection of such an edict.[25] However, we lack evidence for such an edict in relation to Roman Corinth.[26]

Another possibility is that they accused Paul of dishonoring Caesar by encouraging people to worship god (σέβεσθαι τὸν θεόν, 18:13) rather than Caesar. (If so, the accusation would be similar to that made by the Jews of Thessalonica, 17:7.) They were thus accusing Paul of rejecting the imperial cult.[27] This would be rather opportunistic and somewhat ironic for Jews, and there is no explicit indication that this was their charge.

A third possibility is that Gallio understood them rightly when he interpreted their charge as being concerned with the "law which governs[28] you" (νόμου τοῦ καθ᾽ ὑμᾶς).[29] If so, Luke is presenting the Corinthian Jews consistently with other Jewish accusers of Paul who attack him for faithlessness toward his ancestral faith (18:6; cf. 13:50–51; 14:2, 19; 17:5; 19:9). Such a charge would certainly not stand up for long in a Roman court and would therefore be consistent with Gallio's speedy dismissal.

A key clue may be the verb used by the Jews concerning Paul's activities: they assert that ἀναπείθει, which is usually translated "he

23. Barrett, *Acts*, 2:872.

24. Josephus *Ant.* 19.5.2–3 §§278–91, esp. 290; Sherwin-White, *Society*, 102–3.

25. Tajra, *Trial*, 56; so also Fitzmyer, *Acts*, 629–30.

26. Schnabel, *Early Christian Mission*, 2:1193; cf. Rajak, "Roman Charter," 107–23, showing that the edicts and decrees we have concerning the Jews in the Roman empire are confined to local situations (Corinth does not come among her examples, which are taken from Josephus and Philo). It should be noted that we have few edicts of *any* kind relating to Roman Corinth (I owe this point to Dr David Gill).

27. Schnabel, *Mission*, 2:1193–94.

28. BDAG 512 κατά §5.a.α.

29. Pesch, *Apostelgeschichte*, 2:150, argues that Paul's encouragement to worship a crucified Messiah was seen as against the Torah, since the Torah recorded a curse on one crucified.

persuades."[30] This is a New Testament *hapax legomenon*. At one level, "persuades" is an adequate translation because this verb is a compound of πείθω, used in 18:4 for Paul's activities in the synagogue "persuading" both Jews and Greeks. But in other places this compound verb carries a negative sense of *deceptive* persuasion, and this is the sense the major New Testament and classical lexica propose here.[31] *The Message* paraphrase of the New Testament renders the verb as "seduce," which certainly gets its "atmosphere" right. On this view, Paul is being accused of being a charlatan who is either deliberately misleading people or misleading people with evil intent—and those would be charges that a Roman court would consider.

A second issue is the meaning and tone of Gallio's ruling (18:14–15). For some, Gallio is very dismissive of the Jews' complaint and handles the situation in a high-handed way.[32] Thus Cassidy asserts that Gallio's address, "O Jews" (18:14) "reflects disdain."[33] However, the phrasing of Gallio's answer seems rather more careful than that, including a number of key legal terms.[34]

Gallio's reply consists of two conditional constructions. The first (18:14b) is a "contrary to fact" conditional which assumes a protasis that is unlikely to be true.[35] As such, this conditional sentence includes two categories of crime which Gallio understands Paul not to have committed: roughly "felony" (ἀδίκημα) and a political misdemeanour (ῥᾳδιούργημα πονηρόν).[36] The apodosis of this conditional construction includes the verb "I would begin a hearing" (ἀνεσχόμην), a technical term which denotes that Gallio would proceed with the case,[37] and the expression κατὰ λόγον, which here refers to the legal basis of their

30. e.g., NRSV, RSV, NIV, TNIV, NASB, NLT, HCSB, ESV.

31. BDAG 70 s.v.; LSJ s.v. §3; examples of this sense include Herodotus 3.148.2; LXX Jer 36:8 [MT 29:8]; 1 Macc 1:11; Winter, "Gallio's Ruling," 216, gives other examples from the papyri. cf. Cassidy, *Society*, 195 n. 30.

32. E.g., Cassidy, *Society*, 91–93.

33. Cassidy, *Society*, 92.

34. I therefore now wish to nuance my earlier comments on Gallio in Walton, "State," 24.

35. Barrett, *Acts*, 2:874.

36. Winter, "Gallio's Ruling," 218; LSJ 1447 πονηρός §III.3.

37. BDAG 78 ἀνέχω §3.

charge.[38] The whole clause thus means, "I would have begun a hearing to consider the legal basis of your complaint."

The second conditional construction (18:15a) has a protasis that is assumed to be true,[39] and here Gallio gives the basis for his ruling in the previous verse. The proconsul assesses that the complaint is merely "concerning words and names and your own law" (περὶ λόγου καὶ ὀνομάτων καὶ νόμου τοῦ καθ᾽ ὑμᾶς). περὶ λόγου may denote a particular legal immunity that the Jews had in relation to the imperial cult, which meant that they were not required to worship or to pray to the emperor.[40] ὀνομάτων may refer to "names" as opposed to deeds, for in Roman law people were held accountable for actions rather than "any name they professed."[41] νόμου τοῦ καθ᾽ ὑμᾶς clarifies that it is under *Jewish* law that the issue exists, rather than being a matter of concern in *Roman* law. Gallio thus grants legal immunity to Paul and the believers against the complaint brought by the Jews and *de facto* treats the group meeting in Titius Justus' house as a subspecies of Judaism. He may thereby be granting the believing community in Corinth an exemption from active participation in the imperial cult.[42]

And what of Gallio's address to the complainants as "O Jews" (ὦ Ἰουδαῖοι, 18:14)? Barrett observes that Luke's usage of ὦ with the vocative is classical rather than hellenistic, so that its inclusion is the "default" form and does not indicate any special warmth. Wallace adds that in Acts a vocative with ὦ at the front of a sentence is emphatic and emotional, but that when it is in the middle of a sentence (as here), it is merely polite, and that applies here.[43] Certainly the term "Jews" (Ἰουδαῖοι) is neutral, neither warm nor distant—how else could Gallio address a group of Jewish people collectively? In any case, the polite address using the classical form underlines the sense that Gallio is giving a formal ruling.[44]

---

38. Winter, "Gallio's Ruling," 219; cf. BDAG 601 λόγος §2.d; LSJ λόγος §III.1; in spite of Barrett, *Acts*, 2:873–74.

39. Barrett, *Acts*, 2:874 calls it an "open" condition.

40. Winter, "Gallio's Ruling," 219.

41. Cotter, "*Collegia*," 82.

42. Winter, "Gallio's Ruling," 222–23.

43. Barrett, *Acts*, 2:874; Wallace, *Greek Grammar*, 69; cf. Moulton, *Grammar*, 3:33.

44. cf. Winter, "Rehabilitating Gallio," 301.

The third key consideration in assessing how Gallio is presented here involves his actions subsequent to his ruling. He first ἀπήλασεν them from the tribunal (18:16); NRSV translates this word as "dismissed," but this is rather mild for this verb. Its meaning is closer to "drove away."[45] As yet another New Testament *hapax legomenon,* it may also have a legal sense. It implies that Gallio called his lictors with their rods to eject the Jewish accusers forcibly.[46]

Following the expulsion, "all" (πάντες)[47] turned on Sosthenes the "synagogue ruler" (ἀρχισυνάγωγος) and Gallio "did not concern himself with any of these things" (18:17).[48] "All" (πάντες) could refer to the Jewish community, disappointed at the failure in the tribunal under Sosthenes' leadership,[49] or it could refer to the people of the city who are either expressing antisemitism[50] or expressing support for Caesar's recent expulsion of the troublesome Jews from Rome (Acts 18:2),[51] or some combination of the two.[52] From poor Sosthenes' point of view, events probably *felt* little different! The natural referent of "these things," (τούτων) of which Gallio took no notice, appears to be the attack on Sosthenes[53] rather than a continuing reference to the same τούτων that the Jewish delegation had brought up in the tribunal and which Gallio declined to judge (18:15).[54] This (in-)action by Gallio is widely reckoned to show at least his collusion with antisemitism, if not active anti-

---

45. BDAG 101 ἀπελαύνω; so also Haenchen, *Acts*, 536 (citing Zahn).

46. Even Winter, "Rehabilitating Gallio," 302 concedes this point, seeing Gallio's forceful action as illustrative of Gallio's unwillingness to be manipulated.

47. This is the likeliest reading in light of support by p74 א A B; so Metzger, *Commentary* (2nd ed.), 411; Barrett, *Acts*, 2:875.

48. Taking οὐδέν as accusative of respect, rather than as nominative subject of the verb ἔμελεν; see discussion in Barrett, *Acts*, 2:876; Moule, *Idiom-Book*, 28.

49. Fitzmyer, *Acts*, 630–31. The minuscules 36 and 453 read "all the Jews" πάντες οἱ Ἰουδαῖοι.

50. Cassidy, *Society*, 92; cf. Haenchen, *Acts*, 536–37. This is the interpretation of Western and later Byzantine manuscripts, which read "all the Greeks" πάντες οἱ Ἕλληνες (so D E H L P Ψ 33 1739 *Byz*, as well as numerous versions and Fathers; see Rius-Camps and Read-Heimerdinger, *Message of Acts*, 3:368).

51. Suggested by Winter, "Rehabilitating Gallio," 303.

52. Barrett, *Acts*, 2:875.

53. So Haenchen, *Acts*, 537.

54. So Winter, "Rehabilitating Gallio," 303, tentatively.

semitic action.[55] Winter proposes that Gallio acted properly in ignoring events outside his tribunal,[56] but this seems overstated given the proper concern a proconsul should have for order within his province. Gallio's collusion with Sosthenes' beating may thus represent the antisemitism that was widespread in Roman society, even if a little below the surface much of the time[57] There may thus be an element of antisemitism behind his judgement cited in 18:14–15, expressed in Roman legalese.

Given this conclusion, how should we see these events? Luke gives the key in 18:9–10, where the Lord appears to Paul to encourage him to continue his ministry in Corinth, saying, "No-one will lay hands on you to do you harm" (οὐδεὶς ἐπιθήσεταί σοι τοῦ κακῶσαί σε). Paul is not promised that no-one will attack him, but that no harm will come to him. This incident shows the Lord's protection of Paul,[58] for Paul is almost completely peripheral to the tribunal scene in 18:12–17 and yet is freed and vindicated. Indeed, Paul can be said to be a passive participant, for on the only two occasions he is named in this story, he is inactive: he is accused by the Jews (18:12) and he is about to speak when Gallio gives his ruling (18:14).

Thus Luke's literary focus in presenting this incident appears less on the role of the Roman proconsul and more on God's action in taking the mission forward, and thus in protecting his servants. Gallio is one chess piece in God's hands who ends up serving God's purposes by giving a legal ruling that benefits the renewed people of God, even if Gallio's actions and motives may be questionable. In presenting the story this way, from God's point of view, Luke is very much in tune with the biblical tradition.[59] Such a conclusion puts the Roman empire very much in its place, for it operates under the sovereign power of God and

55. e.g., Tannehill, *Unity*, 2:228.

56. Winter, "Rehabilitating Gallio," 305.

57. Haenchen, *Acts*, 541 observes that Gallio's brother, Seneca the Younger, was known for his antisemitic views. The main evidence for this is Augustine, *Civ.* 6.11, citing Seneca's lost work *De Superstitione*, stating that the Jews were "a most criminal race" (*sceleratissima gens*; discussion: Lichtenberger, "Jews and Christians," 2155).

58. So also Haenchen, *Acts*, 540; Tannehill, *Unity*, 2:229; Johnson, *Acts*, 334.

59. cf. (for example) Isa 45:1, where God calls the pagan king Cyrus "my anointed." See my survey of the whole book of Acts from this point of view in Walton, "Acts, Book of."

thus (implicitly) its officials should not have an exaggerated sense of their own importance.[60]

Paul before Felix in Caesarea (Acts 23–24)

In Jerusalem, Paul is taken into custody (presumably in the Fortress Antonia on the boundary of the temple precincts[61]) by the tribune Claudius Lysias, initially to quell an apparent riot (21:31–33). When examined, Paul discloses to the centurion that he is a Roman citizen, thus making it illegal for the tribune to chain him or to flog him (22:24–29, esp. 29).[62] Lysias seeks to find out the basis of the accusation against Paul by seeking advice from the Sanhedrin (22:30),[63] but the hearing falls into chaos when Paul identifies himself as a Pharisee, thus dividing the council along party lines (24:6–9). Lysias again steps in to subdue the violence and takes Paul to safety in the barracks (24:10). Luke then writes that the Lord appears to Paul and encourages him to keep up his courage and to keep testifying for the Lord (23:11), in broadly similar terms to the Lord's encouragement to Paul in Corinth (18:9–10).

On learning from Paul's nephew of a plot to assassinate Paul (23:12–22), the tribune decides to send Paul to the Roman administrative capital of Caesarea Maritima, for Paul's own safety (23:23–24). Lysias writes to the governor Felix (23:25–30) in order to brief him. The letter is rather economical with the truth because Lysias wanted to present himself in the best possible light.[64] Lysias makes it clear that he sees the issue as an intra-Jewish debate that does not merit any serious penalty for Paul (23:29).[65]

60. The similarity of thought concerning God's sovereignty over the state in Rom 13:1–7 is striking.

61. Rapske, *Book*, 137–38.

62. Thus, for example, Cicero protests against the tribune Titus Labienus allowing a Roman citizen to be beaten before a proper trial, *Rab. Perd.* 4.12; see the full and helpful discussion in Rapske, *Book*, 47–56.

63. It is not therefore a Sanhedrin *trial*, but simply a means of advising Lysias of the nature of the charges against Paul, with Rapske, *Book*, 146–47; Barrett, *Acts*, 2:1091.

64. For example, it was not on learning that Paul was a Roman citizen that Lysias rescued him (24:27b). More fully, see Rapske, *Book*, 152–53; Witherington, *Acts*, 700–701.

65. Judge in *NewDocs* 1:77–78, on the basis of the use of τύπος (23:25), plausibly suggests that Luke may be drawing on material from official sources in quoting Claudius Lysias' letter.

At this point Felix steps into the story as "governor" (ἡγεμών), technically "procurator."[66] What we know of Felix from extra-biblical sources suggests that he could be a harsh governor who did not hesitate to use military means to keep the peace, and who was willing to cooperate with the *sicarii* terrorists to have the high priest killed.[67] That said, Tertullus' positive introduction that seeks Felix's goodwill and attention (*captatio benevolentiae*, 24:2b–3) is neither mere flattery nor simply disingenuous. Ananias, the high priest who led the delegation to Felix (24:1), and Ananias' predecessor Jonathan had pressed Claudius to appoint Felix as procurator.[68] It was an unusual appointment for a mere freedman rather than someone of equestrian rank.[69] The Jewish delegation was thus compelled to support Felix's administration. Further, not long before this, Felix had brought peace following a rebellion led by an Egyptian.[70] Tertullus' comments (24:2) may allude to this incident.

Luke presents Felix as acting properly, at least initially, in handling Paul's case. First, he establishes whether Paul falls under his jurisdiction by enquiring which province he comes from (23:34). Cilicia was probably at this time under the legate of Syria, Felix's line manager. So for Felix to fail to hear the case and pass it on to the legate of Syria would be to risk appearing to waste the legate's time with a minor matter[71]— even though the transfer of an accused person to his own province was optional at this time.[72]

Second, Felix wishes to hear first-hand from Paul's accusers (23:35a; cf. 25:16).[73] When Tertullus and Paul present their arguments before

66. Greek ἐπίτροπος, see Josephus, *J.W.* 15.11.4 §406 and discussion in Rapske, "Governors," 979; Tajra, *Trial*, 110–13.

67. Respectively, Josephus, *Ant.* 20.8.7 §§173–78; *J.W.* 2.13.7 §§266–70 and *Ant.* 20.8.5 §162; *J.W.* 2.13.3 §§254–57. See the helpful brief treatments in Rapske, "Governors," 982–83; *ABD* 2:783 and, more fully, Gill, "Acts," 21–26.

68. Tacitus, *Ann.* 12.54. Winter, "Importance," 515–16; Bruce, *New Testament History*, 325.

69. Claudius Lysias and Tertullus address Felix as "most excellent" (κράτιστος, 23:26; 24:3), a title undoubtedly used for those of equestrian rank, but not exclusively for such people (Alexander, *Preface*, 133; Foakes Jackson and Lake, *Beginnings*, 2:505–7).

70. Josephus, *J.W.* 2.13.5 §§261–63; Acts 21:38.

71. Sherwin-White, *Society*, 55–57; Rapske, *Book*, 155. Cilicia was probably not formally a province at this time, but this distinction does not affect the point noted.

72. Sherwin-White, *Society*, 55.

73. Sherwin-White, *Society*, 17; Tajra, *Trial*, 115.

Felix (24:1–21), Paul makes the point that at least some of the accusers are not present (24:19), thus implying that the charges were invalid.[74] Their absence is reflected in the reduced claims that Tertullus makes, asserting only that Paul "attempted" to profane the temple (ἐπείρασεν, 24:6), whereas the missing Asian Jews had claimed that Paul "had de-filed" the temple (κεκοίνωκεν, 21:28).

Felix then acts within his powers in deciding to await testimony from the tribune Lysias (24:22), since he needs advice to help him decide between the two contradictory testimonies he has heard.[75] Luke does not tell us whether Felix was never able to consult Lysias or whether a consultation took place but was inconclusive. Whatever the case, Paul remained in custody at governor Felix's pleasure (as the British judicial system charmingly puts it). In the situation of waiting for Lysias' testi-mony, Felix can afford to relax Paul's conditions of detention, and so he does (24:23).[76]

Strikingly, Paul's confinement does not prevent him from testifying to the gospel, for Felix wishes to hear him on the subject on numerous occasions (24:24–26), thus partially fulfilling the Lord's word to Paul (23:11). As Skinner notes, this situation gives Paul access to some of the most powerful people in Judaea.[77] Thus Paul the prisoner is Paul the *missionary*-prisoner.[78]

As well as conducting procedures properly, Felix's response to Paul shows another, less savory, side to his actions; in rapid succession, Luke highlights three issues.[79]

First, Felix becomes fearful at Paul's talk "concerning righteous-ness and self-control and judgement to come" (24:25) and therefore sends Paul away. These qualities imply a call to repent, a key feature of evangelistic proclamation in Acts.[80] However, they may be particularly apposite for Felix as a governor who should act with righteousness and self-control, but had deceptively drawn Drusilla away from her former

---

74. Johnson, *Acts*, 417; Fitzmyer, *Acts*, 737.

75. Sherwin-White, *Society*, 53.

76. On the possible nature of the relaxation of conditions, see Rapske, *Book*, 167–72.

77. Skinner, *Locating Paul*, 137–38.

78. The expression is from Rapske, *Book*, e.g. 429–36.

79. cf. Cassidy, *Society*, 105–6.

80. e.g., 2:38; 3:19; 5:31; 11:18; 17:30; 20:21; 26:20.

husband into his arms.[81] Self-control (ἐγκράτεια) may thus focus on *sexual* self-control.[82] In this light, "judgement to come" would be an unwelcome thought to Felix if his conscience was at all sensitive to what Paul said. Interestingly, Paul is portrayed here as "turning the tables" on Felix, his judge, by speaking to Felix of the values which (ironically) should be guiding his judgement.[83]

Second, Felix hoped for a bribe from Paul, and not just on one occasion, but repeatedly (24:26).[84] This was not uncommon among judges in the Roman empire,[85] although illegal under the *Lex Iulia de Repetundis*.[86] Luke takes a dim view of it,[87] for it results in Paul continuing to be held even though the tribune Lysias had written to Felix that Paul had not committed any crime worthy of death or imprisonment (23:29). As is often the case in Luke-Acts, how possessions are handled is an index of a person's standing with God.[88]

Third, on his departure from office, Felix is motivated to please the Jewish leaders by keeping Paul confined (24:27). This is politically understandable in the sensitive climate of first-century Judaea, particularly because Roman legions based in Syria were occupied with peacekeeping duties on that front and could not be relied upon to help in Judaea.[89] To free Paul would be to arouse the hostility of the Jewish leadership who had sought to persuade Felix to punish him as a troublemaker. Tertullus had darkly hinted at this danger of unrest in stressing the peace that Judaea had enjoyed under Felix's procuratorship (24:2). But to show such bias towards the politically powerful, even against a Roman citizen such as Paul, cannot be seen as good. It

81. Josephus, *Ant.* 20.7.1 §§141–44; Schneider, *Apostelgeschichte*, 2:351–52.

82. BDAG 274 s.v.

83. cf. Cassidy, *Society*, 106.

84. Although πυκνότερον is formally a comparative form, the lack of anything to compare suggests a superlative sense, meaning "very often" (with Moulton, *Grammar*, 3:30; Barrett, *Acts*, 2:1116; *pace* BDF §244[1], who assert it to be ambiguous).

85. e.g., Albinus, as reported by Josephus, *J.W.* 2.14.1 §§272–73. Rapske, *Book*, 65–67 lays out the evidence for such corruption in the judicial system.

86. Introduced in 59 BC to prevent corruption of this kind in the provinces; see Tajra, *Trial*, 131.

87. Gaventa, *Acts*, 330 suggests that Felix is portrayed in the image of the unjust judge of the parable (Luke 18:1–8).

88. For discussion of this theme in Luke, see Johnson, *Literary Function*, 144–58.

89. Gill, "Policy," 22.

is striking, as Tannehill observes, that Felix never declares Paul inno-cent, by contrast with Lysias and, as we shall see, Festus and Agrippa.[90] Felix's appearance in Acts is thus the portrait of a man who is a tragic figure, for he is attracted to Paul and his gospel, and he has the chance (many chances!) to respond positively both to the gospel and to Paul as the Lord's gospel-witness and fails to take it.[91] The resemblance to Pilate's failure to free the innocent Jesus is clear.[92]

Paul before Festus in Caesarea (Acts 25–26)

On Festus' arrival as procurator, he inherits Paul as a prisoner. Presum-ably the procurator's archives contained Lysias' letter and a record of the earlier hearing under Felix, and perhaps also a record of Felix's decision to leave Paul in prison at the end of his governorship.[93]

The Jewish leaders take the opportunity of a new governor to seek a review of Paul's case, to be held in Jerusalem as a favor[94] to them (25:2–3)—in similar manner to the situation with the Corinthian Jews who came to Gallio early in his proconsulship. Festus decides to hear the case in Caesarea, providentially, as Luke notes, because some Jews were planning to ambush and kill Paul *en route* to Jerusalem (25:3b). It seems likely that we should see Festus' decision as an instance of the fulfillment of the Lord's promise of protection for Paul (23:11).

Like Gallio, Festus sits on the raised dais from which he gave judg-ment (ἐπὶ τοῦ βήματος, 25:6; cf. 18:12) and hears the case of the Jewish leaders (25:7) and Paul's defense (25:8). Luke simply states the broad outline of the case and Paul's defense, presumably because we are to fill this gap with information from Tertullus' earlier speech and from Paul's defense before Felix (24:2–8, 10–21). At this point, Luke makes clear Festus' bias: "wanting to do a favor for the Jews" (θέλων τοῖς Ἰουδαίοις

90. Tannehill, *Unity,* 2:304; so also Haenchen, *Acts,* 658–59.

91. A point astutely observed by Tannehill, *Unity,* 2:303. Johnson, *Acts,* 423 sums up Felix's actions as "an altogether shameless performance." cf. Barrett, *Acts,* 2:1092–93.

92. As Bond, *Pilate,* 142–43 notes; see the discussion of Pilate above.

93. Winter, "Official Proceedings," 307–9, provides evidence for careful preservation of court records and argues cogently that such a process went on with hearings of Paul before Felix and Festus.

94. χάριν, echoing Felix's decision to grant the Jews χάριτα (24:27).

χάριν καταθέσθαι, 25:9) is almost a verbatim echo of Felix's motivation (24:27)[95] and a clear echo of the Jewish leaders' desire (25:3).

Luke implies that Paul should not expect justice from such a judge and that he will get injustice if he is handed over to the Jewish authorities. Therefore, Paul appeals to the emperor (25:11c). Paul's thinking in reaching this conclusion is obscured by the NRSV, which rather strangely translates 25:10, "I *am appealing* to the emperor's tribunal," thus making it appear that Paul appeals to the emperor at the beginning of his speech. The verb is "I am *standing*" (the periphrastic ἑστώς εἰμι), referring to Paul's *present* location,[96] and the prepositional phrase "*before* the tribunal of Caesar" (ἐπὶ τοῦ βήματος Καίσαρος) echoes Festus' question, for he asks whether Paul wishes to be tried in Jerusalem "*before* me" (ἐπ᾽ ἐμοῦ)[97] Thus, Paul is asserting that where he now is, before Festus, is the imperial tribunal. That is the correct place for him, as a Roman citizen, to be tried. He does not wish to be handed over to the Jewish authorities, for he has done no wrong to them (25:10b) and they do not have jurisdiction over him (25:11a). Paul's further observation, "no-one is able *to hand* me over [χαρίσασθαι] to them" (25:11b) ironically echoes the uses of the noun χάρις as "favor" (to the Jews) which we have just noted. We might hear the echo by translating, "no-one is able to hand me over to them *as a favor*." Festus is not going to grant Paul justice, and so Paul appeals beyond him to the emperor.

Cassidy detects "a quality akin to outrage" in Paul's words in 25:10–11,[98] but such a tone of voice is hard to recognize without textual signals in support. Certainly, Paul implicitly accuses Festus of dissembling by the phrase "as you yourself [emphatic personal pronoun σύ] know very well" (25:10),[99] but Luke does not say that Paul was angry or that he raised his voice. Johnson may be nearer the mark in seeing desperation on Paul's part,[100] but Gaventa may be the closest of all in identifying

95. The main difference is in the form of χάρις, shifting from one accusative form (χάριτα, 24:27) to another (χάριν, 25:9), with no difference in meaning (Moulton, *Grammar*, 2:132; BDF §47[3]). A's reading χάριτα in 25:9 looks like a scribal harmonization of spelling in the two passages.

96. BDAG 482 ἵστημι §C.2.b; the intransitive perfect of this verb has the force of a present.

97. Gaventa, *Acts*, 334.

98. Cassidy, *Society*, 108.

99. Gaventa, *Acts*, 334.

100. Johnson, *Acts*, 422.

Paul's decision as the outcome of the Lord's word that he will stand before the emperor (23:11)[101]—for these events, as with the earlier meetings with Felix, are under the overarching control of the Lord.

Festus seeks guidance from his advisory council (*consilium*) and grants Paul's appeal to the emperor (25:12). Festus then takes the opportunity of Agrippa and Berenice's visit to seek further advice on what to do with Paul. He presents himself, as Lysias had earlier, as the model of propriety in his handling of the case: he stresses his concern for proper procedure in seeing that the accused meets the accusers face to face and his concern for Paul's right to make a defense (25:16); he intimates that he acted expeditiously in hearing the case ("making no delay," ἀναβολὴν μηδεμίαν ποιησάμενος, 25:17); he recognizes that there was no case to answer under Roman law since the questions were intra-Jewish issues (25:18–19); and thus he offers the accused the chance to be tried before his own people (25:20).

Moreover, when Paul appears before Festus and Agrippa the next day, Festus underlines in this highly public, but Roman, setting (25:23) that he, the just and judicious governor, saved Paul from wild and unsubstantiated attacks—namely, the whole Jewish community (τὸ πλῆθος τῶν Ἰουδαίων) shouting (βοῶντες) for his death (25:24). Festus himself, however (note the emphatic "But I myself," ἐγὼ δέ, 25:25), came to recognize through the proper rational processes of inquiry (κατελαβόμην,[102] 25:25) that Paul had done nothing deserving death. Nevertheless, Festus' hands were now tied by Paul's appeal to Caesar (25:25; cf. 26:32). Festus would therefore like advice from Agrippa in composing his advice to the emperor to accompany the other documents that would be sent to Rome with Paul (25:26–27).[103]

Throughout the encounter with Agrippa, Luke portrays Festus presenting himself in the best possible light,[104] perhaps in contrast to his portrayal of Felix at a number of points. Festus does not mention his real motive, currying favor with the Jewish leaders (25:9), and he somewhat distorts Paul's appeal by implying that Paul *wanted* to stay in Roman custody (25:21). On the contrary, Paul wanted to be free to

---

101. Gaventa, *Acts*, 335.

102. BDAG 519 καταλαμβάνω §4.a.

103. Probably at least Claudius Lysias' letter and the court record of the hearing before Felix; see Winter, "Proceedings," 309.

104. As Cassidy, *Society*, 111–12 recognizes.

proclaim the gospel, and he denied that the charges against him had any substance (24:12–13; 25:8). The story ends with the statement—the third such statement in the trials in Judaea—that Paul has committed no crime under Roman law (26:31; cf. 23:29; 25:25). These three statements parallel Pilate's three declarations of Jesus' innocence in the Gospel (Luke 23:4, 13, 22). Similarly, Agrippa's role as Jewish adviser parallels that of Herod in the trial of Jesus (Luke 23:7–12), coming to the same conclusion of innocence. Luke thus invites his readers to consider Paul's hearings in the light of Jesus' trial.

Festus does not come out of this situation well. However, it should be noted that in at least some aspects of Paul's situation, Festus had been painted into a corner by the actions of his predecessor, Felix. Had Felix dealt summarily and correctly with Paul's case and acted on Lysias' recognition that there was no case to answer, Festus would never have met Paul. We are considering gradations of color here. Rather than clear red (for guilt)[105] or clear white (for innocence), Felix seems considerably deeper pink than Festus.

In the midst of this situation, it is Paul who speaks for God—and thus also for Luke—in identifying what is really going on. Two things are happening in this sequence of events: first, God is helping Paul to testify to the death and resurrection of the Messiah, Jesus (26:22–23a); and second, the exalted Messiah is himself proclaiming the truth to Jew and Gentile alike (26:23b).[106] In relation to the first point, as always in Acts, God is the main actor in the story, and whatever human opposition there is, it cannot ultimately resist God's purposes. In relation to the second point, in speaking to Festus and his Roman court together with Agrippa and Berenice, Paul has a mixed Gentile and Jew audience before him, and thus the Messiah is speaking through Paul to them. As in Corinth, the purposes of God cannot be frustrated by the interference of the empire and its servants.

105. I use "red" on the basis of Isa 1:18.

106. This is one of a number of indications that Jesus is not absent from the story of Acts, as is frequently asserted. More fully, see the excellent discussion of B. R. Gaventa, "The Presence of the Absent Lord: The Characterization of Jesus in the Acts of the Apostles" (Paper given at SBL Annual Meeting, 2003), and her acute observation that here "the proclaimed has become the proclaimer" (Gaventa, *Acts*, 348).

Conclusion

In the four accounts we have considered, we have found significant continuities in the portrayal of the Roman empire and its provincial-level servants—prefects, procurators and proconsuls. Their verdicts on Jesus and Paul are consistently verdicts of innocence. Nevertheless, Pilate finds himself giving sentence for the innocent Jesus to die in order to satisfy the Jewish leaders. Similarly, Felix holds Paul in prison for two years on a charge from the Jewish leaders that is without foundation. Festus is more interested in political expediency, under pressure from the Jewish leaders, than in rejecting what he recognizes to be an insubstantial case. Even Gallio, in many ways nearest to the epitome of Roman justice, may be acting from antisemitic motives—ironically, the reverse of pleasing the Jewish leaders—in finding in favor of Paul. Bond observes insightfully that although the governors as representatives of Roman justice consistently find Jesus and his followers innocent, their character flaws can mean that, in practice, justice is either delayed or denied.[107]

The agents of the Roman Empire are shown to be far from perfect—although not as corrupt as they might be. And yet the center of Luke's attention does not lie with them, but with the purposes of God that the gospel shall reach "the end of the earth" (Acts 1:8). If we consider recent scholarly views of Luke's stance toward the Roman empire,[108] there is something to be said for the claim that Luke is uninterested in politics. Franklin argues that Luke is focused on the triumph of God's purpose in bringing Paul to Rome,[109] and we have seen that there is substance to this point of view. Jervell likewise argues that the empire is no real threat to the gospel's progress to the end of the earth.[110]

But this is not the whole story, because Luke, our omniscient narrator, speaks for God in presenting these servants of the empire in some of the negative ways we have seen. Thus, Cassidy has a point in proposing that Luke is both warning his readers of the grave dangers of Christian testimony and encouraging them to show the same faithful-

---

107. Bond, *Pilate*, 142–43.

108. See my discussion in Walton, "State," 2–12.

109. Franklin, *Christ the Lord*, 134–39.

110. Jervell, *Theology*, 105–6.

ness under trial as Jesus and Paul.[111] And yet, too, there are times when the empire protects believers, of which Gallio's actions in Corinth are a prime example. We might add the freedom Paul had in Rome to speak "unhindered" (28:20), a legal term that implies Paul's innocence.[112]

The portrait of the empire that emerges from this study is thus a mixed one, falling (as I have suggested elsewhere[113]) at *both* ends of the spectrum between the views of the Roman state found in Romans 13 and Revelation 13—the empire can act justly to give gospel proclamation the space to spread and flourish, but it can also act unjustly and thus seek to hinder the gospel's outward movement. It is in the midst of this setting that Luke both tells the story of the spread of the Christian testimony and encourages his readers to become part of the story themselves. Perhaps most notably among his readers, Luke's addressee Theophilus is suggestively addressed as "most excellent" (κράτιστε) in similar manner to both Felix and Festus.[114] Theophilus is thereby invited to consider both how he resembles Felix and Festus, for good or ill, and how he might find himself (as we might say) on the side of the angels in the gospel story through repentance and faith in Jesus—and that would be a true turning of the tables!

111. Cassidy, *Society*, 160.

112. ἀκωλύτως, see Barrett, *Acts*, 2:1253; Tajra, *Trial*, 192–93.

113. Walton, "State," 35.

114. Luke 1:3; Acts 23:26; 24:3; 26:25.

8

Paul's Proclamation of *Lord* Jesus as a Chained Prisoner in Rome

Luke's Ending Is in His Beginning [1]

Richard J. Cassidy

THERE ARE TWO MAJOR PIECES OF INFORMATION THAT LUKE SURELY possessed as he composed Luke and Acts. Luke knew that Jesus was crucified by the Roman governor assigned to Judea only to rise from the tomb three days later. Luke also knew that Paul, auspiciously converted/ commissioned by the risen Jesus, subsequently testified to Jesus as an imperial prisoner in Rome.

These two items, as well as countless other items of comparable and lesser import, influenced Luke to present the compelling narrative that he has fashioned in the two volumes of Luke and Acts. When these two books are carefully considered in the light of narrative criticism, it becomes evident that Luke's description of the mission that Paul completed in Rome resonates beautifully with the presentation regard-

---

1. This essay builds upon my previous work in Luke-Acts and expands my argument that "political apologetic" was *not* one of Luke's purposes (see Cassidy, *Jesus, Politics, and Society*; *Political Issues in Luke-Acts*; *Society and Politics*; *Christians and Roman Rule*). Loveday Alexander's seminal essay ("Reading Luke-Acts") has encouraged me to a greater appreciation for Luke's care in integrating the Gospel and Acts. While I differ with her about what to focus upon in the concluding verses of Acts, I want to underscore the value of the stimulating perspective that she has brought forward in her article. The insights of Mark Stibbe regarding "paradigmatic readers" who read and re-read a text from beginning to end (see Stibbe, *John*) and the insights of David Rhoads regarding narrative criticism and the Gospels (see Rhoads, *Mark as Story*; and Rhoads and Syreeni, eds., *Characterization in the Gospels*) have influenced my recent narra-tive critical study of the Gospels (see Cassidy, *Four Times Peter*) and have also directly benefited this essay.

ing Jesus and his kingdom that Luke set forth at the beginning of his Gospel.

Nevertheless, within Lukan scholarship for more than a century, the character of Luke's endeavor has frequently been misapprehended. This misapprehension manifests itself at a number of points, but especially in mistaken interpretations of Luke's ending in Acts. When the ending of Acts is misinterpreted, the consequence is almost invariably a distorted view regarding one of Luke's principal topics: the topic of Christian discipleship within the Roman world.

In effect, Luke's ending carefully meshes with his beginning(s). Any failure to be clear regarding the character of Acts' ending will result in a diminished clarity regarding Luke's overall presentation regarding the missions of Jesus and Paul within the context of the Roman imperial order.

Misapprehensions of Luke's Ending—As a prelude to a sustained investigation of Luke's ending, it is useful to identify three interpretations that minimize the importance of the verses that constitute the canonical ending of Acts. First it has been conjectured that a fragment containing a "more complete" ending has broken off from Luke's original scroll. Second it has been suggested as an explanation for Luke's "clumsy" ending that Luke came to the end of his scroll and simply stopped writing. A third conjecture is that Luke was not especially concerned with how he ended Acts because he actually envisioned the continuation of his work onto a third scroll.

The consequence of conjectures such as these is to diminish attention to the seriousness of Luke's purpose as he composed the ending of Acts. In effect, those who advance such proposals disrespect Luke's careful concern to fashion a substantive ending for the second volume of his work and for his two-volume work as a whole.

An even more egregious way of disrespecting Luke's ending is to misrepresent it as Luke's final effort to curry favor with the Roman authorities. Such an interpretation takes seriously the ending of Acts but mistakenly argues that Luke's final words portray the Roman authorities as allowing Paul to advance the Christian Gospel without hindrance.

In this view, Luke has been striving all along to convince the Roman authorities to view the Christian movement with a favorable perspective. And Luke now advances this purpose in the final words that he pens. Commonly described as "the political apologetic interpretation," this interpretation, in effect, attributes a certain cravenness to Luke. The evangelist is said to have *consciously* downplayed the challenge that the Christian movement posed to the Roman imperial system in order to influence Roman officials to view Christians favorably.

ANTICIPATIONS OF THE ENDING OF ACTS—From Acts 28:14 to Acts 28:29, Paul is portrayed arriving in Rome and continuing his proclamation of the Gospel there. As will be explicated below, it is highly significant that Paul is in the capital of the empire and is testifying to Jesus there. Speaking broadly, once Paul reaches Rome and witnesses to Jesus there, Luke is drawing Acts to a close. More specifically, the ending of Acts occurs with Luke's final summary of Paul's conduct in Rome in verses 28:30–31. Luke is describing Paul carefully in these verses and this closing image of Paul constitutes the formal ending of Acts.

Before concentrating upon Luke's achievement in these final two verses, it is useful to consider three earlier instances of "predictive prolepsis" that prepare the way for what Luke wants to impart to his readers through his ending. Through the use of these narrative anticipations, Luke has alerted his readers to the importance of having apostolic testimony reach "the end of the earth," to Paul's general mission to preach in Rome, and to Paul's specific mission to testify before Caesar.

In Acts 1:2 the risen Jesus addresses momentous words to "the apostles whom he had chosen." His prediction to them in Acts 1:8b is famously as follows: " and you shall be my witnesses in Jerusalem and in all Judea and Samaria and to the end of the earth." This predictive prolepsis is *internal*, that is, it is fulfilled prior to the end of Acts. According to Luke's narrative, others before Paul have witnessed to Jesus in Rome (28:15). Nevertheless, Paul's arrival in the capital in chapter 28 represents, within the framework of Acts, the first witness by an apostle. (Recall Luke's designation of Paul and Barnabas as "apostles" at Acts 14:4 and 14:14).

In addition to the prediction concerning apostolic witness "to the end of the earth," there is also an internal predictive prolepsis indicating that Paul himself will reach Rome. At Acts 19:21, under the influence of the Spirit, Paul projects his own itinerary, concluding with the words: "After I have been there, I must ($\delta\epsilon\bar{\iota}$) also see Rome."

The nuanced portrayals of Acts concerning Paul's Roman citizenship and Luke's clearly delineated portrayal of the corruption exhibited by Antonius Felix and Porcius Festus in adjudicating Paul's case fly in the face of the proponents of political apologetic who contend that Luke is tailoring his narrative to curry favor with Roman officialdom. Yet within the confines of this essay, these scenes cannot be investigated but only mentioned as scenes that supply the context for the appeal to Caesar that the still chained Paul boldly makes as a risky counter to Festus' manipulations of his case.

As the vessel that is carrying him toward Caesar's tribunal approaches shipwreck, Paul receives a vision and message from an angel of God that is a classic combination of both internal and external predictive prolepsis. The angel's message that Paul and his colleagues will be spared from death is soon fulfilled. In contrast, the prediction that Paul will appear before Caesar is only approached but not fulfilled within Acts. The angel's two predictions occur in the following way: "And he said, "Do not be afraid, Paul, because you must (δεῖ) stand before Caesar; and lo, God has granted you all those who sail with you" (Acts 27:24).

PAUL'S MINISTRY IN ROME—In emphasizing that the ending of Acts presents a closing scene that speaks powerfully to the question of Christian discipleship in the context of Roman imperium, it is important to emphasize that Luke also has other interests in view as he details Paul's years in Rome. Thus, in Acts 28:17–28, Luke reports Paul's interactions with the Jews of Rome.

In delineating Paul's interactions with the Jewish community at Rome, what does Luke highlight? Principally, Luke is concerned to show that Paul continues his steadfast effort to bring his fellow Jews to faith in Jesus. As in many previous episodes in which Paul has striven to evangelize Jews, Luke portrays a divided response on the part of the Jews at Rome. This response vexes Paul and causes him to indict those who reject his witness on behalf of Jesus with harsh words from the prophet Isaiah. Nevertheless, it will be seen below that Paul continues to offer welcome to any Jews who visit him in his lodgings.

In contrast to the eleven full verses that he addresses to Paul's ministry with the Jewish community, Luke only includes one verse (28:15) to describe the welcome that some members of the Christian community at Rome accorded to Paul when he first drew near to the city. Why is Luke's description of Paul's interactions with the Christians who were living at Rome prior Paul's arrival there so sparing?

This question cannot be answered within the framework of narrative criticism. Yet in an effort to shed light upon the "minimal" (in comparison with the way Paul has previously interacted with Christian communities in Acts) interactions that Luke portrays Paul having with the Christians of Rome a brief departure from the methodology governing this paper may be appropriate.

Parenthetical reference to Philippians—In order to provide an exposition ancillary to the principal exposition of this paper, let it be assumed that Paul's Letter to the Philippians was written from Rome and let it be recalled that he authored this letter as a prisoner in chains. If Luke knew of the controversy that Paul describes in Philippians, he might have highlighted Paul's positive welcome by the Christians of Rome and elected not to try to describe the complex situation that Philippians references. Here then are Paul's words concerning a divided response *among Christians*: "Some indeed preach Christ from envy and rivalry, but others from good will. The latter do it out of love, knowing that I am put here for the defense of the gospel; the former proclaim Christ out of partisanship, not sincerely but thinking to afflict me *in my chains*" (Phil 1:15–18; my trans.).

In his major delineation of Paul's interactions with Jews and his minor delineation of Paul's interactions with Christians in Rome Luke continues to advert to Paul's status as a chained Roman prisoner whose case is under appeal to Caesar. Paul has remained under a centurion's custody throughout his sea voyage and, as Acts 28:16 indicates, Paul continues to be guarded by a Roman soldier upon his arrival in Rome. Indeed, in speaking to the Jewish delegation, Paul makes the following dramatic reference to his status as a chained prisoner (28:20): "since it is because of the hope of Israel that *I am bound with this chain*."

The final scene of Acts—For his narrative-ending finale, Luke has elected to shine his spotlight upon a noble disciple of Jesus, Paul himself, who is now alone *at center stage*. Far from not knowing how to end, or far from running out of the space necessary for an appropriate ending, Luke's intention is to impart to his readers an appealing image of Paul faithful to Jesus Christ *usque ad mortem*. In two extremely well crafted sentences, Luke accomplishes this objective: "And he lived there two whole years at his own expense, and welcomed all who came to him, preaching the kingdom of God and teaching about the Lord Jesus Christ with all boldness; un-intimidated" (Acts 28:30–31; my trans.).

What are the specific elements that Luke's spotlight identifies for his audience? First, Paul is in his lodging welcoming "all" (πάντας) who come to him. Who are included within this circumscribing term? Are the members of the Jewish community being welcomed by Paul? Are the members of the Christian community being welcomed by him? Are any imperial officials among those to whom Paul extends a welcome? Luke's choice of the encompassing "all" means that in this final scene *no one* is excluded from Paul's hospitality.

Second, the geographical site for this closing scene continues to be the very capital of the empire. Paul's ministry of welcoming and proclaiming is no longer being done in a Roman colony such as Philippi. It is no longer being done in a provincial capital such as Ephesus. It is no longer being done in a governor's praetorium in Caesarea. Nothing less than the capital of the empire is now Paul's location.

Third, Paul is at center stage in chains. For Luke, Paul is a noble and courageous figure. Yet in contrast to the Roman generals whose triumphs in Rome occur in magnificent splendor, Luke's Paul has arrived as a far different type of hero. Paul's triumph is a triumph of faithful witness. It is a triumph achieved precisely in and through his chains. In their triumphs Roman generals paraded the prisoners they had taken in their military campaigns. Although Paul has waged extensive campaigns for Jesus Christ, he now wears the chains that conquered figures wear. Yet Paul is not conquered!

Fourth, what is the content of Paul's preaching? It is "the kingdom of God" (βασιλείαν τοῦ θεοῦ). Again where is Paul preaching concerning God's βασιλεία? He is preaching at the political center of the Roman βασιλεία. Inevitably, this question arises from the scene that Luke is depicting: do the two kingdoms make competing claims for allegiance?

Fifth, Paul is in the capital precincts of an emperor who styles himself as "lord." Yet he does not cease to proclaim that Jesus is Messiah and *Lord*. It is significant to note that Luke has prepared for Paul's proclamation that Jesus is Lord by reporting the governor Festus' perplexity due to the fact that, in sending Paul to the emperor, he does not know how to present Paul's case to "*my lord*" (25:26; emphasis added). Now, having arrived at Festus' lord's very doorstep, Paul does not cease to teach about *the* Lord Jesus Christ" (28:31).

The penultimate words of Acts thus portray Paul conducting two related types of discourse. Paul is both preaching and teaching. Presumably he is doing so in interaction with "all" who come to his quarters. In the heart of the dominant kingdom of the world, Paul continues preaching about the kingdom of God and teaching about the Lord Jesus Christ. Far from being bedazzled or cowed by the signs and accoutrements of Roman power that are all around him, Paul boldly directs attention to the kingdom of God in which Jesus reigns as Lord.

LUKE'S TWO-CHORD ENDING—Luke's ultimate four words remain to be considered: μετὰ πάσης παρρησίας ἀκωλύτως. Luke uses these words to emphasize the moral conviction with which Paul is testifying and then, to employ a cinematographic image, Luke "freezes the frame." Far from being at a loss as to how to close his narrative, Luke is well satisfied to close it precisely with these words. Μετὰ πάσης παρρησίας ἀκωλύτως identify two important facets within Luke's closing portrayal of Paul. In effect, these words delineate the enduring image of Paul that Luke wants his readers/hearers to carry with them when they finish with the scroll of Acts.

"Boldness" must be insisted upon as the correct translation for παρρησίας. Luke has used this noun and its cognates repeatedly in Acts is describing the clear, forthright, courageous testimony that Jesus' disciples are called to manifest. Indeed these precise words appear at 4:29 when the apostles specifically pray not to be intimidated by the political rulers but rather to have it granted to them to speak God's word "with all boldness."

In effect (to make reference now to the art of musical composition) "with all boldness" is the first chord of the two-chord ending that Luke has conceived as the conclusion for his entire work. Paul is preaching the kingdom of God and teaching about the lordship of Jesus Christ and he is doing so *with all boldness*. Does Luke intend his readers to observe a double rest before he sounds his second and final chord?

The meaning of ἀκωλύτως, the word that sounds Luke's final chord, has historically been misinterpreted by commentators on Acts and it is still being misinterpreted by twenty-first-century commentators. As a consequence of this misapprehension of ἀκωλύτως, the inspiring character of the ending that Luke has carefully labored to construct becomes obfuscated.

If the meaning ascribed to ἀκωλύτως is that the imperial authorities are not "hindering" Paul, then Luke's actual meaning is turned inside out! For Luke has shown that the Roman authorities most certainly are hindering Paul! They have kept him in chains and under military guard for over four years preventing him from his normal missionary activity and the strengthening, through his personal presence, of the churches he has founded. In writing ἀκωλύτως as the concluding word for his lengthy second volume, Luke does not intend to undermine the logic of the narrative that he has unfolded up until this point. He intends no concluding-word "sop" to the Roman authorities.

Again, the final word of Acts is *not* about favorable conduct on the part of Roman officials. Rather it is a final favorable word about Paul! In effect, ἀκωλύτως states negatively the fundamental concept that μετὰ πάσης παρρησίας states positively. Far from being a word of appreciation for the Roman officials (that they are not hindering Paul), ἀκωλύτως is actually a word of affirmation for Paul. Paul exhibits strength of character and does not let Roman chains intimidate him.

When ἀκωλύτως is correctly interpreted as a descriptive term for the quality of Paul's witness, the brilliant achievement that Luke has made in his ending emerges for the acclaim it deserves. Positively, Paul continues to preach and teach regarding Jesus his Lord *with all boldness.* (Pause for effect.) Negatively, Paul is *un-intimidated* by any blandishment or any persecution made against him by the Roman authorities even should death result. (Freeze frame.) Luke has composed a highly nuanced two-volume work that encompasses fifty-two chapters. His final four words bring this magnum opus to a truly satisfying conclusion.

LUKE'S FIRST CHAPTERS ANTICIPATE THE ENDING OF ACTS—The remaining task for this paper is to elaborate, in a necessarily abbreviated treatment, that Luke's ending is not only a satisfying close for the Book of Acts. It is an ending that comports well with the first chapters of the Gospel. Here too the ending is tied to the beginning. Just as the ending of Acts effectively fulfills the program indicated in Acts 1:8, so does the ending of Acts felicitously resonate with the beginning of the Gospel.

What did Luke know when he began to compose the Gospel? The opening paragraph for this essay affirmed that Luke certainly knew of

Jesus' death by Roman crucifixion in Jerusalem. Further Luke surely knew that, approximately three decades later, Paul faced Roman chains and the prospect of Roman execution in Rome.

Because he is cognizant of what has transpired in Paul's case and because he is cognizant of the complex events that resulted in Jesus' condemnation by Pilate, did Luke try to anticipate these outcomes in composing the first chapters of his Gospel? In other words, in his opening chapters did Luke try to anticipate the "Roman factors" that impacted both Jesus and Paul?

When they are read from the perspective of Paul's chains and his appeal to Caesar, Luke's opening chapters do indeed disclose perspectives regarding the sovereign status of Jesus and the nature of Jesus' kingdom that contrast dramatically with the claims of Caesar and the nature of Caesar's kingdom.

LUKE'S OPENING AFFIRMATIONS THAT JESUS IS LORD AND SAVIOR—As noted previously, near the end of Acts Festus refers to the emperor as "my lord." In contrast, at the very end of Acts Paul is resolutely testifying on behalf of "Lord" Jesus. Near the beginning of the Gospel, Luke recognizes the power of the emperor, Caesar Augustus, to order a census of "all the world" (2:1). However, Luke then accords a superior status to Jesus when angels from heaven acclaim the new-born child as "Savior" and "Lord."

Nothing is said by Luke's angels to indicate that allegiance to Lord Jesus will be in tension with allegiance to lord Caesar. Nevertheless, the implicit but real consequence of the angels' proclamation is to engender among Luke's paradigmatic readers the question: Who truly is "Lord?" In the pages of Acts, this is indeed one of the central questions that Luke is addressing as he details Paul's interactions with various Roman officials.

JESUS AS HEIR TO A KINGDOM WITHOUT END—God who is in heaven possesses ultimate sovereignty over all of heaven and all of earth and the angels presumably accord these sovereign titles to Jesus according to God's purposes. Yet in what ways will Jesus manifest his sovereign power? In the angel Gabriel's annunciation to Mary a startling disclosure about Jesus' kingdom is given. Gabriel's words are that "of his kingdom there will be *no end*" (τῆς βασιλείας αὐτοῦ οὐκ ἔσται τέλος).

How is this clause to be understood? Certainly Luke intends to affirm that Jesus is the heir to David's throne for he has expressly connected Jesus with David in the preceding verse (1:32).

Is this eternal kingdom also geographical in scope? If so, then how does this kingdom comport with other existing geographical kingdoms? Could the announcement that Jesus will have unending rule over David's territories mean that he will rule over them as an enclave with the "world" controlled by Caesar? If this kingdom is not geographical in the way that David's was, then how can it be measured? An inability to be precise about the scope of Gabriel's announcement does not mean that Luke envisions the kingdom Jesus possesses to be free from tension with the kingdom over which Caesar presently rules.

An additional point to be noted is that, while Gabriel's announcement says not a word about Caesar's kingdom, the proclamation that Jesus' kingdom is *eternal* may implicitly raise a question about the duration of Caesar's kingdom.

MARY ON KINGS AND KINGDOMS—There are two additional references in Luke's opening chapters that bear upon the topic of how the Luke views worldly kings/kingdoms. The first reference occurs in Mary's Magnificat. In Luke's description, Mary joyfully acclaims the majesty of God. As a part of her prayer, she then boldly proclaims that one aspect of God's greatness lies in God's facility for putting down "the mighty from their thrones" (1:52).

To whom do these words apply? Do they pertain only to those who have occupied the seats of power in the past? No, in Mary's perspective, God's capacity for pulling down the mighty is ongoing. Who sits upon thrones in Mary's own day? The inference is never drawn. Are the Romans and their client kings somehow exempt from God's power to pull rulers from their thrones?

SATAN'S INFLUENCE ACCORDING TO LUKE—In Luke 3:1–2 Luke delineates the administrative structure of Roman rule at the time when Jesus enters upon his public ministry naming the new emperor, the new governor, several tetrarchs, and the reigning high priests. In Luke 3:19–20 Luke indicates that one of these Roman rulers, Herod Antipas took the step of casting John the Baptist, acclaimed by Luke as the forerunner of Jesus, into prison! It is in the context of these two references that Luke then narrates the second temptation that Jesus faced.

At 4:5–8 Luke relates that the devil brought Jesus to view "all the kingdoms of the world" (πάσας τὰς βασιλείας τῆς οἰκουμένης). Note the vastness of this scene: not simply a kingdom as vast as the Roman empire, but rather *all* kingdoms, seemingly past as well as present are included.

Luke's Satan then places before Jesus an astonishing proposal and claim: "To you I will give all this authority (τὴν ἐξουσίαν ταύτην ἅπασαν) and their glory (καὶ τὴν δόξαν αὐτῶν) for it has been delivered to me and I give it to whom I will" (4:6). Truly an astonishing statement: that *all* the kingdoms of the world have been delivered to Satan! Luke's Jesus does not dispute this assertion. His response is rather to reject that Satan's prerogatives are so compelling as to justify Jesus' worship of Satan.

In delineating this second temptation, does Luke understand that it takes in the Roman kingdom whose census of the world he has just referenced in chapter two? Two other factors afford additional support for the view that Luke does indeed have the Roman kingdom within his sights in this temptation scene. The first factor is more easily assessed since it emerges from Luke's use of the modifier, "all" (πάσας). Satan's influence is not restricted to *some* of the kingdoms of the world but rather reaches to *all* of them.

The second factor pertains to the ending of the Acts as it has been analyzed above. As Acts ends Paul is chained by the authorities of the Roman kingdom but continues to preach resolutely regarding the kingdom of God. In Luke's view, is the kingdom that is confining Paul in chains a kingdom influenced by Satan? What types of behavior are exhibited by a kingdom in which Satan holds the levers of power? The kingdom of God that Paul twice references while he is in Rome (at 28:23 as well as at 28:31) is uncontaminated by such evil conduct.

THE CONSISTENCY OF LUKE'S PRESENTATION—The thesis of this essay has now been delineated. In composing the beginning of the Gospel and in portraying Jesus' commission in Acts 1:8, Luke had Paul's witness as a chained prisoner in Caesar's Rome fully in view. Because he presents the angel's acclaim of Jesus as *Lord* and *Savior* and because he presents Jesus' kingdom as unending, what Luke subsequently presents, forty chapters later at the end of Acts, is fully plausible to Luke's paradigmatic readers.

Throughout the chapters of the Gospel and throughout the chapters of Acts, Luke has presented a carefully woven narrative that motivates his readers toward an ever deepening allegiance to Jesus. In Acts itself, Paul's uncompromised testimony to Jesus before various Roman authorities and in Rome itself serves as a model for all of Luke's readers.

Because they know unalterably that Jesus is Lord and because they also know that earthly kingdoms and empires are subject to Satan's orchestrations, Luke's paradigmatic readers are well prepared to appreciate the nobility of Acts' final scene in which chained Paul continues to preach about God's kingdom and to teach that Jesus Christ is *Lord*—with all boldness; not intimidated!

Bibliography

Africa, Thomas. "Worms and the Death of Kings: A Cautionary Note on Disease and History." *Classical Antiquity* 1 (1982) 1–17.

Alexander, L. *The Preface to Luke's Gospel: Literary Convention and Social Context in Luke 1.1–4 and Acts 1.1.* SNTSMS 78. Cambridge: Cambridge University Press, 1993.

Alexander, Loveday. "The Acts of the Apostles as an Apologetic Text" in *Acts in its Ancient Literary Context.* Edinburgh: T. & T. Clark International, 2007.

———. "Reading Luke-Acts from Back to Front." In *Acts in Its Ancient Literary Context*, 207–229. New York: T. & T. Clark, 2007.

Allen, Brent. "Luke-Acts and the Imperial Cult in Asia Minor." *JTS* 48 (1997) 411–38.

Allen, O. Wesley, Jr. *The Death of Herod: The Narrative and Theological Function of Retribution in Luke-Acts.* SBLDS 158. Atlanta: Scholars, 1997.

Bachmann, Michael. *Antijudaismus im Galaterbrief?: Exegetische Studien zu einem polemischen Schreiben und zur Theologie des Apostels Paulus.* NTOA 40. Göttingen: Vandenhoeck & Ruprecht, 1999.

———. *Anti-Judaism in Galatians?: Exegetical Studies on a Polemical Letter and on Paul's Theology.* Translated by Robert L. Brawley. Grand Rapids: Eerdmans, 2009.

———. *Jerusalem und der Tempel: Die geographisch-theologischen Elemente in der lukanischen Sicht des jüdischen Kultzentrums.* BWANT 109. Stuttgart: Kohlhammer, 1980.

———. "Die Stephanusepisode (Acts 6,1–8,3): Ihre Bedeutung für die lukanische Sicht des jerusalemischen Tempels und des Judentums." In *The Unity of Luke-Acts*, edited by Jozef Verheyden, 545–62. BEThL 122. Leuven: Peeters, 1999.

———. "Tempel III: Neues Testament." In *TRE* 33 (2002) 54–65.

———. "Zur Entstehung (und zur Überwindung) des Christlichen Antijudaismus." *ZNT* 10 (2002) 44–52.

———. Review of *Gemeinde ohne Tempel/Community without Temple*, edited by Beate Ego et al. *OLZ* 98 (2003) 251–69.

Backhaus, Knut. "Mose und der *Mos Maiorum*: Das Alter des Judentums als Argument für die Attraktivität des Christentums in der Apostelgeschichte." In *Josephus und das Neue Testament: Wechselseitige Wahrnehmung: II. Internationales Symposium zum Corpus Judaeo-Hellenisticum, 25.–28. Mai 2006, Greifswald,* edited by Christfried Böttrich and Jens Herzer (in cooperation of Torsten Reiprich), 401–428. WUNT 209. Tübingen: Mohr/Siebeck, 2007.

Barrett, C. K. *A Critical and Exegetical Commentary on the Acts of the Apostles.* 2 vols. ICC. Edinburgh: T. & T. Clark, 1994, 1998.

———. *Luke the Historian in Recent Study.* Facet Books Biblical Series 24. Philadelphia: Fortress, 1970.

Bauckham, Richard. "Anna of the Tribe of Asher." *RB* 104 (1997) 161–91.

———. "The *Restoration* of Israel in Luke-Acts." In *Restoration: Old Testmanent, Jewish, and Christian Perspectives,* edited by James M. Scott, 435–87. JSJSup 72. Leiden: Brill, 2001.

Becker, Adam, and Annette Yoshiko Reed, editors. *The Ways that Never Parted: Jews and Christians in Late Antiquity and the Middle Ages.* Minneapolis: Fortress, 2007.

Bendemann, Reinhard von. "Paulus und Israel in der Apostelgeschichte des Lukas." In *Ja und Nein: Christliche Theologie im Angesicht Israels: Festschrift zum 70. Geburtstag von Wolfgang Schrage,* 291–303. Neukirchen-Vluyn: Neukirchener, 1998.

Berg, Elizabeth. "Iconoclastic Moments: Reading the *Sonnets for Helene,* Writing the *Portugese Letters.*" In *The Poetics of Gender,* edited by Nancy Miller. New York: Columbia University Press, 1986.

Blinzler, Josef. *Der Prozess Jesu: Das jüdische und das römische Gerichtsverfahren gegen Jesus Christus auf Grund der ältesten Zeugnisse dargestellt und beurteilt.* 4th ed. Regensburg: Pustet, 1969.

Bock, Darrell L. *Acts.* Baker Exegetical Commentary on the New Testament. Grand Rapids: Baker, 2007.

Bond, Helen K. *Pontius Pilate in History and Interpretation.* SNTSMS 100. Cambridge: Cambridge University Press, 1998.

Bozzoli, Belinda. *Theatres of Struggle and the End of Apartheid.* Athens: Ohio University Press, 2004.

Brawley, Robert L. "Abrahamic Covenant Traditions and the Characterization of God in Luke-Acts." In *The Unity of Luke-Acts,* edited by Jozef Verheyden, 109–32. BEThL 142. Leuven: Peeters, 1999.

———. *Centering on God: Method and Message in Luke-Acts.* Louisville: Westminster John Knox, 1990.

———. *Character Ethics and the New Testament: Moral Dimensions of Scripture.* Louisville: Westminster John Knox, 2007.

———. "Ethical Borderlines between Rejection and Hope: Interpreting the Jews in Luke-Acts." *CTM* 27 (2000) 415–23.

———. "The God of Promises and the Jews in Luke-Acts." In *Literary Studies in Luke-Acts: Essays in Honor of Joseph B. Tyson,* edited by Richard P. Thompson and Thomas E. Phillips, 279–96. Macon, GA: Mercer University Press, 1998.

———. *Luke-Acts and the Jews: Conflict, Apology, and Conciliation.* SBLMS 33. Atlanta: Scholars, 1987.

———. *Text to Text Pours Forth Speech: Voices of Scripture in Luke-Acts.* Bloomington: University of Indiana Press, 1995.

Brooke, George J. "A Long-Lost Song of Miriam." *BAR* 20.3 (1994) 62–65.

Brown, Raymond E. *The Birth of the Messiah.* Garden City, NY: Doubleday, 1977, 1993.

———. *The Death of the Messiah.* 2 vols. ABRL. London: Chapman, 1994.

Bruce, F. F. *The Acts of the Apostles: The Greek Text with Introduction and Commentary.* 3rd ed. Grand Rapids: Eerdmans, 1990.

———. *New Testament History.* Rev. ed. London: Oliphants, 1971.

Brunt, Peter. "Procuratorial Jurisdiction." In *Roman Imperial Themes,* 163–87. Oxford: Clarendon, 1990.

————. "The Romanization of the Local Ruling Classes." In *Roman Imperial Themes*, 267–81. Oxford: Clarendon, 1990.

Burfeind, Carsten. "Paulus *muß* nach Rom: Zur politischen Dimension der Apostelgeschichte." *NTS* 46 (2000) 75–91.

Burns, Rita J. *Has the Lord Indeed Spoken Only through Moses? A Study of the Biblical Portrait of Miriam*. SBLDS 84. Atlanta: Scholars, 1987.

Burrus, Virginia. "The Gospel of Luke and the Acts of the Apostles." In *A Postcolonial Commentary on the New Testament Writings*, edited by Fernando F. Segovia and R. S. Sugirtharajah, 133–55. New York: T. & T. Clark, 2007.

Butler, Judith, and G. Spivak, *Who Sings the Nation State?* London: Seagull. 2007.

Cadbury, Henry. *The Making of Luke-Acts*. London: Macmillan, 1927.

Caputo, J. *More Radical Hermeneutics: On Not Knowing Who We Are*. Studies in Continental Thought. Bloomington: Indiana University Press, 2000.

Carter, Warren. "Evoking Isaiah: Why Summon Isaiah in Matthew 1:23 and 4:15–16?" In *Matthew and Empire: Initial Explorations*, 93–107. Harrisburg, PA; Trinity, 2001.

————. *Matthew and Empire: Initial Explorations*. Harrisburg, PA: Trinity, 2001.

————. *Pontius Pilate: Portraits of a Roman Governor*. Collegeville, MN: Liturgical, 2001.

————. *The Roman Empire and the New Testament. An Essential Guide*. Nashville: Abingdon, 2006.

Cassidy, Richard. "Aspects of Narrative Criticism in the Four Gospels." In *Four Times Peter: Portrayals of Peter in the Four Gospels and at Philippi*, 1–12. Interfaces. Collegeville, MN: Liturgical, 2007.

————. *Christians and Roman Rule in the New Testament*. New York: Crossroad, 2001.

————. *Jesus, Politics, and Society: A Study of Luke's Gospel*. Maryknoll, NY: Orbis, 1978.

————. *Political Issues in Luke-Acts*. Maryknoll, NY: Orbis, 1983.

————. "Saint Luke Does Not Apologize!" *The Bible Today* 45 (2007) 17–21.

————. *Society and Politics in the Acts of the Apostles*. Maryknoll, NY: Orbis, 1987.

Chance, J. Bradley. *Jerusalem, the Temple, and the New Age in Luke-Acts*. Macon, GA: Mercer University Press, 1988.

Chibici-Revneanu, Nicole. "Ein himmlischer Stehplatz: Die Haltung Jesu in der Stephanusvision (Acts 7.55–6) und ihre Bedeutung." *NTS* 53 (2007) 459–88.

Clarke, William K. L. "The Use of the Septuagint in Acts." In *The Beginnings of Christianity: The Acts of the Apostles*, edited by F. J. Foakes-Jackson and Kirsopp Lake, 2:66–105. 5 vols. London: Macmillan, 1920–1933.

Cohen, Shaye J. D. *From the Maccabees to the Mishnah*. Library of Early Christianity 7. Louisville: Westminster John Knox, 1989.

Conzelmann, Hans. *Acts of the Apostles*. Translated by James Limburg et al. Hermeneia. Philadelphia: Fortress, 1987.

————. *Die Mitte der Zeit: Studien zur Theologie des Lukas*. BHTh 17. 6th ed. (= 4th ed. [of 1962]). Tübingen: Mohr/Siebeck, 1977 (7th ed.: 1993).

————. *The Theology of St Luke*. Translated by Geoffrey Buswell. London: Faber & Faber, 1960.

Cotter, Wendy. "The *collegia* and Roman Law: State Restrictions on Voluntary Associations." In *Voluntary Associations in the Graeco-Roman World*, edited by John S. Kloppenborg and Stephen G. Wilson, 74–89. London: Routledge, 1996.

Croatto, J. Severino. "Jesus, Prophet Like Elijah, and Prophet-Teacher Like Moses." *JBL* 124 (2005) 451–65.

Crossan, John Dominic. *God and Empire: Jesus against Rome, Then and Now*. San Francisco: HarperSanFrancisco, 2007.

———. *The Historical Jesus: The Life of a Mediterranean Jewish Peasant*. San Francisco: HarperSanFrancisco, 1991.

Cruz, Jon. *Culture on the Margins: The Black Spiritual and the Rise of American Cultural Interpretation*. Princeton: Princeton University Press, 1999.

D'Angelo, Mary Rose. "Women in Luke-Acts: A Redactional View." *JBL* 109 (1990) 441–61.

Dahl, Nihls Alstrup. "The Purpose of Luke-Acts." In *Jesus in the Memory of the Early Church: Essays*, 87–98. Minneapolis: Augsburg, 1976.

Danker, Frederick W. *A Greek-English Lexicon of the New Testament and other Early Christian Literature*. Chicago: University of Chicago Press, 2000.

Davison, Lisa Wilson. *Preaching the Women of the Bible*. St. Louis: Chalice, 2006.

de Man, Paul. *Allegories of Reading: Figural Language in Rousseau, Nietzsche, Rilke, and Proust*. New Haven: Yale University Press, 1979.

Demandt, Alexander. *Hände in Unschuld: Pontius Pilatus in Geschichte*. Cologne: Böhlau, 1999.

Derrida, Jacques. *The Gift of Death*. Chicago: University of Chicago Press, 1995.

deSilva, David A. *Introducing the Apocrypha: Message, Context, and Significance*. Grand Rapids: Baker, 2002.

Dittenberger, W. *Orientis graeci inscriptiones selectee*. Vol. 2. Leipzig: Hirzel, 1905.

Dixon, Suzanne. *The Roman Mother*. London: Croom Helm, 1988.

Douglass, Frederick. "Life and Times of Frederick Douglass Written by Himself." In *Autobiographies*. New York: Library of America, 1994.

du Bois, W. E. B. *The Souls of Black Folks*. 1903. Reprinted, New York: Knopf, 1993.

Dunn, James D.G. "ΚΥΡΙΟΣ in Acts." In *Jesus Christus als die Mitte der Schrift: Studien zur Hermeneutik des Evangeliums*, edited by Christof Landmesser et al., 363–78. BZNW 86. Berlin: de Gruyter, 1997.

———. *Jews and Christians: The Parting of the Ways, A.D. 70 to 135: The Second Durham-Tübingen Research Symposium on Earliest Christianity and Judaism*. Grand Rapids: Eerdmans, 1999.

During, Simon. "Postmodernism or Postcolonialism?" *Landfall* 39 (1985) 366–80.

Egger, P. *"Crucifixus sub Pontio Pilato": Das "Crimen" Jesu von Nazareth im Spannungsfeld römischer und jüdischer Verwaltungs- und Rechtsstrukturen*. Neutestamentlich Abhandlungen 32. Münster: Aschendorff, 1997.

Ego, Beate, et al. *Gemeinde ohne Tempel/Community without Temple. Zur Substituierung und Transformation des Jerusalemer Tempels und seines Kults im Alten Testament, antiken Judentum und frühen Christentum*. WUNT 118. Tübingen: Mohr/Siebeck, 1999.

———. *Im Himmel wie auf Erden. Studien zum Verhältnis von himmlischer und irdischer Welt im rabbinischen Judentum*. WUNT II/34. Tübingen: Mohr/Siebeck, 1987.

Eisen, Ute E. *Die Poetik der Apostelgeschichte: Eine narratologische Studie.* NTOA/ StUNT 58. Göttingen: Vandenhoeck & Ruprecht, 2006.

Eissfeldt, Otto. "'Juda' und 'Judäa' als Bezeichnung nordsyrischer Bereiche." In *Kleine Schriften*, edited by Rudolf Sellheim and Fritz Maass, 4:121–32. Tübingen: Mohr/ Siebeck, 1962–1973 (orig. 1964).

———. "'Juda' in 2. Könige 14,28 und 'Judäa' in Apostelgeschichte 2,9." In *Kleine Schriften*, edited by Rudolf Sellheim and Fritz Maass, 4:99–120. Tübingen: Mohr/ Siebeck, 1962–1973 (orig. 1963).

———. "Kreter und Araber." In *Kleine Schriften*, edited by Rudolf Sellheim and Fritz Maass, 3:28–34. Tübingen: Mohr/Siebeck, 1962–1973 (orig. 1947).

Elliott, John H. "Temple versus Household in Luke-Acts: A Contrast in Social Institutions." In *The Social World of Luke-Acts*, edited by Jerome H. Neyrey, 211– 40. Peabody, PA: Hendrickson, 1991.

Elliott, Neil. *The Arrogance of Nations: Reading Romans in the Shadow of Empire.* Minneapolis: Fortress, 2008.

Epstein, Dena. *Sinful Tunes and Spirituals: Black Folk Music to the Civil War.* Urbana: University of Illinois Press, 1977.

Esler, Philip F. *Community and Gospel in Luke-Acts: The Social and Political Motivations of Lucan Theology.* SNTSMS 57. Cambridge: Cambridge University Press, 1987.

Farris, Stephen. *The Hymns of Luke's Infancy Narratives: Their Origin, Meaning, and Significance.* JSNTSup 9. Sheffield: JSOT Press, 1985.

Fishwick, Duncan. *The Imperial Cult in the Latin West: Studies in the Ruler Cult of the Western Provinces of the Roman Empire.* Religions in the Greco-Roman World 145–148. Leiden: Brill, 1991.

Fitzmyer, Joseph A. *The Acts of the Apostles: A New Translation and Commentary.* AB 31. New York: Doubleday, 1998.

———. *The Gospel according to Luke I–IX.* AB 28. Garden City, NY: Doubleday, 1981.

Flusser, David. *Entdeckungen im Neuen Testament 2: Jesus—Qumran—Urchristentum.* Neukirchen-Vluyn: Neukirchener, 1999.

Foakes Jackson, F. J., and K. Lake. *The Beginnings of Christianity, Part I: The Acts of the Apostles.* 5 vols. London: Macmillan, 1920–33.

Foxhall, L. and H. Forbes. "*Sitometreia*: The Role of Grain as a Staple Food in Classical Antiquity." *Chiron* 12 (1982) 41–90.

Franklin, Eric. *Christ the Lord: A Study in the Purpose and Theology of Luke-Acts.* Philadelphia: Westminster, 1975.

Fredriksen, Paula. *Jesus of Nazareth, King of the Jews: A Jewish Life and the Emergence of Christianity.* New York: Vintage, 1999.

Freire, Paulo. *Pedagogy of the Oppressed.* 20th Anniversary rev ed. New York: Continuum, 1993.

Friesen, Steven J. "Injustice of God's Will: Explanations of Poverty in Proto-Christian Texts." In *A People's History of Christianity: Christian Origin*, 240–60. Minneapolis: Fortress, 2005.

———. "Poverty in Pauline Studies: Beyond the so-called New Consensus." *JSNT* 26 (2004) 323–61.

Fulkerson, Mary McClintock. *Changing The Subject: Women's Discourses and Feminist Theology.* Minneapolis: Fortress, 1994.

Fuller, Michael, E. *The Restoration of Israel: Israel's Re-gathering and the Fate of the Nations in Early Jewish Literature and Luke-Acts*. BZNW 138. Berlin: de Gruyter, 2006.

Gafney, Wilda C. *Daughters of Miriam: Women Prophets in Ancient Israel*. Minneapolis: Fortress, 2008.

Gallagher, Susan. "Introduction." In *Postcolonial Literature and the Biblical Call for Justice,* 3–33. Jackson: University of Mississippi Press, 1994.

Ganser-Kerperin, Heiner. *Das Zeugnis des Tempels: Studien zur Bedeutung des Tempelmotivs im lukanischen Doppelwerk*. NTA NF 36. Münster: Aschendorff, 2000.

Garnsey, Peter. "The Bean: Substance and Symbol." In *Cities, Peasants, and Food in Classical Antiquity,* 214–25. Cambridge: Cambridge University Press, 1988.

———. *Famine and Food Supply in the Graeco-Roman World: Responses to Risk and Crisis*. Cambridge: Cambridge University Press, 1988.

———. *Food and Society in Classical Antiquity*. Cambridge: Cambridge University Press, 1999.

———. *Social Status and Legal Privilege in the Roman Empire*. Oxford: Clarendon, 1970.

Gauger, Jörg-Dieter. "Der 'Tod des Verfolgers': Überlegungen zur Historizität eines Topos." *JSJ* 33 (2002) 42–64.

Gaventa, Beverly R. *Acts*. ANTC. Nashville: Abingdon, 2003.

———. *From Darkness to Light: Aspects of Conversion in the New Testament*. Overtures to Biblical Theology. Philadelphia: Fortress, 1986.

———. "The Overthrown Enemy: Luke's Portrait of Paul." In *SBL Seminar Papers, 1985,* 439–49. SBL Seminar Papers 24. Atlanta: Scholars, 1985.

———. "The Presence of the Absent Lord: The Characterization of Jesus in the Acts of the Apostles." Paper presented at SBL Annual Meeting, 2003

Gilbert, Gary. "Luke-Acts and Negotiations of Authority and Identity in the Roman World." In *The Multivalence of Biblical Texts and Theological Meanings,* edited by Christine Helmer, 83–104. Symposium Series 37. Atlanta: Society of Biblical Literature, 2006.

Gilbert, Shirli. "Singing Against Apartheid." *Journal of South African Studies* 33 (2007) 421–47.

Gill, D. W. J. "Acts and Roman Policy in Judaea." In *The Book of Acts in its Palestinian Setting,* edited by Richard Bauckham, 15–26. A1CS 4. Grand Rapids: Eerdmans, 1995.

Goldstein, Jonathan A. *II Maccabees: A New Translation with Introduction and Commentary*. AB 41A. Garden City, NY: Doubleday, 1983.

Goodman, Martin. *Rome and Jerusalem: The Clash of Ancient Civilizations*. New York: Knopf, 2008.

Goulder, M. *Luke: A New Paradigm*. Vol. 2. JSNTSup 20. Sheffield: Sheffield Academic, 1989.

Green, J. B. *The Death of Jesus: Tradition and Interpretation in the Passion Narrative*. WUNT II/33. Tübingen: Mohr/Siebeck, 1988.

———. *The Gospel of Luke*. NICNT. Grand Rapids: Eerdmans, 1997.

———. *The Theology of the Gospel of Luke*. Cambridge: Cambridge University Press, 1995.

Greenway, John. *American Folksongs of Protest.* Philadelphia: University of Pennsylvania Press, 1953.

Haacker, Klaus. "Das Bekenntnis des Paulus zur Hoffnung Israels nach der Apostelgeschichte des Lukas." *NTS* 31 (1985) 437–51.

———. *Versöhnung mit Israel: Exegetische Beiträge.* Veröffentlichungen der Kirchlichen Hochschule Wuppertal NF 5. Neukirchen-Vluyn: Neukirchener, 2002.

Haenchen, Ernst. *The Acts of the Apostles.* Translated by Bernard Noble et al. Oxford: Blackwell, 1971.

———. *Die Apostelgeschichte.* KEK 3 (16th ed.). 7th ed. of this new interpretation. Göttingen: Vandenhoeck & Ruprecht, 1977.

Haensch, Rudolf. "Die römische Provinzialverwaltung im Frühen Prinzipat/Das römische Heer und die Heere der Klientelkönige im Frühen Prinzipat." In *Neues Testament und Antike Kultur 1,* edited by Kurt Erlemann and Karl Leo Noethlichs, 149–58; 158–65. Neukirchen-Vluyn: Neukirchener, 2004.

Hannah, Darrell D. "The Throne of His Glory: The Divine Throne and Heavenly Mediators in Revelation and the Similitudes of Enoch." *ZNW* 94 (2003) 68–96.

Harnack, Adolf [von]. *Die Apostelgeschichte: Untersuchungen.* Beiträge zur Einleitung in das Neue Testament 3. Leipzig: J. C. Hinrichs, 1908.

Harvey, A. E. *Jesus on Trial: A Study in the Fourth Gospel.* London: SPCK, 1976.

Hawn, C. Michael. *Gather into One: Praying and Singing Globally.* Grand Rapids: Eerdmans, 2003.

———. "Singing with the Faithful of Every Time and Place: Thoughts on Liturgical Inculturation and Cross-Cultural Liturgy." *Yale Institute of Sacred Music Colloquium Journal* 2 (Autumn 2005) 109–24.

———. "Siyahamba, South African Freedom Song." *The Chorister* 51.6 (1999) 23–27.

Heckel, Ulrich. *Der Segen im Neuen Testament: Begriff, Formeln, Gesten: Mit einem praktisch-theologischen Ausblick.* WUNT 150. Tübingen: Mohr/Siebeck, 2002.

Hendrickx, Herman. *The Third Gospel for the Third World.* Vol. 1. Collegeville, MN: Liturgical, 1996.

Hengel, Martin. *Crucifixion in the Ancient World and the Folly of the Message of the Cross.* Translated by John Bowden. Philadelphia: Fortress, 1977.

———. "ʾΙουδαία in der geographischen Liste Acts 2,9–11 und Syrien als ʾGroßjudäa.'" *RHPhR* 80 (2002) 51–68.

Herzog II, William R. *Jesus, Justice, and the Reign of God: A Ministry of Liberation.* Louisville: Westminster John Knox, 2000.

Hoffmann, Michael. "Das eschatologische Heil Israels nach den lukanischen Schriften." PhD diss., Universität Heidelberg, 1988.

Holtz, Traugott. "δώδεκα." In *EWNT* I (1980) 874–80.

Horn, Friedrich Wilhelm. "Die Haltung des Lukas zum römischen Staat im Evangelium und in der Apostelgeschichte." In *The Unity of Luke-Acts,* edited by Jozef Verheyden, 203–24. BEThL 122. Leuven: Peeters, 1999.

Horsley, Richard, editor. *Hidden Transcripts and the Arts of Resistance: Applying the Work of James C. Scott to Jesus and Paul.* Semeia Studies 48. Atlanta: Society of Biblical Literature, 2004.

———. *Jesus and Empire: The Kingdom of God and the New World Disorder.* 2003. Reprinted, Minneapolis: Fortress, 1993.

————. *Jesus and the Spiral of Violence: Popular Jewish Resistance in Roman Palestine.* San Francisco: Harper & Row, 1987.

————. *The Liberation of Christmas: The Infancy Narratives in Social Context.* 1989. Reprinted, Eugene, OR: Wipf & Stock, 2006.

————, editor. *Paul and Empire: Religion and Power in Roman Imperial Society.* Harrisburg, PA: Trinity, 1997.

————, editor. *Paul and Politics: Ekklesia, Israel, Imperium, Interpretation. Essays in Honor of Krister Stendahl.* Harrisburg, PA: Trinity, 2000.

————, editor. *Paul and the Roman Imperial Order.* Harrisburg, PA: Trinity, 2004.

Horst, P. W. van der. "Drohung und Mord schnaubend (Acta IX 1)." *NovT* 12 (1970) 257–69.

Howell, Justin. "The Imperial Authority and Benefaction of Centurions and Acts 10.34–43: A Response to C. Kavin Rowe." *JSNT* 31/1 (2008) 25–51.

Janzen, J. Gerald. "Song of Moses, Song of Miriam: Who is Seconding Whom?" *CBQ* 54 (1992) 211–20.

Jennings, Theodore. *Reading Derrida: Thinking Romans.* Cultural Memory in the Present. Stanford: Stanford University Press, 2006.

Jervell, Jacob. *Die Apostelgeschichte.* Kritisch-exegetischer Kommentar über das Neue Testament 3. Göttingen: Vandenhoeck & Ruprecht, 1998.

————. "God's Faithfulness to the Faithless People: Trends in the Interpretation of Luke-Acts." *Word & World* 12 (1991) 29–37.

————. "Gottes Treue zum untreuen Volk." In *Der Treue Gottes trauen: Beiträge zum Werk des Lukas: Für Gerhard Schneider,* edited by Claus Bussmann and Walter Radl, 15–27. Freiburg: Herder, 1991.

————. *Luke and the People of God: A New Look at Luke-Acts.* Minneapolis: Augsburg, 1972.

————. *Luke and the People of God.* Minneapolis: Augsburg, 1979.

————. *The Theology of the Acts of the Acts of the Apostles.* New Testament Theology. Cambridge: Cambridge University Press, 1996, 2008.

Jeska, Joachim. *Die Geschichte Israels in der Sicht des Lukas: Apg 7,2b–53 und 13,17–25 im Kontext antik-jüdischer Summarien der Geschichte Israels.* FRLANT 195. Göttingen: Vandenhoeck & Ruprecht, 2001.

Johnson, Luke Timothy. *The Acts of the Apostles.* Sacra Pagina 5. Collegeville, MN: Liturgical, 1992.

————. *The Gospel of Luke.* Sacra Pagina 3. Collegeville, MN: Liturgical, 1991.

————. *The Literary Function of Possessions in Luke-Acts.* SBLDS 39. Missoula, MT: Scholars, 1977.

Johnson, Terry, and Christopher Dandeker. "Patronage: Relation and System." In *Patronage in Ancient Society,* 219–41. New York: Routledge, 1989

Jones, A. H. M. *The Herods of Judaea.* Oxford: Clarendon, 1967.

Karrer, Martin. *Der Gesalbte: Die Grundlagen des Christustitels.* FRLANT 151. Göttingen: Vandenhoeck & Ruprecht, 1990.

Kirk-Duggan, Cheryl A. *Exorcizing Evil: A Womanist Perspective on the Spirituals.* Maryknoll, NY: Orbis, 1997.

Klauck, Hans-Josef, "Die Heilige Stadt: Jerusalem bei Philo und Josephus." In *Gemeinde, Amt, Sakrament: Neutestamentliche Perspektiven,* 101–29. Würzburg: Echter, 1989 (orig.: 1986).

Klein, Richard. "Das Bild des Augustus in der frühchristlichen Literatur." In *Rom und das himmlische Jerusalem: Die frühen Christen zwischen Anpassung und Ablehnung*, edited by Raban von Haehling, 205–236. Darmstadt: Wissenschaftliche Buchgesellschaft, 2000.

Koet, Bart J. "Paul in Rome (Acts 28,16–31): A Farewell to Judaism? " In *Five Studies on Interpretation of Scripture in Luke-Acts*, 119–39. SNTA 14. Leuven: Peeters, 1989 (orig.: 1987).

Kollmann, Bernd. *Einführung in die Neutestamentliche Zeitgeschichte*. Darmstadt: Wissenschaftliche Buchgesellschaft, 2006.

Kratz, Reinhard. *Rettungswunder: Motiv-, traditions- und formkritische Aufarbeitung einer biblischen Gattung*. Europäische Hochschulschriften 23/123. Frankfurt: Lang, 1979.

Kurth, Christina. *"Die Stimme der Propheten erfüllt": Jesu Geschichte und "die" Juden nach der Darstellung des Lukas*. BWANT 148. Stuttgart: Kohlhammer, 2000.

LaGrand, James. "Luke's Portrait of Simeon (Luke 2:25–35): Aged Saint or Hesitant Terrorist?" In *Common Life in the Early Church; Essays Honoring Graydon F. Snyder*, edited by Julian V. Hills, 175–85. Harrisburg, PA: Trinity, 1998.

Lake, Kirsopp, and Henry J. Cadbury. *English Translation and Commentary. The Beginnings of Christianity: The Acts of the Apostles*, vol. 4, edited by F. J. Foakes-Jackson and Kirsopp Lake. 5 vols. London: Macmillan, 1920–1933.

Lang, Manfred. *Die Kunst des christlichen Lebens: Rezeptionsästhetische Studien zum lukanischen Paulusbild*. Arbeiten zur Bibel und ihrer Geschichte 29. Leipzig: Evangelische Verlagsanstalt, 2008.

Lankshear, Colin. "Functional Literacy from a Freirean Point of View." In *Paulo Freire: A Critical Encounter*, edited by P. McLaren and P. Leonard, 90–118. Routledge: London, 1993.

Lehnert, Volker. "Die 'Verstockung Israels' und biblische Hermeneutik: Ein Kabinettsstückchen zur Methodenfrage." *ZNT* 16 (2005) 13–19.

Lenski, Gerhard. *Power and Privilege: A Theory of Social Stratification*. Chapel Hill: University of North Carolina Press, 1984.

Lichtenberger, Hermann. "Jews and Christians in Rome in the Time of Nero: Josephus and Paul in Rome." *ANRW* II.26.3 (1996) 2142–76.

———. "Organisationsformen und Ämter in den jüdischen Gemeinden im antiken Griechenland und Italien." In *Jüdische Gemeinden und Organisationsformen von der Antike bis zur Gegenwart*, edited by Robert Jütt and Abraham Peter Kustermann, 11–27. Aschkenas Beih. 3. Vienna: Böhlau, 1996.

Lincoln, A. T. *Truth on Trial: The Lawsuit Motif in the Fourth Gospel*. Peabody, MA: Hendrickson, 2000.

Lohfink, Gerhard. *Die Himmelfahrt Jesu: Untersuchungen zu den Himmelfahrts- und Erhöhungstexten bei Lukas*. StANT 26. Munich: Kösel, 1971.

Longenecker, R. N. *The Christology of Early Jewish Christianity*. SBT 2/17. London: SCM, 1970.

MacMullen, Ramsay. *Roman Social Relations 50 B.C. to A.D. 284*. New Haven: Yale University Press, 1974.

Maddox, Robert. *The Purpose of Luke-Acts*. FRLANT 126. Göttingen: Vandenhoeck & Ruprecht, 1982.

Malina, Bruce J., and Richard L. Rohrbaugh. *Social-Science Commentary on the Synoptic Gospels*. Minneapolis: Fortress, 1992.

Marcus, Joel. "Crucifixion as Parodic Exaltation." *JBL* 125 (2006) 73–87.

Marguerat, Daniel. *The First Christian Historian: Writing the 'Acts of the Apostles.'* SNTSMS 121. Cambridge: Cambridge University Press, 2002.

Marshall, I. Howard. *Acts.* Tyndale New Testament Commentaries 5. Grand Rapids: Eerdmans, 1980.

—————. *Luke: Historian and Theologian.* Exeter, UK: Paternoster, 1970.

Mattingly, David J. "First Fruit? The Olive in the Roman World." In *Human Landscapes in Classical Antiquity: Environment and Culture,* edited by Graham Shipley and John Salmon, 213–53. London: Routledge, 1996.

McGing, Brian. "Pontius Pilate and the Sources." *CBQ* (1991) 416–38.

Merritt, Robert. "Jesus, Barabbas, and the Pascal Pardon." *JBL* 104 (1985) 58–66.

Metzger, Bruce M. *A Textual Commentary on the Greek New Testament.* 2nd ed. Stuttgart: United Bible Societies, 1994.

Metzger, Paul. *Katechon: II Thess 2,1–12 im Horizont apokalyptischen Denkens.* BZNW 135. Berlin: de Gruyter, 2005.

—————. "Zeitspiegel: Neutestamentliche Handschriften als Zeugnisse der Kirchengeschichte: Die Frage nach einer Hoffnung für Israel bei Lukas." In *The Book of Acts as Church History/Apostelgeschichte als Kirchengeschichte: Text, Textual Traditions and Ancient Interpretation/Text, Texttraditionen und antike Auslegung,* edited by Tobias Nicklas and Michael Tilly, 241–62. BZNW 120. Berlin: de Gruyter, 2003.

Mishra, Vijay and Bob Hodge, "What Is Post(-)colonialism?" In *Colonial Discourse and Post-Colonial Theory: A Reader,* edited by Patrick Williams and Laura Chrisman, 276–90. New York: Columbia University Press, 1994.

Moberly, W. "Proclaiming Christ Crucified: Some Reflections on the Use and Abuse of the Gospels." *Anvil* 5 (1988) 31–52.

Morgenthaler, Robert. *Statistik des neutestamentlichen Wortschatzes.* Zürich: Gotthelf, 1958.

Moule, C. F. D. *An Idiom-Book of New Testament Greek.* 2nd ed. Cambridge: Cambridge University Press, 1959.

Moulton, J. H., et al. *A Grammar of New Testament Greek.* 4 vols. Edinburgh: T. & T. Clark, 1906–76.

Moxnes, Halvor. *The Economy of the Kingdom: Social Conflict and Economic Relations in Luke's Gospel.* Overtures to Biblical Theology. 1988. Reprinted, Eugene, OR: Wipf & Stock, 2004.

Murphy-O'Connor, Jerome. *St Paul's Corinth: Texts and Archaeology.* 3rd ed. Collegeville, MN: Liturgical, 2002.

Nanos, Mark. "Paul and Judaism: Why Not Paul's Judaism?" in *Paul Unbound: Other Perspectives on the Apostle,* 117–60. Peabody, MA: Hendrickson, 2009.

Nestle, Eberhard. "The Vision of Stephen." *ET* 22 (1910–11) 423.

Nestle, Wilhelm. "Legenden vom Tod der Gottesverächter." *AR* 33 (1936) 246–69.

Neubrand, Maria. *Israel, die Völker und die Kirche: Eine exegetische Studie zu Apg 15.* SBS 55. Stuttgart: Katholisches Bibelwerk, 2006.

Nicholson, Linda. "Introduction." In *Feminism/Postmodernism,* edited by Linda J. Nicholson, 1–16. New York: Routledge, 1990.

Nickelsburg, George W. E. *Jewish Literature Between the Bible and the Mishnah: A Historical and Literary Introduction.* 2nd ed. Minneapolis: Fortress, 2005.

Nicklas, Tobias. "Der Historiker als Erzähler: Zur Zeichnung des Seleukidenkönigs Antiochus in 2 Makk. ix." *VT* 52 (2002) 80–92.

Nolland, John. *Luke 18:35—24:53*. WBC 35C. Dallas: Word, 1993.

Nowell, Irene. *Women in the Old Testament*. Collegeville, MN: Liturgical, 1997.

Öhler, Markus. "Die Jerusalemer Urgemeinde im Spiegel des antiken Vereinswesens." *NTS* 51 (2005) 393–415.

Olwage, Grant, editor. *Composing Apartheid: Essays on the Music of Apartheid*. Johannesburg: Wits University Press, 2007.

Omerzu, Heike. "Das Imperium schlägt zurück: Die Apologetik der Apostelgeschichte auf dem Prüfstand." *ZNT* 18 (2006) 26–36.

———. *Der Prozeß des Paulus: Eine exegetische und rechtshistorische Untersuchung der Apostelgeschichte*. BZNW 115. Berlin: de Gruyter, 2002.

Osiek, Carolyn, and Margaret Y. MacDonald. *A Woman's Place. House Churches in Earliest Christianity*. Minneapolis: Fortress, 2006.

Parsons, Mikeal. *Luke: Storyteller, Interpreter, Evangelist*. Peabody, MA: Hendrickson, 2007.

Parsons, Mikeal and Richard Pervo. *Rethinking the Unity of Luke-Acts*. Minneapolis: Fortress, 1993.

Perowne, Stewart. *The Later Herods: The Political Background of the New Testament*. New York: Abingdon, 1959.

Pesch, Rudolf. *Die Apostelgeschichte*. Evangelisch-Katholischer Kommentar zum Neuen Testament 5/1–2. Neukirchen-Vluyn: Neukirchener, 1986, 1995.

Plümacher, Eckhard. "Acta Forschung 1974–1982." *TR* 48 (1983) 1–56.

———. *Lukas als hellenistischer Schriftsterrler: Studien zur Apostegeschichte*. SUNT 9. Göttingen: Vandenhoeck & Ruprecht, 1972.

Powell, Mark Allen. *What Is Narrative Criticism?* Guides to Biblical Scholarship. Minneapolis: Fortress, 1993.

Price, Simon. R. F. *Rituals and Power: The Roman Imperial Cult in Asia Minor*. Cambridge: Cambridge University Press, 1984.

Purcell, N. "Wine and Wealth in Ancient Italy." *Journal of Roman Studies* 75 (1985) 1–19.

Rad, Gerhard von. "δοξα C: *kabōd im NT*." In *ThWNT* 2 (1935) 240–45.

Rajak, T. "Was There a Roman Charter for the Jews?" *JRS* 74 (1984) 107–23.

Ramsay, W. M. *St Paul the Traveller and Roman Citizen*. 17th ed. London: Hodder & Stoughton, 1930.

Rapske, Brian. *The Book of Acts and Paul in Roman Custody*. The Book of Acts in Its First-Century Setting 3. Grand Rapids: Eerdmans, 1994.

———. "Roman Governors of Palestine." In *Dictionary of the Later New Testament and Its Developments*, edited by Ralph P. Martin and P. H. Davids, 979–84. Downers Grove, IL: InterVarsity, 1997.

Ravens, David. *Luke and the Restoration of Israel*. JSNTSS 119. Sheffield: Sheffield Academic, 1995.

Reid, Barbara E. *Choosing the Better Part? Women in the Gospel of Luke*. Collegeville, MN: Liturgical, 1996.

———. *Taking Up the Cross: New Testament Interpretations through Latina and Feminist Eyes*. Minneapolis: Fortress, 2007.

Reinbold, Wolfgang. *Der Prozess Jesu*. Biblisch-theologische Schwerpunkt 28. Göttingen: Vandenhoeck & Ruprecht, 2006.

Reiser, Marius. "Numismatik und Neues Testament." *Bib* 81 (2000) 457–88.

Rese, Martin. "The Jews in Luke-Acts: Same Second Thoughts." In *The Unity of Luke-Acts*, edited by Jozef Verheyden, 185–201. BEThL 142. Leuven: Peeters, 1999.

Rhoads, David, and Kari Syreeni, editors. *Characterization in the Gospels: Reconceiving Narrative Criticism*. JSNTSS 184. Sheffield: Sheffield Academic, 1999.

Rhoads, David et al. *Mark as Story*. 2nd ed. Minneapolis: Fortress, 1999.

Richey, Lance Byron. *Roman Imperial Ideology and the Gospel of John*. CBQMS 43. Washington, DC: Catholic Biblical Association, 2007.

Riesner, Rainer. "Fixpunkte für eine Chronologie des Neuen Testaments." In *Neues Testament und Antike Kultur 1*, edited by Kurt Erlemann and Karl Leo Noethlichs, 214–20. Neukirchen-Vluyn: Neukirchener, 2004.

Ringe, Sharon H. *Jesus, Liberation, and the Biblical Jubilee*. Overtures to Biblical Theology. Philadelphia: Fortress, 1985.

Rius-Camps, J., and J. Read-Heimerdinger. *The Message of Acts in Codex Bezae: A Comparison with the Alexandrian Tradition*. (Projected) 4 vols. LNTS. London: T. & T. Clark International, 2004–.

Robbins, Vernon K. "Luke-Acts: A Mixed Population Seeks a Home in the Roman Empire." In *Images of Empire*, edited by Loveday Alexander, 202–21. JSOTSup 122. Sheffield: JSOT Press, 1991.

Robinson, A. T. *Luke the Historian, in Light of Research*. 1920. Reprint, Grand Rapids: Baker, 1977.

Roloff, Jürgen. *Die Apostelgeschichte*. Neue Testament Deutsch 5. Göttingen: Vandenhoeck & Ruprecht, 1988.

Rose, M. "'Die Juden' im lukanischen Doppelwerk: Ein Bericht über eine längst nötige 'neuere' Diskussion." In *Der Treue Gottes trauen: Beiträge zum Werk des Lukas: Für Gerhard Schneider*, edited by Claus Bussmann and Walter Radl, 61–79. Freiburg: Herder, 1991.

Rowe, C. Kavin. "Luke-Acts and the Imperial Cult: A Way Through the Conundrum?" *JSNT* 27/3 (2005) 279–300.

Sanders, E. P. *The Historical Figure of Jesus*. London: Penguin, 1993.

———. *Paul and Palestinian Judaism: A Comparison of Patterns of Religion*. Minneapolis: Fortress, 1977.

Sanders, Jack T. *The Jews in Luke-Acts*. Philadelphia: Fortress, 1987.

Sandmel, S. "Caiaphas." In *IDB* 1:481–82.

Scaer, Paul. *The Lukan Passion and the Praiseworthy Death*. New Testament Monographs 10. Sheffield: Sheffield Phoenix, 2005.

Schaberg, Jane. *The Illegitimacy of Jesus: A Feminist Theological Interpretation of the Infancy Narratives*. San Francisco: Harper & Row, 1987.

———. "Luke." In *Women's Bible Commentary*, edited by Carol A. Newsom and Sharon H. Ringe, 363–80. Rev. ed. Louisville: Westminster John Knox, 1998.

Schnabel, Eckhard J. *Early Christian Mission*. 2 vols. Downers Grove, IL: InterVarsity, 2004.

Schneider, Gerhard. *Die Apostelgeschichte*. 2 vols. HTKNT. Freiburg: Herder, 1980, 1982.

Schürer, Emil. *The History of the Jewish People in the Age of Jesus Christ (175 B.C.–A.D. 135)*. Revised and edited by Geza Vermes and Fergus Millar. Translated by T. A. Burkill. 3 vols. Edinburgh: T. & T. Clark, 1973.

Schwartz, Daniel R. *Agrippa I: The Last King of Judaea*. Texte und Studien zum antiken Judentum 23. Tübingen: Mohr/Siebeck, 1990.

———. "Pontius Pilate." In *ABD* 5: 396–401.

Schwartz, Seth. *Were the Jews a Mediterranean Society? Reciprocity and Solidarity in Ancient Judaism*. Princeton: Princeton University Press, 2010.

Schweizer, Eduard. *Das Evangelium nach Lukas*. NTD 3. 3rd ed. Göttingen: Vandenhoeck & Ruprecht, 2000.

Scott, James C. *Domination and the Arts of Resistance: Hidden Transcripts*. New Haven: Yale University Press, 1990.

———. *Weapons of the Weak: Everyday Forms of Peasant Resistance*. New Haven: Yale University Press, 1985.

Scott, James M. "Luke's Geographical Horizon." In *The Book of Acts in Its Graeco-Roman Setting*, edited by David W. J. Gill and Conrad Gempf, 483–544. The Books of Acts in Its First Century Setting 2. Grand Rapids: Eerdmans, 1994.

Seim, Turid Karlsen. *The Double Message: Patterns of Gender in Luke-Acts*. Nashville: Abingdon, 1994.

Setel, Drorah O'Donnel. "Exodus." In *Women's Bible Commentary*, 36. Rev. ed. Louisville: Westminster John Knox, 1998.

Sherwin-White, A. N. *Roman Society and Roman Law in the New Testament*. Grand Rapids: Baker, 1963. Reprinted, 1981.

Skinner, M. L. *Locating Paul: Places of Custody as Narrative Settings in Acts 21–28*. AcBib 13. Atlanta: Society of Biblical Literature, 2003. [series]

Smallwood, E. Mary. "High Priests and Politics in Roman Palestine." *JTS* 13 (1962) 14–34.

———. *The Jews under Roman Rule: From Pompey to Diocletian*. Studies in Judaism in Late Antiquity 20. Leiden: Brill, 1976.

Soards, Maron. "Tradition, Composition, and Theology in Luke's Account of Jesus before Herod Antipas." *Bib* 66 (1985) 344–64.

Spivak, Gayatri Chakravorty. *A Critique of Postcolonial Reason: Toward a History of the Vanishing Present*. Cambridge: Harvard University Press, 1999.

———. *Other Asias*. Oxford: Blackwell, 2008.

———. *The Post-Colonial Critic: Interviews, Strategies, Dialogues*. London: Routledge, 1990.

Stegemann, Wolfgang. "'Licht der Völker' bei Lukas." In *Der Treue Gottes trauen: Beiträge zum Werk des Lukas: Für Gerhard Schneider*, edited by Claus Bussmann and Walter Radl, 81–97. Freiburg: Herder, 1991.

———. *Zwischen Synagoge und Obrigkeit: Zur historischen Situation der lukanischen Christen*. FRLANT 126. Göttingen: Vandenhoeck & Ruprecht, 1991.

Stendahl, Krister. "Paul and the Introspective Conscience of the West." In *Paul Among Jews and Gentiles*, 78–96. Minneapolis: Fortress, 1976.

Stern, M. "The Reign of Herod and the Herodian Dynasty." In *The Jewish People in the First Century: Historical Geography, Political History, Social, Cultural and Religious Life and Institutions*, edited by Shemuel Safrai and M. Stern, 216–307. Compendia rerum iudaicarum ad Novum Testamentum 1/1. Philadelphia: Fortress, 1974.

Stibbe, Mark. *John*. Readings. Sheffield: JSOT Press, 1993.

Stolle, Volker. *Der Zeuge als Angeklagter: Untersuchungen zum Paulus-Bild des Lukas*. BWANT 102. Stuttgart: Kohlhammer, 1973.

Strobel, August. "Βαβυλον." In *EWNT* I (1980) 451–53.

Sugirtharajah, R. S. "Introduction." In *Voices from the Margin: Interpreting the Bible in the Third World* edited by R. S. Sugirtharajah, 1–6. Maryknoll, NY: Orbis, 1995.

Tajra, H. W. *The Trial of St Paul: A Juridical Exegesis of the Second Half of the Acts of the Apostles.* WUNT II/35. Tübingen: Mohr/Siebeck, 1989.

Talbert, Charles H. *Literary Patterns, Theological Themes, and the Genre of Luke-Acts.* SBLMS 20. Missoula: Scholars, 1974.

———. "What Is Meant by the Historicity of Acts?" In *Reading Luke-Acts in Its Mediterranean Milieu*, 197–217. NovTSup 107. Leiden: Brill, 2003.

Tannehill, Robert C. *Luke.* Abingdon NT Commentaries. Nashville: Abingdon, 1996.

———. *The Narrative Unity of Luke-Acts: A Literary Interpretation.* 2 vols. Minneapolis: Fortress, 1986, 1990.

———. "The Story of Israel within the Lukan Narrative." In *Jesus and the Heritage of Israel*, 325–39. Harrisburg, PA: Trinity, 1999.

Theissen, Gerd. *Sociology of Early Palestinian Christianity.* Translated by John Bowden. Philadelphia: Fortress, 1978.

Tiffin, Helen. "Post-Colonialism, Post-Modernism and the Rehabilitation of Post-Colonial History." *Journal of Commonwealth Literature* 23.1 (1988) 161–81.

Trible, Phyllis. "Bringing Miriam Out of the Shadows." *BRev* 5 (1989) 14–25.

Trites, A. A. *The New Testament Concept of Witness.* SNTSMS 31. Cambridge: Cambridge University Press, 1977.

Tyson, Joseph B. *Luke, Judaism, and the Scholars: Critical Approaches to Luke-Acts.* Columbia: University of South Carolina Press, 1999.

Walasky, Paul. *And So We Came to Rome: The Political Perspective of St Luke.* SNTSMS 49. Cambridge: Cambridge University Press, 1983.

Wallace, D. B. *Greek Grammar beyond the Basics: An Exegetical Syntax of the New Testament.* Grand Rapids: Zondervan, 1996.

Walters, Patricia. *The Assumed Authorial Unity of Luke and Acts: A Reassessment of the Evidence.* Cambridge: Cambridge University Press, 2009.

Walton, Steve. "Acts, Book of." In *Dictionary for Theological Interpretation of the Bible*, edited by Kevin J. Vanhoozer, 27–31. Grand Rapids: Baker Academic, 2005.

———. *Leadership and Lifestyle: The Portrait of Paul in the Miletus Speech and 1 Thessalonians.* SNTSMS 108. Cambridge: Cambridge University Press, 2000.

———. "The State They Were In: Luke's View of the Roman Empire." In *Rome in the Bible and the Early Church*, edited by Peter Oakes, 1–41. Grand Rapids: Baker Academic, 2002.

Wasserberg, Günter. *Aus Israels Mitte—Heil für die Welt: Eine narrativ-exegetische Studie zur Theologie des Lukas.* BZNW 92. Berlin: de Gruyter, 1998.

Weatherly, J. A. *Jewish Responsibility for the Death of Jesus in Luke-Acts.* JSNTSup 106. Sheffield: Sheffield Academic, 1994.

Whittaker, C. R. "The Poor." In *The Romans,* edited by Andrea Giardina, 272–99. Translated by Lydia G. Cochrane. Chicago: University of Chicago Press, 1993.

Wilk, Florian. "Die Geschichte des Gottesvolkes im Licht jesajanischer Prophetie: Neutestamentliche Perspektiven." In *Josephus und das Neue Testament: Wechselseitige Wahrnehmungen: II. Internationales Symposium zum Corpus Judaeo-Hellenisticum, 25.-28. Mai 2006, Greifswald*, edited by Christfried Böttrich and Jens Herzer, 245–64. WUNT 209. Tübingen: Mohr/Siebeck, 2007.

Wilker, Julia. *Für Rom und Jerusalem: Die herodianische Dynastie im 1. Jahrhundert n.Chr.* Studien zur Alten Geschichte 5. Frankfurt: Antike, 2007.

Winter, B. W. "Gallio's Ruling on the Legal Status of Early Christianity (Acts 18:14–15)." *TynBul* 50 (1999) 213–24.

———. "The Importance of the *Captatio Benevolentiae* in the Speeches of Tertullus and Paul in Acts 24:1–21." *JTS* 42 (1991) 505–31.

———. "Official Proceedings and the Forensic Speeches in Acts 24–26." In *The Book of Acts in Its Ancient Literary Setting*, edited by Bruce W. Winter and A. D. Clarke, 305–36. The Book of Acts in Its First-Century Setting 1. Grand Rapids: Eerdmans, 1993.

———. "Rehabilitating Gallio." *TynBul* 57 (2006) 291–308.

Witherington, Ben, III. *The Acts of the Apostles: A Socio-Rhetorical Commentary.* Grand Rapids: Eerdmans, 1998.

Witherup, Ronald D. "Functional Redundancy in the Acts of the Apostles: A Case Study." *JSNT* 48 (1992) 67–86.

Wolter, Michael. "Israel's Future and the Delay of the Parousia according to Luke." In *Jesus and the Heritage of Israel*, edited by David P. Moessner, 307–24. Luke the Interpreter of Israel 1. Harrisburg, PA: Trinity, 1999.

———. "Israels Zukunft und die Parusieverzögerung bei Lukas." In *Theologie und Ethos im frühen Christentum: Studien zu Jesus, Paulus und Lukas,* 311–33. WUNT 236. Tübingen: Mohr/Siebeck, 2009 (orig. 1997).

———. "Die Juden und die Obrigkeit bei Lukas." In *Theologie und Ethos im frühen Christentum: Studien zu Jesus, Paulus und Lukas,* 388–401. WUNT 236. Tübingen: Mohr/Siebeck, 2009 (orig. 1998).

———. *Das Lukasevangelium.* HbNT 5. Tübingen: Mohr/Siebeck, 2008.

Wright, N. T. *The Climax of the Covenant: Christ and the Law in Pauline Theology.* Minneapolis: Fortress, 1991.

Yamazaki-Ransom, Kazuhiko. "God, People, and Empire: Anti-Imperial Theology of Luke-Acts in Light of Jewish Portrayals of Gentile Rulers." PhD diss., Trinity Evangelical Divinity School, 2006.

———. *The Roman Empire in Luke's Narrative.* Library of New Testament Studies 404. London: T. & T. Clark International, 2010.

Young, Iris Marion. *Justice and the Politics of Difference.* Princeton: Princeton University Press, 1990.

Zanker, Paul. *The Power of Images in the Age of Augustus.* Ann Arbor: University of Michigan Press, 1990.

Zeigan, Holger: *Aposteltreffen in Jerusalem: Eine forschungsgeschichtliche Studie zu Galater 2,1–10 und den möglichen lukanischen Parallelen.* Arbeiten zur Bibel und ihrer Geschichte 18. Leipzig: Evangelische Verlagsanstalt, 2005.

Zimmerman, Georges. *Songs of Irish Rebellion: Irish Political Street Ballads and Rebel Songs, 1780–1900.* Dublin: Four Courts, 2002.

Publications of Robert L. Brawley

Books

Character Ethics and the New Testament: Moral Dimensions of Scripture (editor and Contributor). Louisville: Westminster John Knox, 2007.

Biblical Ethics and Homosexuality: Listening to Scripture (editor and contributor). Louisville: Westminster John Knox, 1996.

Text to Text Pours Forth Speech: Voices of Scripture in Luke-Acts. Indiana Studies in Biblical Literature. Bloomington: Indiana University Press, 1995.

Centering on God: Method and Message in Luke-Acts. Literary Currents in Biblical Interpretation. Louisville: Westminster John Knox, 1990.

Luke-Acts and the Jews: Conflict, Apology, and Conciliation. SBL Monograph Series 33. Atlanta: Scholars, 1987.

• • •

Articles

"Generating Ethics from God's Character in Mark." In *Character Ethics and the New Testament: Moral Dimensions of Scripture*, edited by Robert L. Brawley. Louisville: Westminster John Knox, 2007.

"Identity and Metaethics: Being Justified and Ethics in Galatians." In *Character Ethics and the New Testament: Moral Dimensions of Scripture*, edited by Robert L. Brawley. Louisville: Westminster John Knox, 2007.

"'Have This Mindset among Yourselves': A Way of Reconciliation in Philippians." *Theological Studies* (Hanshin University Press, Korea) 49 (2006) 111–38.

"Complex Enigmas of Complicity: The Human Predicament." In *Gewalt und Gewaltüberwendung: Stationen eines theologischen Dialogs*, edited by Erhard Kampenhausen and Gerhard Köberlin, 128–51. Frankfurt: Lembreck, 2006.

"Meta-Ethics and the Role of Works of Law in Galatians." In *Luterische oder Neue Perspektive: Beiträge zu einem Schlüsselproblem der gegenwärtigen exegetischen Diskussion*, edited by Michael Bachmann, 135–59. WUNT 182. Tübingen: Mohr/ Siebeck, 2005.

"Social Identity and the Aim of Accomplished Life in Acts 2." In *Acts and Ethics*, edited by T. Phillips, 16–33. New Testament Mongraphs 9. Sheffield: Sheffield Phoenix, 2005.

"Evocative Allusions in Matthew: Matthew 5:5 as a Test Case." In *Literary Encounters with the Reign of God*, edited by Sharon Ringe and Paul Kim, 127–48. New York: T. & T. Clark, 2004. [Published simultaneously as in the next entry]

"Evocative Allusions in Matthew: Matthew 5:5 as a Test Case." *Hervormde Teologiese Studies* 59 (2003) 597–619.

"Sexuality in Relation to God and the Christian Community." *Currents in Theology and Mission* 30 (2003) 46–49.

"Exegesis." *Lectionary Homiletics* 13/11 (2002) 1–2, 9–10, 17–18, 25–26.

"Contextuality, Intertextuality, and the Hendiadic Relationship of Promise and Law in Galatians." *Zeitschrift für die neutestamentliche Wissenschaft* 93 (2002) 99–119.

"Exegesis." *Lectionary Homiletics* 12/10 (2001) 1–2, 7–8, 15–16, 22–23, 31–32.

"Ethical Borderlines between Rejection and Hope: Interpreting the Jews in Luke-Acts." *Currents in Theology and Mission* 27 (2000) 415–23.

"The Spirit, the Power, and the Commonwealth in Acts." *The Bible Today* 37 (1999) 268–75.

"Abrahamic Covenant Traditions and the Characterization of God in Luke-Acts." In *The Unity of Luke-Acts*, edited by J. Verheyden, 109–32. BETL 142. Leuven: Peeters. 1999.

"Multivocality in Romans 4." In *Reading Israel in Romans*, edited by Daniel Patte and Cristina Grenholm, 74–95. Harrisburg, PA: Trinity, 2000.

With Thomas D. Parker. "Multivocality and Multiplex Perspectives in the Interpretation of Romans." In *Reading Israel in Romans*, edited by Daniel Patte and C. Grenholm, 96–104. Harrisburg, PA: Trinity, 2000.

"Reverberations of Abrahamic Covenant Traditions in the Ethics of Matthew." *Realia Dei: Biblical and Archaeological Essays in Honor of Edward F. Campbell*, edited by Theodore Hiebert and P. Williams. Atlanta: Scholars, 1999.

"The God of Promises and the Jews in Luke-Acts." In *Literary Studies in Luke-Acts: Essays in Honor of Joseph B. Tyson*, edited by R. Thompson and T. Phillips, 279–96. Macon, GA: Mercer University Press, 1998.

"Offspring and Parent: A Lucan Prolegomena to Ethics." *Society of Biblical Literature 1998 Seminar Papers*, 807–30. Atlanta: Scholars, 1998.

"Multivocality in Romans 4." *Society of Biblical Literature 1997 Seminar Papers*. Edited by E. Lovering, 285–305. Atlanta: Scholars, 1997.

"Scripture Resisting the Carnivalesque in the Lucan Passion." In *Scriptures in the Gospels: Intertextuality. The Use of the Old Testament in the Four Gospels*, edited by Christopher Tuckett, 247–51. BETL 125. Leuven: Leuven University Press, 1997.

"Resistance to the Carnivalization of Jesus: Scripture in the Lucan Passion Narrative." *Semeia* 69/70 (1995) 33–60.

"Exegesis." *Lectionary Homiletics* 7/7 (1996) 3–4, 11–12, 18, 26–27, 33–34.

"Table Fellowship: Bane and Blessing for the Historical Jesus." *Perspectives in Religion* 22 (1995) 13–31.

"For Blessing All Families of the Earth: Covenant Traditions in Luke-Acts." *Currents in Theology and Mission* 22 (1995) 18–26.

"'To Have and to Hold, and—in Time—Let Go': The Ethics of Interpreting the Bible." *Currents in Theology and Mission* 21 (1994) 113–16.

"The Blessing of All the Families of the Earth: Jesus and Covenant Traditions in Luke-Acts." In *Society of Biblical Literature 1994 Seminar Papers*, edited by E. Lovering, 252–68. Atlanta: Scholars, 1994.

"An Absent Complement and Intertextuality in John 19:28–29." *Journal of Biblical Literature* 112 (1993) 427–43.

"Discoursive Structure and the Unseen in Hebrews 2:8 and 11:1: A Neglected Aspect of the Context." *Catholic Biblical Quarterly* 55 (1993) 81–98.

"Canon and Community: Intertextuality, Canon, Interpretation, Christology, Theology, and Persuasive Rhetoric in Luke 4:1–13." *Society of Biblical Literature 1992 Seminar Papers*, edited by E. Lovering, 419–34. Atlanta: Scholars Press, 1992.

"Exegesis." *Lectionary Homiletics* 3/6 (1992) 1, 7, 12, 20, 27.

"*Anamnesis* and Absence in the Lord's Supper." *Biblical Theology Bulletin* 20 (1990) 139–46.

"Joseph in Matthew's Birth Narrative and the Irony of Good Intentions." *Memphis Theological Seminary Journal* 28 (1990) 69–76.

"Response to Robert Hann." *Journal of Ecumenical Studies* 26 (1989) 343–44.

"Paul in Acts: Aspects of Structure and Characterization." In *Society of Biblical Literature 1987 Seminar Papers*, edited by David Lull. Atlanta: Scholars, 1987.

"Paul in Acts: Lucan Apology and Conciliation." In *Luke-Acts: New Perspectives from the Society of Biblical Literature Seminar*, edited by Charles Talbert, 129–47. New York: Crossroad, 1983.

• • •

Translations

Bachmann, Michael. *Anti-Judaism in Galatians?* Translation by Robert L. Brawley. Grand Rapids: Eerdmans, 2009. (Original publication: *Antijudaismus im Galaterbrief?*)

Lampe, Peter. *New Testament Theology in a Secular World: A Constructivist Work in Christian Apologetics.* Translation by Robert L. Brawley. London: Continuum (forthcoming 2010). *Die Wirklichkeit als Bild.*

• • •

Reviews

Review of *The Mystery of Acts: Unraveling Its Story* by Richard Pervo (Santa Rosa: Polebridge, 2008). *Catholic Biblical Quarterly* 71 (2009) 907–8.

Review of *The Sage from Galilee: Rediscovering Jesus' Genius*, by David Flusser with R. Stepehn Notley (Grand Rapids: Eerdmans, 2007). *Review of Biblical Literature* http://www.bookreviews.org/BookDetail.asp?TitleId=6152.

Review of *Studies in Early Christianity* by François Bovon, WUNT 161 (Tübingen: Mohr/Siebeck, 2003). *Catholic Biblical Quarterly* 69 (2007) 396–98.

Review with Ogbu Kalu of *Paul's Concept of Charisma in 1 Corinthians 12: With Emphasis on the Nigerian Charismatic Movement* by Luke Ndubuisi (Frankfurt: Lang, 2003). *Pneuma* 28 (2006) 358–61.

Review of *The Lukan Passion and the Praiseworthy Death* by Peter J. Scaer, New Testament Monographs 10 (Sheffield: Sheffield Phoenix, 2005). *Review of Biblical Literature* http://www.bookreviews.org/BookDetail.asp?TitleId=5112.

Review of *The Exorcism Stories in Luke-Acts: A Sociostylistic Reading* by Todd Klutz (Cambridge University Press, 2004). *Journal of Religion* 85 (2005) 653–54.

Review essay of *The New Testament; Lost Christianities;* and *Lost Scriptures* by Bart Ehrman. *Princeton Seminary Bulletin* 25 (2004) 332–38.

Review of *La Bonne Nouvelle de Dieu: Une analyse de la figure narrative de Dieu dans le discours pétriniens d'écangélisation des Actes de Apôtres* by Christian Dionne. *Catholic Biblical Quarterly* 66 (2004) 644–45.

Review of *Mimesis and Intertextuality in Antiquity and Christianity* edited by D. MacDonald. *Catholic Biblical Quarterly* 64 (2002) 611–13.

Review of *The Bible, Theology, and Faith: A Study of Abraham and Jesus* by R. W. L. Moberly. *Catholic Biblical Quarterly* 63 (2001) 348–49.

Review of *Agape, Eros, Gender: Towards a Pauline Sexual Ethic* by Francis Watson. *Theology Today* 58 (2001) 132–33.

Review of *Homoeroticism in the Biblical World: A Historical Perspective*, by Martti Nissinen. Translated by Kirsi Stjerna. Minneapolis: Fortress, 1998. *Review of Biblical Literature* (2000).

Review of *Mark as Story: An Introduction to the Narrative of a Gospel*, by David Rhoads, Joanna Dewey, and Donald Mitchie. Second Edition. *Currents in Theology and Mission* 27 (2000) 127–29.

Review of *The Gospel of Luke*, by Joel B. Green. *Interpretation* 53 (1999) 89–90.

Review of *The Jewish Heroes of Christian History: Hebrews 11 in Literary Context*, by Pamela Michelle Eisenbaum. *Shofar* 17/4 (1999) 151–52.

Review of *The Things Accomplished Among Us: Prophetic Tradition in the Structural Pattern of Luke-Acts*, by Rebecca I. Denova. *Journal of Biblical Literature* .

Review of *The Blind, the Lame, and the Poor: Character Types in Luke-Acts*, by S. John Roth. *Currents in Theology and Mission.*

Review of *Hebrews*. Interpretation: A Bible Commentary for Teaching and Preaching, by Thomas G. Long. *Princeton Theological Seminary Bulletin* 19 (1998) 62–63.

Review of *Jesus The Liberator: Nazareth Liberation Theology (Luke 4.16–30)*, by Michael Prior. *Currents in Theology and Mission* 24 (1997) 492.

Review of *Feasting and Social Rhetoric in Luke 14*, by Willi Braun. *Journal of Biblical Literature.*

Review of *Household Conversion Narratives in Acts: Pattern and Interpretation*, by David Matson. *Journal of Biblical Literature* 10 (1997) 194–96.

Review of Mary: Glimpses of the Mother of Jesus, by Beverly Roberts Gaventa. *Interpretation* 51 (1997) 314.

Review of *The Theology of the Gospel of Luke*, by Joel B. Green. *Journal of Religion* 77 (1997) 125–26.

Review of *The Postmodern Bible*, by the Bible and Culture Collective, George Aichele et al. *Theology Today* 53 (1996) 129–31.

Review of *Post Structuralism and the New Testament: Derrida and Foucault at the Foot of the Cross*, by Stephen D. Moore. *Theology Today* 52 (1995) 134–36.

Review of *Reading Luke-Acts: Dynamics of Biblical Narrative*, by William S. Kurz. Critical Review of Books in Religion 8 (1995) 240–43.

Review of *Stewardship and the Kingdom of God: An Historical, Exegetical, and Contextual Study of the Parable of the Unjust Steward in Luke 16:1–13*, by Dennis J. Ireland. *Journal of Biblical Literature* 113 (1994) 541–43.

With E. Campbell review of *The Anchor Bible Dictionary*, edited by David Noel Freedman. *Christian Century* 110 (1993) 426–29.

Review of *Bursting the Bonds? A Jewish Christian Dialogue on Jesus and Paul*, by Leonard Swidler, Lewis John Eron, Gerard Sloyan, and Lester Dean. *Journal of Ecumenical Studies* 29 (1992) 277–78.

Review of *Das Sondergut des Evangeliums nach Lukas*. Zürcher Werkkommentare zur Bibel, by Gerd Petzke. *Journal of Biblical Literature* 111 (1992) 724–26.

Review of *Luke. A Bible Commentary for Teaching and Preaching*. Interpretation, by Fred B. Craddock. *Theology Today* 48 (1991) 261–62.

Review of *The Narrative Unity of Luke-Acts: A Literary Interpretation*, by Robert C. Tannehill. *Theology Today* 47 (1991) 452–55.

Review of *Echoes of Scripture in the Letters of Paul*, by Richard B. Hays. *Memphis Theological Seminary Journal* 28 (1990) 94–95.

Review of *Interpreting Difficult Texts: Anti-Judaism and Christian Preaching*, by Clark M. Williamson and Ronald J. Allen. *Theology Today* 47 (1990) 225–26.

Review of *Lord of the Banquet: The Literary and Theological Significance of the Lukan Travel Narrative*, by David P. Moessner. *Memphis Theological Seminary Journal* 37 (1990) 53–54.

Review of *Die Rezeption der Paulusbriefe in der Miletrede (Apg 20:18–35)*, by Lars Aejmelaeus. *Journal of Biblical Literature* 108 (1989) 532–34.

Review of Luke-Acts and the Jewish People: Eight Critical Perspectives, edited by Joseph Tyson. *Perkins (School of Theology) Journal* 42/2–3 (1989) 15–16.

Review of *The Jews in Luke-Acts*, by Jack T. Sanders. *Memphis Theological Seminary Journal* 26 (1988) 106–9.

Review of *Reading Luke*, by Charles Talbert. *Memphis Theological Seminary Journal* 21 (1983) 25–27.

Review of *The Purpose of Luke-Acts*, by Robert Maddox. *Memphis Theological Seminary Journal* 21 (1983) 24–25.

Review of *Evangelio de la esperanza: evangelio de la unidad*, by Francisco Marin. *Religious Studies Review* 6 (1980) 149.

• • •

Dissertation

"The Pharisees in Luke-Acts: Luke's Irenic Purpose and His Address to Jews." PhD diss., Princeton Theological Seminary, 1978.

30290868R00105

Made in the USA
Middletown, DE
19 March 2016